LIVING WITH THE FLOOD

LIVING WITH THE FLOOD

Mesolithic to post-medieval archaeological remains
at Mill Lane, Sawston, Cambridgeshire

A wetland/dryland interface

*Samantha Paul, Kevin Colls
and Henry Chapman*

Oxbow Books
Oxford & Philadelphia

Published in the United Kingdom in 2016 by
OXBOW BOOKS
10 Hythe Bridge Street, Oxford OX1 2EW

and in the United States by
OXBOW BOOKS
1950 Lawrence Road, Havertown, PA 19083

Softcover Edition: ISBN 978-1-78297-966-1
Digital Edition: ISBN 978-1-78297-967-8

A CIP record for this book is available from the British Library

Library of Congress Cataloging-in-Publication Data

Paul, Samantha.
  Living with the flood : mesolithic to post-medieval archaeological remains at Mill Lane, Sawston, Cambridgeshire : a wetland/dryland interface / Samantha Paul, Kevin Colls, and Henry Chapman. -- Softcover edition.
     pages cm
  ISBN 978-1-78297-966-1
  1. Sawston (England)--Antiquities. 2. Excavations (Archaeology)--England--Sawston. 3. Water-saturated sites (Archaeology)--England--Sawston. I. Colls, Kevin. II. Chapman, Henry, 1973- III. Title.
  DA690.S253P38 2015
  942.6'57--dc23
                         2015020108

Printed in the United Kingdom by Hobbs the Printers Ltd, Totton, Hampshire

For a complete list of Oxbow titles, please contact:

UNITED KINGDOM
Oxbow Books
Telephone (01865) 241249, Fax (01865) 794449
Email: oxbow@oxbowbooks.com
www.oxbowbooks.com

UNITED STATES OF AMERICA
Oxbow Books
Telephone (800) 791-9354, Fax (610) 853-9146
Email: queries@casemateacademic.com
www.casemateacademic.com/oxbow

Oxbow Books is part of the Casemate Group

Front cover: Reconstruction of the small early Anglo-Saxon village at the site, looking northwest © Nigel Dodds
Back cover: (top) Excavations at Mill Lane under snow looking north-west © Birmingham Archaeology, University of Birmingham; (bottom, left to right) Clipped Roman coin from 1088; broken slender leaf-shaped arrowhead from 1459; Buckle loop from 1067.

CONTENTS

CHAPTER 1: INTRODUCTION

CHAPTER 2: METHODOLOGIES

CHAPTER 3: THE EXCAVATIONS

CHAPTER 4: PREHISTORIC LITHICS (*by Barry John Bishop*)

CHAPTER 10: PREHISTORIC AND ROMAN ACTIVITY

CHAPTER 11: ANGLO-SAXON, MEDIEVAL AND POST-MEDIEVAL ACTIVITY

CHAPTER 12: CONCLUSIONS: LIFE ON THE WETLAND EDGE

LIST OF FIGURES AND TABLES

LIST OF CONTRIBUTORS

SUE ANDERSON
Freelance archaeological specialist,
Spoilheap Archaeology, Norfolk, UK.

BARRY JOHN BISHOP
Freelance lithic specialist,
Cambridge, UK.

HENRY CHAPMAN
Senior lecturer in Archaeology and Visualisation,
Department of Classics, Ancient History and Archaeology,
University of Birmingham, UK.

KEVIN COLLS
Archaeological project manager, Centre of Archaeology,
Staffordshire University, UK.

CECILY CROPPER
Freelance forensic archaeologist and glass specialist,
Wiltshire, UK.

VAL FRYER
Freelance environmental archaeologist,
Norfolk, UK.

BENJAMIN GEAREY
Lecturer in Archaeology,
University College Cork, Ireland.

MATILDA HOLMES
Consultant archaeozoologist,
Leicester, UK.

EMMA-JAYNE HOPLA
Postgraduate researcher,
Geography and Environment,
University of Southampton, UK.

KRISTINA KRAWIEC
Environmental archaeologist,
Archaeology South-East, Brighton, UK.

ROSALIND MCKENNA
Freelance environmental archaeologist,
Greater Manchester, UK.

SAMANTHA PAUL
Research Fellow in Archaeology and Heritage,
Department of Classics, Ancient History and Archaeology,
University of Birmingham, UK.

ROB PERRIN
Freelance Roman pottery specialist,
Salisbury, UK.

D. JAMES RACKHAM
The Environmental Archaeology Consultancy,
York, UK.

EILEEN REILLY
School of Archaeology,
University College Dublin, Ireland.

PENELOPE WALTON ROGERS
The Anglo-Saxon Laboratory,
York, UK.

ROGER WHITE
Senior lecturer,
Ironbridge International Institute for Cultural Heritage,
University of Birmingham, UK.

ANN WOODWARD
Independent archaeologist and prehistoric pottery specialist,
Dorchester, UK.

ACKNOWLEDGEMENTS

The Mill Lane excavations and subsequent analysis and report were sponsored by Spicers Limited. Sincere thanks to Neil Bramall (Spicers) and Mike Cronin (Spicers) who ensured the archaeological investigations were smoothly integrated into the pre-development programme and helped make the project a success. The archaeological investigations were monitored by Kasia Gdaniec for Cambridgeshire County Council. The Mill Lane investigations and post-excavation programme were also monitored by Dan Slatcher of RPS Planning and Development on behalf of Spicers Limited. The fieldwork was managed by Kevin Colls of Birmingham Archaeology.

The fieldwork staff were; Bob Burrows (director), Anthony Aston, David Brown, Ellie Buttery, Liz Charles, Mark Charles, Emma Collins, Paul Collins, Emily Hamilton and Phil Mann. The archaeoenvironmental field team comprised Ben Gearey, Kristina Krawiec and Emma Hopla.

The post-excavation assessment was managed by Kevin Colls with the final publication managed by Samantha Paul. Processing of artefacts was managed by Erica Macey-Bracken and Emma Collins. The illustrations were produced by Nigel Dodds and Henry Chapman. The reconstruction artwork was produced by Nigel Dodds. Henry Chapman and Samantha Paul undertook the formatting and technical editing and Malcolm Hislop undertook the final copy editing.

Samantha Paul would especially like to thank Henry Chapman for his guidance and support throughout the end stages of this project. Thanks also to the archaeological specialists who have contributed to this publication and have helped to enhance our understanding of a site at a wetland/dry land interface.

SUMMARY

River valleys have been a focus for human activity since the early Holocene and, in addition to providing abundant archaeological evidence for this interaction, the proximity to water also highlights the potential for the preservation of archaeological remains and palaeoenvironmental source material. However, human activity within the areas of river valleys also commonly bridges locals of both wetland and dryland; ecological areas that are often approached using quite different archaeological methods and which present considerable differences in levels of archaeological visibility and preservation. Hence, there have been few studies that have explored the interface between these two different zones as a single archaeological landscape.

This book details the results of the study at a wetland/dryland interface on the edge of palaeochannels from the River Cam in Cambridgeshire. Through the integrated archaeological and palaeoenvironmental analysis of a site to the east of Sawston, a detailed picture of life on the edge of the floodplain from the late glacial to the post-Medieval periods has been developed. At the heart of this is the relationship between people and their changing environment; a shifting pattern of occupation and more transitory activity as the riparian landscape in a wooded setting became a wetland within a more openly grazed environment. The high levels of preservation, owing to the masking effects of alluviation and colluviation, mean that the site has revealed a range of building construction processes during a variety of different periods, along with complex patterns of artefact and waste deposition.

The research at Sawston has reinforced the value of studying the archaeology of river valley landscapes, and has highlighted how, despite the challenges of archaeological visibility using traditional methods, the processes of accretion within these environments can result in considerable preservation, presenting a more detailed and complete picture of past human activity at the wetland/dryland interface.

Chapter 1

Introduction

1.1 Background to the project

The richness of human activity within floodplain environments is well known (Brown 1997). Previous investigations within such landscapes have demonstrated how the floodplains of river systems provide considerable potential for dense levels of human activity, as seen within the valleys of the Thames (Sidell and Wilkinson 2004), the Trent (Knight and Howard 2004; Buteux and Chapman 2009) and the rivers surrounding the Humber estuary (Van de Noort 2004). In addition to the basic human need for proximity to water, rivers and their floodplains continue to demonstrate how many other human activities took place within these landscapes. From river crossings to ceremonial landscapes the wealth of landscape archaeology in these environments is well known (*e.g.* Chapman *et al.* 2010), as is the potential for these landscapes to provide wet-preservation of organic remains (*cf.* Menotti 2012). In particular, the interfaces between the wetlands of the floodplains and the adjacent drylands provide considerable opportunity to explore the interaction between two ecosystems.

Despite the considerable archaeological potential of floodplain environments, the same factors that can result in preservation can also restrict the visibility of remains. The accreting nature of alluvium and other wetland deposits within floodplain environments typically results in the concealment of earlier layers of activity, and this can be further impacted upon by the build up of colluvial deposits derived from adjacent areas due to ploughing. Such processes of sedimentation can result in deeply buried deposits that conceal surface features such as earthworks or surface finds. Combined with high water tables, this can result in poor visibility of archaeological remains when approached using conventional methods of archaeological prospection. Whilst there has been considerable success in the application of aerial photography within river valleys, and particularly within gravel landscapes (Whimster 1989), the reliance on natural drainage for the formation of crop marks (Riley 1944; Wilson 1982) means that the identification of sites within alluvial environments is more restricted. Similarly, the application of geophysical techniques within alluvial landscapes can be equally challenging (Schleifer *et al.* 2002). Despite recent developments in the application of other approaches such as Ground Penetrating Radar and the use of airborne Light Detection and Ranging (LIDAR) technologies (Carey *et al.* 2006), the reliable identification of archaeological sites and deposits in these landscape remains challenging.

The prospect of studying the archaeology of wetland/dryland interfaces on the edge of a river floodplain through open area excavation became available in 2001–2009 at the site of Mill Lane on the western side of the village of Sawston in Cambridgeshire (NGR TL 4712 4984). The excavation area stretched across this interface, with the floodplain covering its western and northern sides (Fig. 1.1). Previous archaeological research in the wider area had demonstrated the potential for human activity from the Neolithic period through to the post-medieval period, although detail for some periods was limited and quite fragmentary. The geographical location of the site, on the floodplain of the River Cam, but also within an area to the south of its confluence with the River Granta, strengthened the potential for archaeological remains. Hence, this was seen as a significant opportunity to investigate such an area in detail to establish the chronological range of human activity at the site, to determine the earliest evidence for occupation there and to explore themes of change and continuity relating to human activity. It was also an opportunity to explore the potential barriers to archaeological visibility which might have accounted for the largely fragmentary evidence from the area. From the detailed study of such a well-positioned site, this also provided the opportunity to put the results of the work at Mill Lane into the wider context of the River Cam network and of floodplain environments more generally.

1.2 Location, geology and preservation potential

The site of Mill Lane lies within a bend of the River Cam approximately a kilometre to the west of Sawston village in Cambridgeshire, centred on NGR TL 4712 4984 (Fig. 1.1). The site is bounded to the west and north by woodland, to the east by a hedgerow and to the south by an arable field, although it lies on a slight spur of land comprising gleyic brown calcareous earths with deep fine loams over chalk drift and chalk falling from about 19m AOD in the east to about 16.7m AOD in the west. Surrounding the western and southern sides of the site, the alluvial floodplain of the River Cam is between 300m and 1km wide, with extensive outcrops of river terrace deposits, particularly on its western side (Fig. 1.2). While the site is proximally most closely associated with the River Cam, which lies just 250m away to the south, a tributary running from Whittlesford joins the

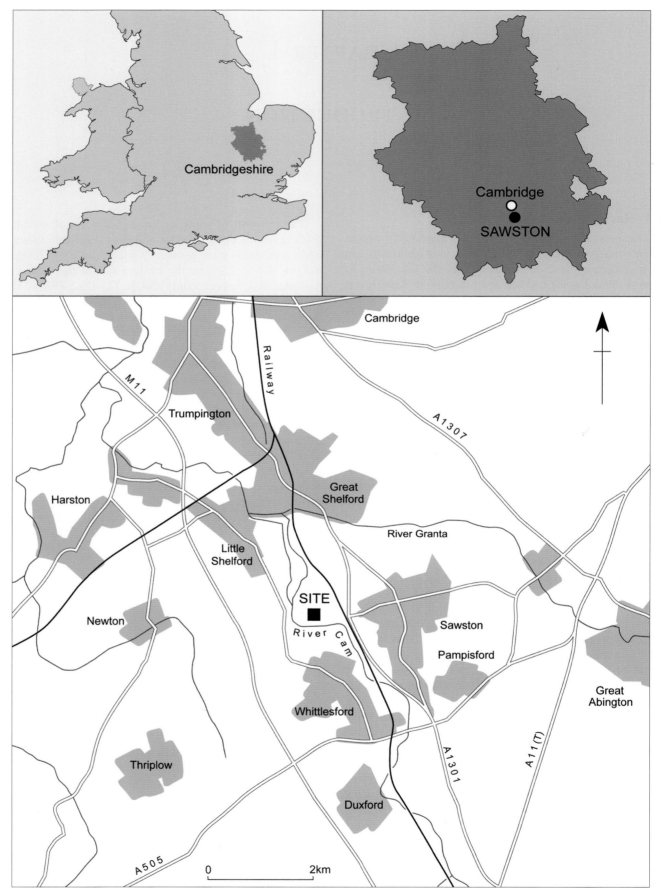

Figure 1.1 Location of the Mill Lane site.

Cam about 800m to the south of the site, and the confluence with the River Granta lies approximately 2km to the north. The village of Sawston occupies the area of dryland between the Rivers Cam and Granta.

The site of Mill Lane bridges the floodplain edge of the River Cam, as defined by the mapped extent of alluvium (Fig. 1.2). As such the potential for wet-preservation of organic archaeological remains and palaeoenvironmental source material from the site was considered high. However, the area has been subjected to considerable water abstraction such as through the Sawston Mill borehole between 1976 and 1983, although this was shut down for reasons relating to industrial contamination (Wilkinson 2011). Furthermore, there had been no previous investigations of past river migration within the area and so it was not clear whether there was any potential for the erosion of buried deposits. Hence, prior to investigation, the state of preservation of organic matter at the site was unknown.

1.3 Archaeological and historical background

The large parish of Sawston lies approximately seven miles south of Cambridge. The western boundary of the parish is formed by the River Cam, which has had a dominant effect upon the development of the settlement (Taylor 1998). Culturally, perhaps the most significant feature has been the Icknield Way, which is likely to have been the major prehistoric thoroughfare bisecting the county of Cambridgeshire from east to west, and which crossed the River Cam in four places within the Parish boundary. Whilst the precise prehistoric origins of the Icknield Way remain debated (Harrison 2003), the potential significance of these river crossings during prehistory is demonstrated by find spots of lithic material dating to the Neolithic period including blades and scrapers. It is also indicated more broadly by the presence of eleven ring ditch features, the surviving remains of Bronze Age barrow monuments, identified from aerial photography in the immediate landscape around the northernmost river crossing. Furthermore, to the north of the site, previous excavations have revealed an extensive middle Bronze Age field system (Mortimer 2006).

Later prehistoric activity within the area is more significant than for earlier periods. Dominating the landscape during this period is the site of Borough Hill, a late Iron Age multivallate fort measuring 8 hectares in extent, which occupies a slight promontory of chalk immediately to the southeast of the excavation area on the banks of the River Cam. The site of Borough Hill was first recognised as an archaeological feature in 1980 and was subsequently identified as a late Iron Age multivallate fort (JSAC 2003). In 1995, the fort was assigned protection as a Scheduled Ancient Monument (SAM No. 24407) and between 1993 and 1997 a number of small archaeological investigations took place in the vicinity of the site including a geophysical survey, an evaluation, fieldwalking, and a watching brief (JSAC 2003). These investigations confirmed the presence of buried archaeological remains but did not provide conclusive dating evidence or significantly increase understanding of the site.

In 2000 an assessment of aerial photographs of a period covering 50 years from 1949 was undertaken (Air Photo Services 2000). This assessment further clarified the layout of Borough Hill through the identification of a 'ringwork' to the south of the site formed by double ditches and banks that was interpreted as forming a defensive enclosure, with the River Cam as its southern boundary. However, no internal features were identified within the enclosure during this assessment. In the same year, a geophysical survey was undertaken in the area of Borough Hill (Fig. 1.3) which also detected a large curving enclosure consisting of two large ditches with a lesser more discontinuous ditch between them (GSB Prospection 2000). This survey also identified internal features including ditches, smaller enclosures and pits. To the northwest and north of the enclosed area (south and east of the site) the survey also detected rectangular enclosures, one of which was cut by the main defences, therefore reflecting earlier activity.

In 2003 an archaeological evaluation was completed within the scheduled monument of Borough Hill to further characterise features identified through the previous aerial photographic and geophysical surveys (JSAC 2003, see Fig. 1.4). The results of this evaluation revealed a chronological sequence of three phases of activity across the three ditches and bank's of what was interpreted as a multivallate Iron Age hillfort. Evidence for domestic occupation, in the form of bone and pottery, was obtained from within the area enclosed by the fort's inner defensive ditch. The evaluation also investigated a rectangular ditched enclosure identified by the geophysical survey. Dating evidence from a period ranging from the Neolithic through to the Bronze and Iron Ages was recovered from the ditches, most of which appeared residual. The enclosure was interpreted as being a small prehistoric settlement or farmstead (JSAC 2003).

The evidence for Roman occupation within the area is sparse, although occasional scatters of artefacts dating to this period such as the Dernford Farm pottery scatter and the rectangular enclosures identified on aerial photographs on the eastern side of the parish, indicate activity was taking place, as does the continued use of the Icknield Way along which many enclosures, villas and settlements were established during this period (Taylor 1998). However, the Anglo-Saxon origins of Sawston are better documented. The first documentary reference to the settlement dates to 970 in the Chronicles of Ramsey Abbey where it was referred to as Salsingetune, a name derived from 'farm of Salse' or 'farm of Salse's people'. One of the predominant factors in deciding the locations of early Anglo-Saxon settlements was their proximity to running water, often following on from a Romano-British settlement on prime fertile land in river valleys (Hamerow 1991), and the earlier Roman river crossings at Sawston may have been a significant factor in the selection of this location for the Anglo-Saxon settlers. In 1816, a single Anglo-Saxon burial was found during excavations at Huckridge Hill, on the Cambridge Road to the north of the village (Taylor 1998). The richly furnished burial containing sword, shield, bronze bowl, and a buckle shaped like a snake head, may have related to the settlement

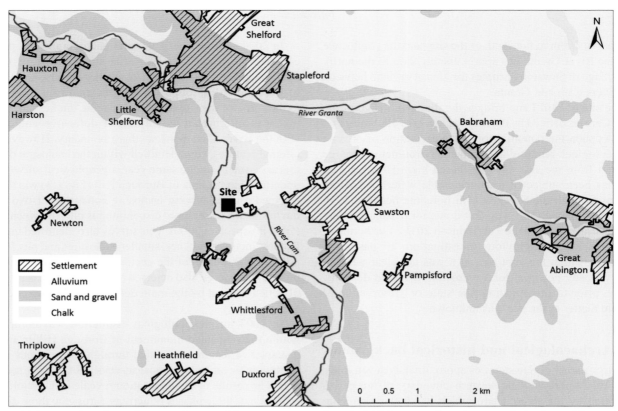

Figure 1.2 Principal geological units and rivers of the region surrounding the Mill Lane site (based on British Geological Survey data).

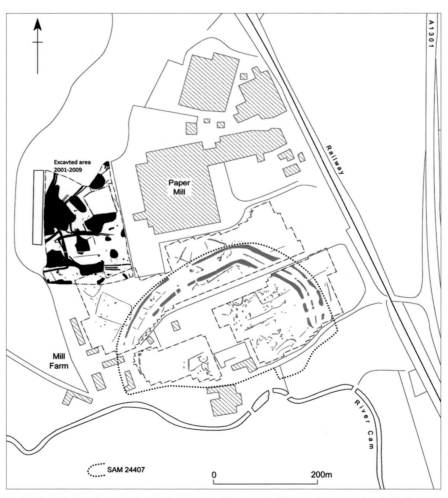

Figure 1.3 Results of the geophysical survey of Burrough Hill undertaken by GSB Prospection.

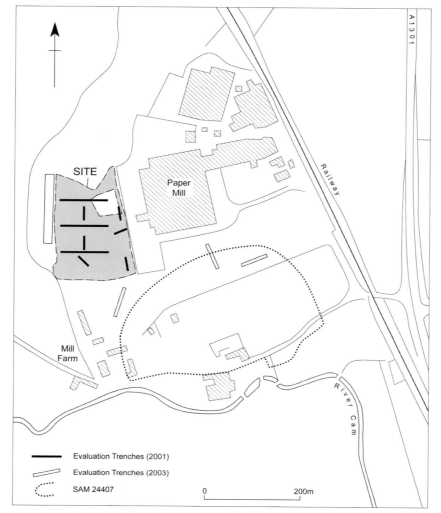

Figure 1.4 Locations of previous excavations within the study area and outline of the SAM.

at Sawston or occupation closer to the river. By the end of the Anglo-Saxon period, the 1086 Domesday Book records three substantial holdings that included three mills.

The parish was largely agricultural from the 11th century until the mid-19th century when the existing paper and leather industries expanded, adding an industrial dimension to the economy with associated mills along the course of the Cam. By the late 19th century, Burrough or Borough Mill (Sawston Mill), grounded on medieval origins, was well established on the north side of the river. It probably derived its name from the Old English *burh* or fortified place, also reflecting the earlier hillfort. Drainage around the mill was quite extensive, attesting to the wet nature of the site. One attempt to deal with the common problem of flooding within the parish is detailed on the Sawston Enclosure Award map of 1811 which depicts a network of existing channels with an additional three planned to be constructed. Waterlogging following a severe flood in 1918 caused a whole row of clay-bat cottages to collapse, while in 1943, 'Italian POWs were used to clear ditches on Deal Moor as they were full and the area was flooding regularly' (Taylor 1998, 74).

The only archaeological investigation within the boundaries of the current site prior to this excavation was

an evaluation in 2001 (Poppy *et al.* 2006; Fig. 1.4). Within the eastern section of the site the evaluation located a series of north–south aligned ditches across the site that appeared to be part of a medieval and post-medieval pattern of drainage and field boundaries. The western part of the site was dominated by palaeochannels associated with the River Cam. Significant palaeoenvironmental remains were recovered which produced evidence ranging from the Mesolithic period through to post-medieval period (JSAC 2001).

The wider landscape context

Within the wider area surrounding the village of Sawston a wealth of archaeological evidence has been unearthed in the last decade building on evidence representing all periods from the Mesolithic onwards (Medlycott and Brown 2008). These have included Neolithic causewayed enclosures at Great Wilbraham and Haddenham (Evans 1988), where a long barrow with a preserved wooden chamber was also discovered. Similarly at Eynesbury a multi-phased monumental landscape on the River Ouse has also been investigated (Ellis *et al.* 2004), and at Haverhill a late Bronze Age rectilinear enclosure has been excavated and a late Bronze Age founder's hoard unearthed (Medlycott and Brown 2008).

At Over, Neolithic occupation and a later Bronze Age paddock system with associated settlement complex lie within the floodplain terraces of the River Great Ouse, as does the Over barrow group. Also falling within the Ouse floodplain, a post-built Neolithic longhouse within a C-shaped enclosure has been excavated at Needingworth alongside a Romano-British field system. At Longstanton Neolithic pit clusters with structured deposition have been recorded as part of a multi-phase landscape that includes evidence for seasonal Bronze Age occupation, an Iron Age farmstead, a Romano-British enclosure, an Anglo-Saxon cemetery and late Anglo-Saxon and medieval field systems (Paul and Hunt 2015). Anglo-Saxon cemeteries have been found at Girton, Haslingford, Barrington and Melbourn and elsewhere, though fewer settlements of the same date have been unearthed.

The village of Sawston lies approximately equidistant between the Roman settlements of Duroliponte (Cambridge) to the north and Great Chesterford to the south, and is surrounded by the network of Roman roads including the named roads of Worstead Street (Via Devana) to the northeast and Ermine Street further to the west (Fig. 1.5).

1.4 Research context and aims

As has been previously demonstrated, river valleys provide considerable potential for the survival of well-preserved archaeological remains reflecting multiple periods of human activity (Knight and Howard 2004; Buteux and Chapman 2009). Furthermore, the interface between the alluvial wetlands and the adjacent drylands provides opportunities for exploring the dynamic interaction between the two through time. Evidence from the previous investigations at Sawston has indicated a high potential for continuous occupation within the landscape, further strengthened by the evidence of past river crossings in the area. Hence, investigations at Mill Lane were focused primarily on understanding the landscape evolution of this area of Cambridgeshire through the identification and recording of archaeological remains. They were also aimed at assessing the potential for wet preservation of organic material, particularly within the context of previous water abstraction near to the site (Wilkinson 2011).

In addition to the broader questions relating to the evolution of this landscape, and within the context of the Research Agenda for Cambridgeshire (Medlycott 2011), three specific research aims relating to the Mill Lane area were defined:

Aim 1: Chronology of occupation at the wetland/ dryland interface

The importance of riparian environments for human activity has been well documented (see above). The location of the site on the edge of the floodplain of the River Cam, in addition to the wider landscape context including the confluence with the River Granta to the north, indicates the high potential for human activity across earlier periods. Previous research in the wider area of Sawston has demonstrated this potential, with evidence for human activity recorded from the Neolithic through to the post-medieval period, although at varying levels of density and certainty. The research framework for the eastern counties (Medlycott 2011) highlights the challenges in understanding the chronology and processes of change through the archaeology of the region. In particular, whilst broad chronologies are understood, the specifics for different periods are less well known. Hence, the project aimed to obtain detailed information relating to chronology through both the application of relative and absolute methods of dating. In particular, the project sought to address the following questions:

- What is the chronological range for human activity at the site? Does it extend earlier than the Neolithic period?
- What evidence is there for continuity of settlement at the site? Specifically, is there evidence for structures relating to the different phases of activity? Are there periods of abandonment? What was the impact (if any) of the Borough Hill fort during later prehistory and succeeding periods?
- What is the nature of waste at the site (*e.g.* the comparison between lithic debitage and tools), and how does this relate to the wider concerns of the local community?

Aim 2: Landscape and environmental context

Similar to the value of establishing tighter chronological information for the area of Sawston, the importance of understanding the landscape and environmental context of the archaeology of different periods has been noted as a strategic research priority for the region (Medlycott 2011). Given the location of the site on the floodplain of the River Cam, the potential for environmental change through time is significant through factors such as river migration and re-working, shifts in groundwater levels, and vegetation change. In terms of human occupation of the area, there is currently no understanding of the relationship between people and their environment during periods of environmental change or stasis. Floodplain deposits commonly provide the potential for the preservation of palaeoenvironmental source material for the reconstruction of past environments, and so the work at Mill Lane provided the potential to address this gap in our understanding through an assessment of the landscape, the palaeoenvironment and the changing relationships between landscape and the human populations who occupied it. Specifically, the following questions were considered throughout the project:

- To what extent has the environment changed throughout the Holocene and how does this relate to human occupation and activities during this period?
- What is the relationship between the River Cam and early human activity during prehistory? To what extent has environmental change (*e.g.* river migration, vegetation change) impacted upon human choice in the area?

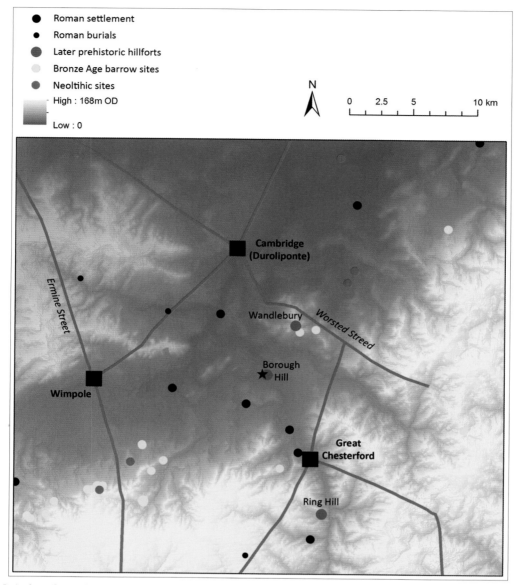

Figure 1.5 Archaeological sites and Roman roads within the wider landscape. Contains OS data © Crown Copeyright.

- To what extent have environmental processes concealed archaeological deposits?
- What is the nature and date of palaeochannels of the River Cam within the study area?

Aim 3: Preservation and archaeological visibility

In addition to the cultural questions relating to the temporal and spatial occupation of the area of Mill Lane, the final aim of the project was to establish baseline data that might assist in the understanding the state of preservation of the site. Furthermore, it provided an opportunity to explore the visibility of archaeology within accreted environments to establish the relationship between the scant evidence from aerial photography and the material remains identified through open area excavation. The potential for the preservation of organic archaeological remains and palaeoenvironmental source material was considered high due to the position of the site crossing the edge of the floodplain. Elsewhere, such environments have produced good evidence for preservation (Brown 1997). However, evidence of groundwater abstraction during the 1970s and early 1980s (Wilkinson 2011) indicated that regional levels might have dropped and this might have had a detrimental impact on the *in situ* preservation of wet-preserved archaeological deposits at the site, although the level of any such impact was unknown.

The physical assessment of the preservation of deposits at Mill Lane therefore had the potential for interpreting the likely levels of wet-preservation within the river system more generally through extrapolation. Hence, this project also aimed to assess the preservation of organic material on site to establish the likely potential along the river network in the region more generally. In particular the project aimed to answer the following questions:

- To what extent are archaeological, wet-preserved organic remains present on the site?

- To what extent are deposits with palaeoenvironmental potential preserved on site? How useful are these for the assessment of different palaeoenvironmental proxies?
- Is there variation in the levels of preservation laterally (*i.e.* with proximity to the River Cam) or vertically with depth?
- Are there factors influencing the archaeological visibility of some periods, such as concealment under colluviation, or factors influencing the efficacy of techniques such as aerial photography?

1.5 Structure of this book

The project design focused on the intensive investigation of the area of the site in relation to the research aims outlined above, and within the context of regional strategic priorities and agendas (Medlycott 2011). The book is essentially divided into three sections. The first section (Chapters 1 and 2) outlines the research background, the aims of the project, and the methodologies applied to address these aims. The next section (Chapters 3–9) presents the results of the work, beginning with an overview of the results of the excavations, presented chronologically (Chapter 3). The finds are presented in the succeeding chapters as follows: prehistoric (4–5), Roman (6), early Anglo-Saxon (7), late Anglo-Saxon to medieval (8). Palaeoenvironmental analyses are presented in Chapter 9.

The third section of the book (Chapters 10–12) presents a discussion of these results. Chapters 10 and 11 explore the results and their significance chronologically, with chapter 10 discussing the prehistoric and Roman period occupation of the wetland/dryland interface, and Chapter 11 the re-occupation of the site during the Anglo-Saxon and later periods, including craft activities, lifestyle, industry and trade activities. The final chapter (Chapter 12) provides an integrated discussion and synthesis of the evidence from all periods and returns to the original aims of the project. It also outlines the wider significance of this research for the region and more broadly.

Chapter 2

Methodologies

2.1 Introduction

This chapter details the methodologies used in the investigation of the site in relation to the aims outlined in Chapter 1. In the following section, the methodologies are mapped directly onto the aims of the project. Within the rest of this chapter, the methods themselves are presented.

At the time of investigation, the site was under arable agriculture. Experience on site and through recent historical records (see Chapter 1) demonstrated that the site had been and remained prone to flooding. Previous land use has been mixed, with potential influence from the woodland of Borough Grove, which, until the late 1970s, covered the northwestern portion of the site. To the east of the site a sewage works is recorded on 1980s Ordnance Survey mapping as 'disused'. These activities had the potential of impacting upon archaeological preservation within adjacent areas of the site. In addition, the evidence of groundwater abstraction between 1976 and 1983 within the vicinity (Wilkinson 2011) may have lowered groundwater levels locally, with the possibility of drying out *in situ* deposits leading to negative effects on any buried wet-preserved remains.

2.2 Mapping aims onto methods

The aims outlined in Chapter 1 comprised the assessment of diachronic human occupation and other activities within the area and, specifically, the refinement of chronology, the exploration of the landscape and environmental context, and the assessment of preservation across the site. Due to the limitations of traditional methods of aerial photography and remote sensing within accreting landscapes, the project centred on an open-area excavation strategy that would reveal all archaeological deposits. In addition to excavation, a range of other methods were applied to the site including the analysis of finds, palaeoenvironmental research and a programme of absolute dating. The specifics of the different approaches used within the project can be explored in relation to each of the aims.

Aim 1: Chronology of occupation at the wetland/dryland interface

As outlined in Chapter 1, the objectives underlying this aim were to explore the chronological range of human activity at the site, including the earliest activity, and to establish whether this occupation was continuous or punctuated by periods of abandonment. It was also intended to explore the spatial patterns of waste and tools and to establish whether there were any environmental factors influencing archaeological visibility, such as resulting from alluviation or colluviation.

In order to address these objectives, the open area excavation methodology was chosen in order to gain a continuous understanding of the site so that it might be possible to identify whether it reflected continuous or punctuated occupation. It also provided the opportunity to identify all archaeological deposits within the area to establish the full chronological range of human activity. In order to better understand the chronology of the site and to have the potential for investigating the more subtle phasing within periods, a range of relative and absolute dating methods were used. In addition to stratigraphic analysis, all finds, including lithics, ceramics, animal bone, antler, coins and building materials were analysed by specialists. Absolute dating methods focused on the application of radiocarbon dating. No suitable objects for dendrochronological dating were recovered during excavation.

Aim 2: Landscape and environmental context

In order to address the objectives around the landscape and environmental context of the site, a programme of onsite and laboratory-based palaeoenvironmental approaches were used, in addition to cartographic analysis. These approaches comprised onsite stratigraphic analysis from excavation and boreholes to establish the geoarchaeology of palaeochannels and other features (including levels of alluviation and colluviation). Laboratory methods included the analysis of pollen, coleoptera, charcoal and plant macrofossils sampled from different locations and depths across the site. In addition, the programme of radiocarbon dating was applied to establish the dates of the palaeochannels and other features and to establish the chronology for environmental change.

Aim 3: Preservation, management and archaeological visibility

The assessment of preservation focused on the survival of both archaeological remains and palaeoenvironmental source material. The excavation provided the potential for identifying wet-preserved organic archaeological remains and, where found, the state of their preservation was assessed by the relevant specialist. For palaeoenvironmental source material, deposits were assessed visually in the field, but a more detailed study was carried out on samples for the assessment of the preservation of pollen, coleoptera and plant macrofossils.

2.3 Methods

2.3.1 Excavation and recording

Previous work around the Mill Lane site included an aerial photographic survey (Air Photo Services 2000) and geophysical survey (GSB Prospection 2000) in 2000 (see Fig. 1.3), and excavations in 2003 (JSAC 2003; see Fig. 1.4), all focused on the area of Burrough Hill. The only previous investigations within the study area consisted of an archaeological evaluation in 2001 (JSAC 2001; Poppy *et al.* 2006) which explored a sample of the site through the excavation of nine trenches (see Fig. 1.4). This work identified palaeochannels of the River Cam on the western side of the site and evidence of medieval and post-medieval drains and field boundaries, but the sampling nature of the trench array restricted detailed understanding of these features.

Building on this previous work, the approach at Mill Lane focused on open area excavation of the site. This excavation exposed more than 3ha (approximately 31,350 square metres)

of land, encompassing areas of both floodplain deposits and the adjacent dryland. One area, measuring approximately 2,300 square metres was not excavated towards the north of the site due to contamination.

The process of excavation commenced with the removal of all topsoil and modern overburden in strips using two 360° tracked mechanical excavators with toothless ditching buckets, under direct archaeological supervision, down to the top of the uppermost archaeological horizon or the subsoil. Subsequent cleaning and excavation was by hand (Fig. 2.1). All archaeological features were sampled to define their character, stratigraphic relationships and to recover artefactual remains using the following strategy:

- 100% of structural remains and areas of significant and specific activity
- 50% of pits under 1.5m or postholes
- 25% of pits over 1.5m including a complete section
- 25% sample of linear/curvilinear features under 5m in length
- 10% sample of linear/curvilinear features over 5m in length

The area of the excavation was set out and subsequently mapped using a Leica Differential GPS system accurate to sub-centimetre allowing all records to be referenced to the Ordnance Survey National Grid. Within this reference system, features were planned by hand at a scale of 1:20 or 1:50 as appropriate, and sections drawn of all cut features and significant vertical stratigraphy at a scale of 1:10.

Figure 2.1 Photograph of the site following initial stripping, facing northwest.

A comprehensive written record was maintained using a continuous numbered context system on *pro-forma* cards. Written records and scale plans were supplemented by photographs using black and white monochrome, colour slide and digital photography.

Single context recording enabled the construction of a Harris matrix detailing all chronological relationships across the site which was augmented throughout the project following radiocarbon dating and the identification and typological dating of finds.

All recovered archaeological finds were cleaned, marked, documented and stored, and where any remedial conservation work was required it was undertaken. Treatment of all finds conformed to appropriate guidance, such as *First Aid for Finds* (Watkinson and Neal 1998). All artefacts were subsequently assessed, analysed and reported on by an appropriately qualified specialist (see below).

2.3.2 On-site sampling

The importance of establishing the relationship between people and their environment through time (Aim 2) and of understanding the nature of preservation across the site (Aim 3), was felt critical for specialist advice and sampling on-site. Therefore, all buried soils and sediment sequences were inspected and recorded on site by specialists from Birmingham Archaeo-environmental (BAe). On-site examination of soil sediments conformed to guidelines set out in *Geoarchaeology: using earth sciences to understand the archaeological record* (English Heritage 2004).

Deposits were sampled for retrieval and assessment of the preservation conditions and potential for analysis of biological remains. The environmental sampling policy followed the guidelines outlined in *Environmental Archaeology: a guide to the theory and practice of methods, from sampling and recovery to post-excavation* (English Heritage 2002). Sampling strategies for wooden structures conformed to guidelines set out in *Waterlogged wood: Guidelines on the recording, sampling, conservation and curation of waterlogged wood* (Brunning 1996). The palaeochannel monolith and column samples were taken by specialists from BAe.

2.3.3 Analysis of lithic material
(by Barry John Bishop)

As with all finds analyses, the lithic analysis was undertaken over two stages. The first assessed the research potential of lithic material (Bishop 2010), whilst the second consisted of full analysis and reporting (see Chapter 4). Each piece of struck flint was examined by eye and at 10× magnification, and catalogued by context according to its basic typological/ technological attributes. All measurements of the lithic material followed the methodology outlined by Saville (1980). The characteristics of each of the industries were identified and described, and then these were assessed in terms of their wider significance in relation to broader themes of prehistoric occupation and flintworking practices within

the area. In addition to the assessment reporting in Chapter 4, further details of the assemblage are contained within the catalogue of the struck material, detailed by individual context, and presented as Appendix 1.

2.3.4 Analysis of the prehistoric pottery
(by Ann Woodward)

The pottery was recorded and analysed according to the *Guidelines* of the Prehistoric Ceramics Research Group (PCRG 1995). A detailed record of the occurrence of pottery, including information on context type, number of sherds, weight, sherd type, fabric, rim and base diameters, conjoins and abrasion, was undertaken and is summarised in a series of Excel databases. The colour of exterior surface, core and interior surface was also recorded for each vessel or sherd.

The system of fabric codes employed included an initial letter for each inclusion type: F for flint, G for grog, S for sand and Sh for shell. Density was coded as sparse, medium or dense (1 to 3) and fragment size as small, medium or large (S, M, L). Also recorded was the degree of hardness for each vessel or sherd, and the incidence of soapy and other unusual fabric textures. Most of the Earlier Neolithic fabrics contained inclusions which were angular in shape and ill-sorted within the matrix, and this diagnostic feature could be employed to assign small and otherwise undiagnostic sherds to that period. A series of eight samples of pottery was selected for petrographic examination, the aim being to investigate the nature and possible origin of the perceived fabric types in more detail. The samples included seven from Earlier Neolithic vessels, and one from a Beaker of Late Neolithic/Early Bronze Age date; full discussion of this material is provided in Chapter 5.

2.3.5 Analysis of the post-Roman pottery
(by Sue Anderson)

Quantification of the post-Roman pottery was carried out using sherd count, weight and estimated vessel equivalent (EVE). The minimum number of vessels (MNV) within each context was also recorded, but cross-fitting was not attempted unless particularly distinctive vessels were observed in more than one context. A full quantification by fabric, context and feature is available in the archive. All fabric codes were assigned from the author's post-Roman fabric series, which includes East Anglian and East Midlands fabrics, as well as imported wares. Early Anglo-Saxon fabric groups have been characterised by major inclusions. Form terminology and dating for early Anglo-Saxon pottery follows Myres (1977) and Hamerow (1993). Form terminology for medieval and later pottery follows guidelines from the Medieval Pottery Research Group (MPRG 1998). Recording uses a system of letters for fabric codes together with number codes for ease of sorting in database format.

In total, 853 sherds of post-Roman pottery, weighing a collective total of 9108g, were collected during the evaluation and excavation. The pottery was generally in good condition, although almost a third of the assemblage showed a degree of abrasion. The average sherd weight for the whole assemblage was relatively high at 10.7g. The full reporting on the post-Roman pottery assemblage is provided in Chapters 7 and 8.

2.3.6 The ceramic building material
(by Sue Anderson)

The ceramic building material collected during the excavations was quantified by context, fabric and type, using fragment count and weight in grams. Fabrics were identified on the basis of macroscopic appearance and main inclusions. The thicknesses of bricks were measured, but roof tile thicknesses were only measured when another dimension was available. Roman forms were identified with the aid of Brodribb (1987). The presence of burning, combing, finger marks and other surface treatments was recorded. Roman tile thicknesses were measured and for flanged tegulae, the form of flange was noted and its width and external height were measured.

In total, 103 fragments of ceramic building material, weighing a total of 10,186g and representing 76 bricks/tiles, were collected from 25 contexts on the site during the evaluation and excavation. The ceramic building material collected from site primarily represents Roman period activity, although medieval and post-medieval material was also identified. Table 2.1 shows the quantification of all of the ceramic building material by type and form.

This ceramic building material was divided into basic fabric groups based on major inclusions. Fifteen different fabrics were identified in this assemblage:

Estuarine fabrics (medieval)

These fabrics are extremely variable in colour, density and degree of firing/hardness; bricks made from estuarine clays are common throughout the southeast of England and have been described in detail by Drury (1993b). They were rare in this assemblage.

est   Coarse estuarine fabric in varying colours (pink, purple, yellow, often within a single brick), tempered with coarse organic (voids), ferrous and calcareous inclusions. Brick and roof tile. 7 pieces, 334g.

Red sandy fabrics (Roman and medieval to post-medieval)

These fabrics generally have a similar range of coarse, naturally occurring, local inclusions (ferrous oxide, clay pellets, flint, chalk), often as a background scatter, and have been divided on the basis of quartz sand grain size or abundance. Fabrics 'ms' and 'fs' were generally allocated unless pieces showed a clear difference in size or abundance of other inclusions.

fs   Fine sandy red fabric with few coarse inclusions. Includes Roman, box flue and roof tile. Mainly Roman, some post-medieval. 24 pieces, 1065g.

ms   Medium sandy red fabric with few other inclusions. Roman tile of all types and some roof tile. Roman and later. 23 pieces, 2859g.

fsc   Fine sandy with sparse calcareous inclusions. Roman tile and flanged *tegulae*. Roman. 5 pieces, 801g.

fscp/mscp   Fine/medium sandy red fabric with common red clay pellets, often soft with mica. Roman tile of all types. Roman. 20 pieces, 3332g.

fsf/msf   Fine sandy red fabrics coarse flint. Roof tile, late brick and Roman tile. Roman and post-medieval. 8 pieces, 790g.

fsm   Fine sandy soft pale orange-red fabric with common mica. Roman and box flue tile. Roman. 2 pieces, 100g.

msfe   Medium sandy with moderate to common small red ferrous inclusions. Roman tile. Roman. 1 piece, 36g.

msffe   As 'msf' with occasional coarse ferrous inclusions. Roman, box flue and roof tile. Roman and later. 6 pieces, 327g.

msv   As 'ms' with common voids, possibly from leached calcarous inclusions. Roman tile. 1 piece, 118g.

Table 2.1 Ceramic building material by type and form.

Type	Form	Code	No.	Wt (g)	Min No.
Roman	Roman tile	RBT	49	5396	39
	Box flue tile	BOX	16	1822	12
	Flanged *tegula*	FLT	8	1125	6
	Imbrex	IMB	3	65	2
Post-Roman	Roof tile	RT	15	670	12
	Early brick	EB	6	309	2
	Late brick	LB	5	625	2
	Air brick	AB	1	174	1
Total			103	10,186	76

Red sandy with 'grog' (post-medieval)

Tiles of this type often have the same background scatter of local inclusions as noted above, but with the addition of varying degrees of 'grog'.

fsg   Fine sandy red fabric with sparse to moderate fine to coarse angular 'grog'. Roof tile. post-medieval. 1 piece, 55g.

White fabrics (late medieval to post-medieval)

Gault clay fabrics with varying degrees of ferrous inclusions.

wfs/wms   White-firing fine/medium sandy fabrics with few inclusions. Roof tile and air brick. Post-medieval. 4 pieces, 297g.

In addition to the above, 14 red-firing fragments recovered from samples were too small to be assigned to any fabric.

2.3.7 The palaeoenvironmental analyses
(by E-J Hopla, B. Gearey, E. Reilly and R. McKenna)

Laboratory analyses of palaeoenvironmental samples focused on the examination of Coleoptera (beetles), plant macrofossils and sub-fossil pollen. The processes of sample preparation and analyses followed established guidelines:

Coleoptera and plant macrofossils

Seven bulk samples were processed using methods described by Kenward *et al.* (1980). This involved paraffin flotation in order to extract any insect remains, with plant remains then being extracted by means of a 'washover' to concentrate the lighter, organic fraction. Insect identification was carried out using published keys, online resources, the author's own specimens and the Gorham and Girling collections of Coleoptera housed at the Department of Classics, Ancient History and Archaeology at the University of Birmingham. The full species list appears in Appendix 2 (Table A2.1). Taxonomy follows Böhme (2005) (a revision of Lucht 1987) as used by BugsCEP, the Coleopteran Ecology Package, designed and maintained by Philip and Paul Buckland (Buckland 2007; Buckland and Buckland 2006).

Insect species were subsequently grouped into habitat groups, related on ecology or major food source, primarily using BugsCEP as a source for ecological/habitat data (Buckland and Buckland 2006) along with other published keys. Basic statistics for these groups are given in Appendix 2 (Table A2.2), and all subsequent analysis is based on these results

The aquatic element of the assemblages was excluded from the final calculations. This is in order to remove the 'swamping' effect of such species on assemblages accumulating in features thought to have once contained bodies of water. Insects that have not been identified to species and whose genera are highly eurytopic in habitat terms were also excluded ('varied' group). The index of diversity, a statistical representation of the species diversity within an assemblage, was also calculated (Appendix 2; Table A2.2). Due to the small number of samples no further statistical tests were deemed appropriate for these assemblages.

The components of the fraction were recorded whilst wet and the flots were examined for plant remains under a low-power binocular microscope at magnifications between 12× and 40×. A four point semi quantitative scale was used, from '1' – one or a few remains (less than an estimated six per kg of raw sediment) to '4' – abundant remains (many specimens per kg or a major component of the matrix). Data were recorded on paper and subsequently using an MS Access database. For technical reasons the convention 'sp(p)' to denote that more than one species was or may have been present, is used throughout, even where only one specimen of the taxon was recorded (and thus only one species could have been present). For plant remains, '*cf.*' is used to indicate a 'best guess' as to the identity of fossil specimens (Appendix 2; Tables A2.3, A2.4 and A2.5).

Pollen

A total of 18 subsamples (Appendix 2, Table A2.6) were prepared for pollen assessment using standard techniques including potassium hydroxide (KOH) digestion, hydrofluoric acid (HF) treatment and acetylation (Moore *et al.* 1991). At least 125 total land pollen (TLP) grains excluding aquatics and spores were counted for each sample. However, pollen concentrations were very low in eleven of the samples (TpD: 0.50, 0.66 and 0.88m; TPB: 0.24 and 0.40m; TPC: 0m, 0.16m, 0.96m, 1.12m, 1.28m and 1.43m) for which full counts were not possible. The results of the assessments are detailed in Chapter 9.

2.3.8 Analysis of the animal bones
(by Matilda Holmes)

Animal bones from securely dated Anglo-Saxon contexts were recorded and analysed (see Appendix 3). All those of early Anglo-Saxon date were from a pit within sunken featured building (SFB) 1073 (see Chapter 3). Bones were also recovered from other possible SFBs that could only be dated to the Anglo-Saxon period as a whole. Because the animal economy of the *c.* 600 years that the Anglo-Saxon period spans was so varied, only the bones of early Anglo-Saxon date were considered in detail.

Bones were identified using the author's reference collection. Due to anatomical similarities between sheep and goat, bones of this type were assigned to the category 'sheep/goat', unless a definite identification (Prummel and Frisch 1986; Payne 1985) could be made. Bones that could not be identified to species were, where possible, categorised according to the relative size of the animal represented (small – rodent/rabbit sized; medium – sheep/pig/dog size; or large – cattle/horse size). The maxilla, zygomatic arch and occipital areas of the skull were identified from cranial fragments.

Tooth wear and eruption were recorded using guidelines from Grant (1982) and Silver (1969), as were bone fusion (Amorosi 1989; Silver 1969), metrical data (von den Driesch 1976), anatomy, side, zone (Serjeantson 1996) and any evidence of pathological changes, butchery (Lauwerier 1988; Sykes 2007) and working. The condition of bones was also noted on a scale of 1–5, where 1 is perfectly preserved and 5, where the bone is so badly degraded to be unrecognisable (Lyman 1994, 355). Other taphonomic factors were also recorded, including the incidence of burning, gnawing, recent breakage and refitted fragments. All fragments were recorded, although articulated or associated fragments were entered as a count of 1, so they did not bias the relative frequency of species present. Details of articulated bones were recorded in a separate table.

A number of sieved samples were collected but because of the highly fragmentary nature of such samples a selective process was undertaken, whereby fragments were recorded only if they could be identified to species and/or element, or showed signs of taphonomic processing.

2.3.9 Radiocarbon dating

Six sub-samples from the palaeoenvironmental analyses were submitted for radiocarbon dating to BETA, Florida (see Appendix 2; Table A2.8). Sub-samples were taken from the peat in Test Pit B at 0.03–0.05m, 0.25–0.27m, 0.38m and 0.58–0.63m (base), and from the peat in Test Pit D at 0.64m and 0.91m (base). Each sample underwent acid/alkali/acid pre-treatment prior to dating and was calibrated using INTCAL04.

CHAPTER 3

THE EXCAVATIONS

3.1 Introduction: phasing and chronology

This chapter provides an overview of the results of the evaluation and excavation at Mill Lane, Sawston. The archaeological remains are presented in terms of phases of activity, informed by the combination of methods outlined in Chapter 2, including artefactual and stratigraphic data collected throughout the archaeological investigations. Full descriptions of the artefacts are provided in subsequent chapters (Chapters 4–8). Overall site phasing was established through the generation of stratigraphic matrices which also highlighted any obvious residual finds. The occupational remains across the site are briefly described in this chapter, but are more comprehensively discussed and interpreted in Chapters 10–11.

Seven phases of complex archaeological activity were identified ranging from the Mesolithic to the post-medieval periods. These phases are:

- Phase 1 – Mesolithic (*c.* 10,000–4,000 BC)
- Phase 2 – early to middle Neolithic (*c.* 4,000–2,700 BC)
- Phase 3 – late Neolithic/early Bronze Age (*c.* 2,400–1,800 BC)
- Phase 4 – Roman (*c.* AD 43–410)
- Phase 5 – early Anglo-Saxon (5th and 6th centuries AD)
- Phase 6 – medieval (11th to 14th centuries AD)
- Phase 7 – post-medieval (15th to 20th centuries AD)

3.2 Survival and preservation

The features demonstrated a varied degree of preservation and the clarity of the interface between feature cuts and the natural geology was moderate at best, potentially reflecting processes of bioturbation, but also the similarities in materials. The shallow depth of subsoil could indicate that truncation has occurred due to medieval and post-medieval episodes of ploughing. The site was frequently inundated with standing water caused by a high water table and wet weather conditions. Evidence suggesting that the site had been subjected to frequent flooding, included a network of re-cut drainage ditches apparently dating to between the 12th and 14th centuries (Poppy *et al.* 2006). However, due to the significant periods of water extraction (*e.g.* the Sawston Mill borehole, Wilkinson 2011) the level of organic preservation at the site was greatly affected.

3.3 Site narrative

3.3.1 Phase 1 – Mesolithic (10,000–4,000 BC)

Mesolithic activity was identified in the northern part of the excavation (Fig. 3.1). Although no cut features which specifically related to this period were uncovered, a number of significant residual finds were retrieved, including a tranchet axe, two microliths and a micro burin (see Chapter 4). Radiocarbon dating from the humic peat deposits at the base of palaeochannel 1585 also suggests this material began to aggrade during this phase (see Chapter 9 for discussion of the palaeochannel features).

3.3.2 Phase 2 – early to middle Neolithic (4,000–2,700 BC)

The earliest archaeological features within the excavated area relate to a number of concentrations of pottery sherds which have been spot-dated to the early-mid Neolithic period (Chapter 5). A distinctive, irregularly shaped arcing spread of material (1066, Fig. 3.2) situated in the extreme southwestern area of the site along with four postholes (1103, 1327, 1329 and 1338) contained pottery and a large quantity of worked lithics. The presence of two east–west aligned gullies (1113/1115 and 1338) situated immediately to the south of spread 1066 may suggest further evidence of contemporaneous activity. The shallow depth of subsoil afforded little protection to the archaeology in that area of the site and other features may have been lost during ploughing.

Another possible example of human activity dating to this period was provided by an irregular curving feature which may have represented the remains of a shallow ditch (1254/1532/1547) aligned roughly northeast–southwest close to the eastern edge of the excavated area. A strip representing approximately 10m of the ditch had survived; it generally measured 3m in width and the edges sloped very gradually to a flattish base. The potential ditch was filled by a mid grey-brown sandy clay-silt which contained a number of pieces of burnt flint. The feature measured between 0.23–0.38m in depth and significant quantities of pottery and worked flint were recovered (1511, 1512, 1545, 1546 and 1583). It was also noted during excavation that some of the pieces of pottery appeared to have worked flint directly beneath them.

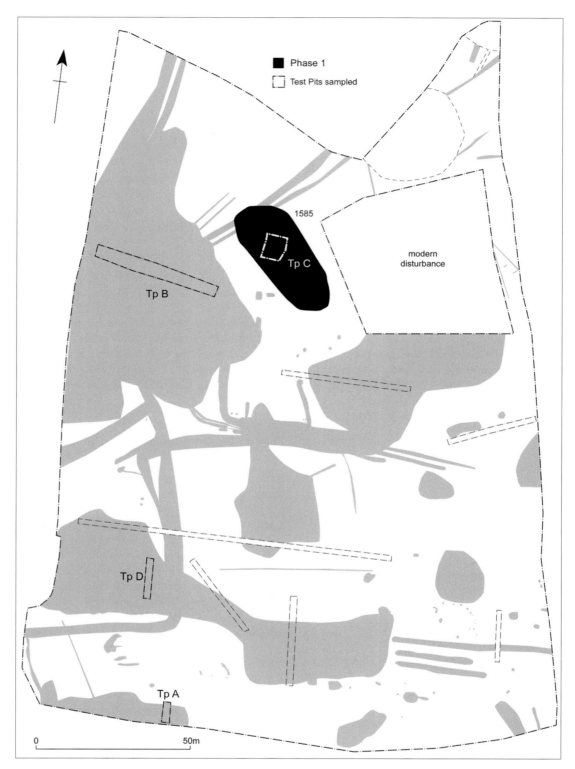

Figure 3.1 Areas of Mesolithic activity identified on site.

It is probable that peat accumulation continued in palaeochannel 1585 through the Neolithic, and radiocarbon dating of the lower sequence from palaeochannel 1299/1302 suggests accumulation of peat deposits began in this phase and that this feature became cut off (perhaps as an oxbow lake) from the main channel of the River Cam (see Chapter 9).

3.3.3 Phase 3 – late Neolithic to early Bronze Age (2,400–1,800 BC)

Further evidence of possible archaeological activity was provided by a shallow linear feature (1187/1189, Fig. 3.3) situated in the southeastern area of the site and following a northwest–southeast alignment. It appeared to be the

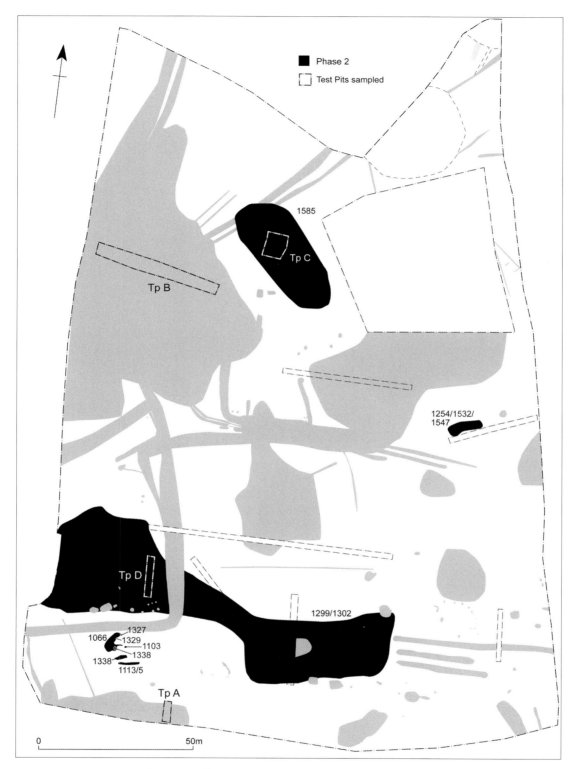

Figure 3.2 Areas of early to middle Neolithic activity identified on site.

remains of a ditch, although the slope at the edges was almost imperceptible, perhaps indicating the impression created by a walkway. The light brown silty clay-sand infill (1186) contained a number of pottery sherds spot-dated to the late Neolithic period (see Chapter 5). A narrow, undated ditch (1063/1076) ran parallel to this feature. Both appeared to continue in a southeasterly direction beyond the edge of the excavated area.

The eastern side of the excavated area appeared to be characterized by shallow archaeological remains, as evidence of activity during this period had been reduced in depth by subsequent ploughing. To the north of ditch 1187/1189

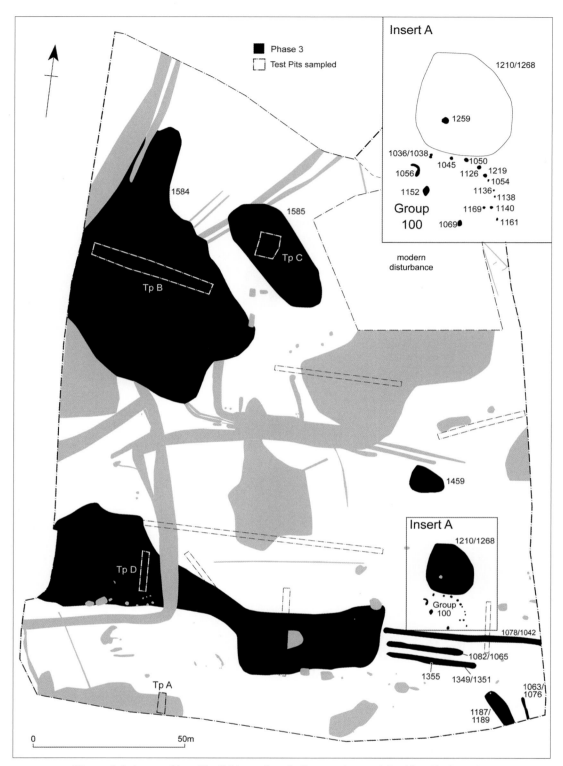

Figure 3.3 Areas of late Neolithic and early Bronze Age activity identified on site.

three equidistant, east–west aligned shallow ditches were uncovered. The two shorter and less well defined features (1349/1351 and 1082/1065) had apparently been truncated by ploughing, although possible structural evidence was provided by a shallow posthole (1355) on the southern edge of ditch 1351. Pottery dating to the late Neolithic and worked flint was retrieved from the fill of one of the ditch sections (1081) and

the most northerly ditch (1078/1042/1008/1024) contained a large amount of worked flint including tools, notably a superbly worked Mesolithic axe head (1041). The ditch, which continued to the east beyond the excavated area and which may represent a boundary line, may have demarcated the southern border of an area of settlement signified by a distinctive arc of postholes and small post pits (Group 100; Fig. 3.3).

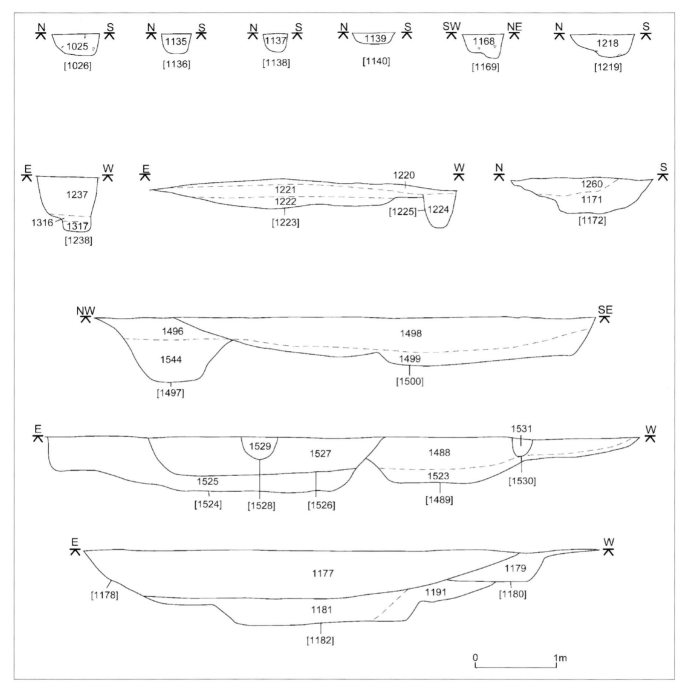

Figure 3.4 Sections through late Neolithic and early Bronze Age features.

The sub-circular and circular features ranged between 0.30–0.65m in diameter and 0.09–0.30m in depth and appear to denote the northern and eastern edges of a possible roundhouse. A number of the features contained pieces of late Neolithic flint, notably possible post-pit (1045) which was filled with dark grey charcoal rich silty sand (1043), probably signifying the remains of a degraded post, positioned against the southern edge of the cut. A number of the postholes on the eastern edge of the structure (1136, 1138, 1140, 1169 and 1219; Fig. 3.4) were sealed by a shallow orange brown layer of silty sand (1141) which contained a number of flint blades

and flakes. No evidence of an internal structure or any signs of a hearth were revealed within the arc of postholes. The slight remains of a possible shallow curvilinear gully (1056) were situated to the northwest of pit 1052 although it had been heavily truncated, apparently by ploughing.

A sub-circular layer/spread of mid grey-brown sandy clay-silt (1210/1268) measuring approximately 18 × 23m in diameter was located immediately to the north of the arc of pits and postholes. The layer possibly represented a buried soil or ploughed out barrow or midden and was investigated with a series of test pits which produced worked flints and pottery. The finds were evenly distributed throughout layer 1210/1268 which measured between 0.23–0.34m in depth. The edges sloped very gradually and perhaps implied that the material had been preserved as it had accumulated in the remains of a hollow. A solitary irregularly shaped pit (1259) was exposed on removal of layer 1210/1268. It measured 1.15m × 0.85m and 0.48m in depth and was filled with dark grey-brown silty sand (1258) which contained a worked flint

Another comparable layer/spread of a possible buried soil (1459) was uncovered approximately 30m to the northwest of layer 1210/1268. A number of worked flints and pottery sherds were recovered from layer 1459 during cleaning. Four test pits were cut through the mid grey-brown sandy clay-silt (1465–1468) which was sealed by a shallow layer of subsoil (1001) and directly overlay the natural reddish orange silty sand (1002). Despite the fact that the layer measured no more than 0.08–0.10m in depth, a significant amount of flint and pottery was retrieved.

It is probable that peat accumulation continued in palaeochannels 1585 and 1299/1302 and radiocarbon dating of the lower sequence from palaeochannel 1584 suggests accumulation of peat deposits began in this phase (see Chapter 9).

3.3.4 Phase 4 – Roman (AD 43–410)

The vast majority of the Roman finds recovered across the site were residual, notably those retrieved from the infills of the early Anglo-Saxon sunken-featured buildings (see section 3.3.5 below). However a large ditch (1485) which ran on a northeast–southwest alignment beyond the western edge of the site (Fig. 3.5), and had been truncated by a post-medieval (phase 7) enclosure ditch (group 104), did produce Roman finds, notably a large piece of mortarium combined with small fragments of possible Roman pottery and two small pieces of pottery dated to the 11th–12th century. In the absence of other datable finds and the differing alignment from the ditches dated to the medieval period, ditch 1485 can perhaps be given a provisional Roman date. A small number of Roman pottery sherds were also retrieved from a spread/layer of brown sandy silty clay (1390), which was excavated in the central-southern area of the site.

3.3.5 Phase 5 – early Anglo-Saxon (5th and 6th centuries AD)

Four features interpreted as Anglo-Saxon sunken-featured buildings were located to the south of the site, close to the large palaeochannel 1299/1302 (Fig. 3.6). The mid brown sandy clay-silt (1064), which formed the uppermost layer in the sequence of alluvial deposits of 1299/1302, had been cut by the northern edge of the smallest of the buildings (1170; Fig. 3.7). It measured 3.00m in length and 2.60m wide; three postholes (1208, 1289 and 1291) were exposed, aligned east–west and positioned down the centre of the structure. The posts had apparently rotted away, as only the bases of the cuts were visible, and a number of sherds of pottery were retrieved (1207, 1288 and 1290). The sunken-featured

building had been filled with dark grey-brown silty clay sand (1067) measuring 0.35m in depth and containing frequent sherds of early Anglo-Saxon pottery, along with animal bone and brick/tile. A small amount of residual Roman pottery and tile was also recovered, dating to the later period of Roman occupation (see Chapter 6).

A second, larger sunken-featured building (1132; Fig. 3.7) was located 3.50m to the east of 1170. The sub-rectangular structure (1132) measured 3.90m by 3.00m and 0.34m in depth and, in common with structure 1170 had quite steeply sloping sides and a flat base (see Fig. 3.8). Here too, the associated postholes had rotted away and were not visible during excavation until the bottoms of the cuts were identified below the level of sunken floor. The bases of five circular and sub-circular postholes were uncovered cut through the dark grey-brown silty clay sand (1088) which filled the feature. Three of the posthole cuts (1134, 1250 and 1293) were positioned towards the western end of the structure, and two (1252 and 1383) were located at the eastern side. A small truncated pit (1304) had cut the eastern edge of the building and had in turn been cut by posthole 1383 and small pit 1385. An assemblage of finds was recovered from the structure. The infill (1088) of the sunken-featured building contained a large amount of pottery dating to the early Anglo-Saxon period.

The largest of the sunken-featured buildings (1074; Fig. 3.9) was uncovered approximately 35m to the east of sunken-featured building 1132. It was sub-circular in shape and measured 5.10m in length, 3.50m in width and 0.27m in depth. It had been cut into the natural silty sand (1002). Sunken-featured building 1074 was filled with mid grey-brown silty clay-sand (1073) which contained a significant amount of early Anglo-Saxon pottery in addition to a small amount of residual late Neolithic and Roman pottery. The bases of four posthole cuts (1101, 1110, 1119 and 1149 were uncovered in close proximity at the western end of the sunken-featured building Three more postholes (1245, 1247 and 1270 were grouped at the eastern end and a single posthole (1243) towards the northern edge. The postholes were sub-circular and sub-rectangular with 'U'-shaped profiles and ranged between 0.23–0.50m in diameter with between 0.20–0.35m of the depth visible in section. The eastern side of the sunken-featured building (1074) had clipped the edge of an east–west aligned linear gully (1344). The gully was probably directly associated with the structure and may have served as drainage. It was filled with a dark grey-brown clay-silt (1343) which contained early Anglo-Saxon pottery, animal bone and a residual sherd of Roman pottery dating to the 1st or 2nd century.

A group of features (group 103) comprising sub-circular and circular pits was identified in the immediate vicinity of the sunken-featured building 1074 (Fig. 3.6). The majority of the features were comparable in size and profile, ranging between 0.45–0.65m in diameter and 0.15–0.20m in depth with bowl-shaped profiles. One of the pits of particular interest (1238) was situated to the northeast of structure 1074. It was much deeper than the aforementioned pits, measuring 0.75m in depth and 0.90 × 0.80m in diameter

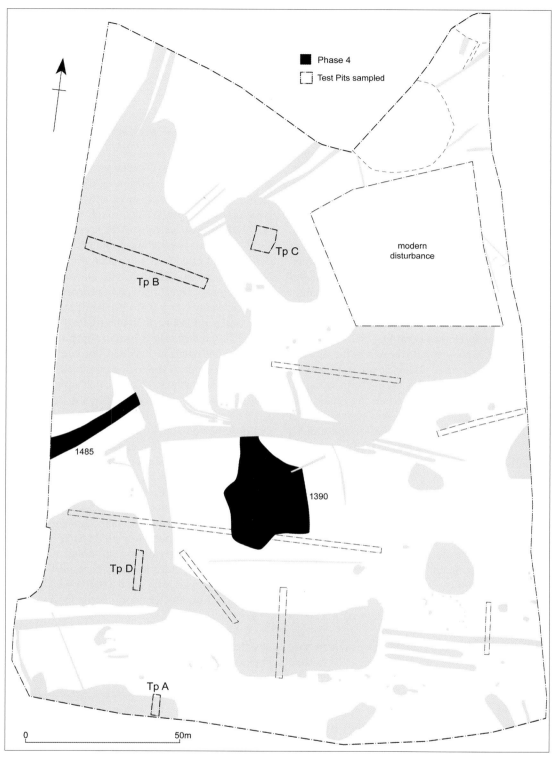

Figure 3.5 Areas of Roman period activity identified on site.

and had very steeply sloping sides with a distinctive stepped profile (Fig. 3.4). The lower fill (1317), re-deposited sandy clay, was sealed by dark-grey silty sand (1316) which was high in charcoal and ash content and included animal bone. The upper pit fill (1237) contained a significant amount of pottery spot-dated to the early Anglo-Saxon period,

also frequent pieces of animal bone. A shallow elongated northwest–southeast-aligned feature (1205) situated between sunken-featured buildings 1132 and 1074 might have been the base of a hearth. It was filled with light grey silty sand (1206) and contained a sherd of early Anglo-Saxon pottery.

A fourth sunken-featured building (1223; Fig. 3.10) was

located approximately 30m to the north of the others. It was comparable in shape and size with sub-circular sunken-featured building 1074. The position of the structure was also related to the large 'channel', which meandered east–west across the southern area of the site. However, it had been cut through the northern edge of the uppermost channel deposit 1064. The building measured 4.00m × 3.60m, was 0.30m in depth, and contained a primary and secondary fill (numbered 1222 and 1221 respectively). It had been sealed by a thin layer of mid grey-brown silty clay-sand (1220). A substantial amount of early Anglo-Saxon pottery was recovered from the dark grey-brown upper fill (1221), also residual Roman and late Neolithic pottery, tile and animal bone. Three fairly substantial circular postholes (1225, 1310 and 1357) were exposed aligned east–west and positioned roughly across the middle of the building, measuring between 0.38–0.50m in diameter and 0.30–0.55m in depth. A shallow gully extended along the line of the postholes and could indicate and internal partition or support beam for the floor. The dark grey sandy clay-silt (1224) which filled posthole 1225 contained early Anglo-Saxon pottery

A possible fifth sunken-featured building (1018; see Fig. 3.6) was located approximately 40m to the east of the sunken-featured building 1223 described above. It was sub-circular in shape measured 3.40m by 2.55m and 0.16m in depth. The feature had probably been truncated during ploughing; evidence suggesting a former structure was provided by a posthole (1020) which was located just inside the eastern edge of the cut. The finds retrieved from the mid grey-brown silty clay-sand infill of the structure (1019) indicated an early Anglo-Saxon date.

A sub-circular feature (1381) in association with two postholes (1377 and 1379) possibly represented a sixth sunken-featured building and was evidently contemporary with the aforementioned series of structures. It was situated approximately 70m to the north of possible sunken-featured building 1018 and was comparable in size and composition (Fig. 3.6). It measured 2.90 by 2.80m in diameter and was comprised of mid grey-brown silty clay-sand infill (1380) which contained a number of early Anglo-Saxon pottery sherds.

Evidence relating to the same period was provided by a number of dated and undated features (group 102) located towards the southwestern corner of the site. A sub-circular pit (1307) which had been cut by a posthole (1309) and pit (1313) provided tantalizing signs of possible contemporary structures in this area. The remains of a possible drip gully (1153) and an associated cluster of undated postholes (1151,1155, 1157, 1159, 1161, 1163, 1165, 1167, 1125, 1121 and 1123, Fig. 2.6) situated on the same east–west alignment as many of the early Anglo-Saxon features and similarly close to the edge of palaeochannel 1064, may indicate contemporary activity.

Further archaeological evidence from the period was provided by a wide spread of silty sand (1184) which possibly represented the infill of a shallow ditch (1183) or the remains of a well-worn trackway, aligned northeast–southwest which may have led to the three southernmost sunken-featured

buildings (1074, 1132 and 1170). The latter explanation seemed to be more likely due to the very poorly defined edges and uneven base. A number of sub-circular features (1192, 1194 and 1196), which were perhaps the bases of three postholes, were exposed although extensive root disturbance made identification difficult.

3.3.6 Phase 6 – medieval (11th to 14th centuries AD)

Most of the medieval features were identified within the central and western portion of the site and predominantly took the form of enclosures and field boundaries. Several sections were excavated through the southern and eastern arms of the most westerly of these enclosures, group 109 (Fig. 3.11). The east–west aligned ditch measured generally 4.50m in width, it had steep sides and a bowl-shaped profile and had survived to a depth of 1m. One of the sections through the ditch exposed a distinctive primary deposit of dark grey organic sandy clay silt (1146), while the north–south aligned arm of the enclosure ditch identified grey-brown sandy clay-silt (1280) measuring 0.70m in depth and containing pottery sherds spot-dated to between the late 12th–14th centuries. The eastern side of the enclosure truncated the upper deposits within palaeochannel 1299/1302, indicating that the water channel had completely filled by the medieval period.

The uppermost alluvial layer within palaeochannel 1299/1302 contained medieval pottery and had been cut by a series of sub-circular and circular pits (group 105) which provided evidence of occupation during the medieval period. The features followed an east–west alignment and were situated just inside the southeastern corner of enclosure 109. Pit group 105 produced a small assemblage of pottery sherds spot-dated to between the late 12th to 14th centuries from several features including pit 1172 (Fig. 3.4). One of the features (1071) may have represented a post-pit. It had very steeply sloping sides and had been infilled with distinctive yellowish-brown silty sand (1070) which contained traces of possible organic material, perhaps signs of a post which had rotted *in-situ*.

The eastern arm of enclosure 109 was extend northwards by the western arm of enclosure 106 (Fig. 3.11). The ditch measured a maximum of 5.10m in width and 0.60m in depth and had a bowl-shaped profile. The pottery sherds which were retrieved from the ditch were spot-dated to between the late 12th and 13th centuries (1488 and 1499). The edge of a large steep sided circular pit (1497), which contained a pottery assemblage dated to the same period, was truncated by the northwest corner of the enclosure ditch. Both the ditch and pit had been truncated by a smaller, shallower ditch (1495/1603) which may have acted as a drainage channel for the larger feature (Group 106). Ditch 1495/1603 was filled with a distinctive dark grey sandy clay-silt infill (1602); excavation of the butt-end uncovered animal bone, slag and a number of pottery sherds, which were dated to between the 11th–14th centuries. A large sub-circular pit (1591) with steeply sloping sides and a bowl-shaped profile was exposed immediately to the southeast of ditch

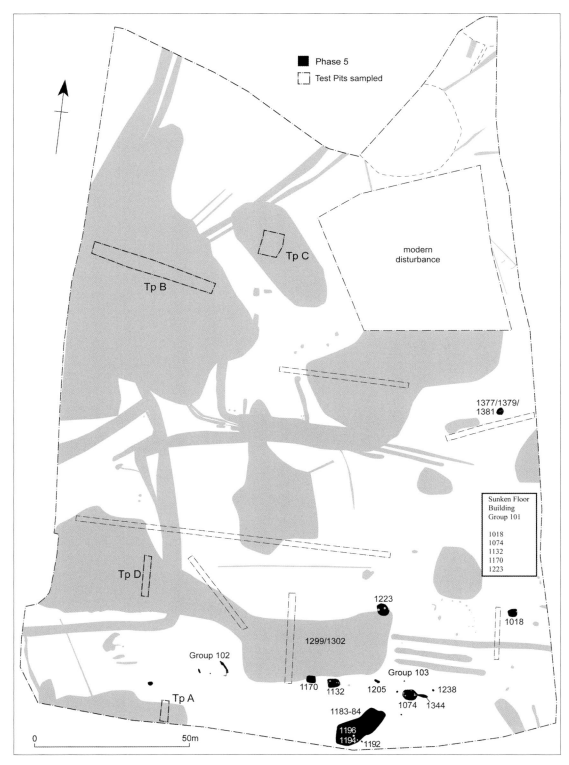

Figure 3.6 Areas of Anglo-Saxon period activity identified on site.

1603, which contained pottery also ranging in date from the 11th–14th centuries. The pit had been cut by a very shallow drainage gully (1587) which ran eastwards from the pit to the edge of the large enclosure ditch (group 106). Two circular probable post pits (1514 and 1518) were also exposed approximately 5m from the western edge of enclosure ditch 106.

The east–west aligned ditch forming the northern side of enclosure 106 was shallower than the western ditch though it still contained 11th–14th century pottery (fill 1440). A number of other east–west aligned ditches were uncovered immediately to the north and northwest of enclosure 106. The earliest of these ditches (1439) contained a notable assemblage of pottery sherds (fill 1438) dated to the mid-12th

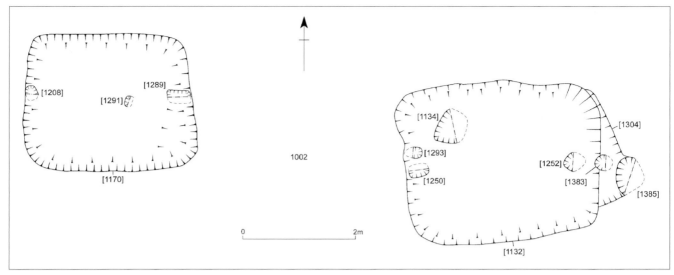

Figure 3.7 Sunken-featured buildings 1170 and 1132.

Figure 3.8 Sieving deposits beside sunken-featured buildings 1170 and 1132, facing northwest.

to mid-13th centuries. These features had created a network of re-cut ditches in an area which had obviously been subject to constant flooding. The features may represent a succession of re-cut drainage ditches that fed into the vast palaeochannel (1584) which occupied the northwestern area of the site. One of the drainage ditches (1502/1474) began at the edge of the palaeochannel (1584) and continued parallel with drainage ditch 1439 to the east where it was re-cut along its length, presumably to improve its drainage properties. To the east of palaeochannel 1584 and west of possible palaeochannel 1594/1597 was located another series of re-cut ditches (group 108). Ditches 108 were on a northwest–southeast orientation and contained ceramic evidence relating to the 12th–14th centuries (fills 1391, 1420 and 1422) and may have acted as further drainage in the area.

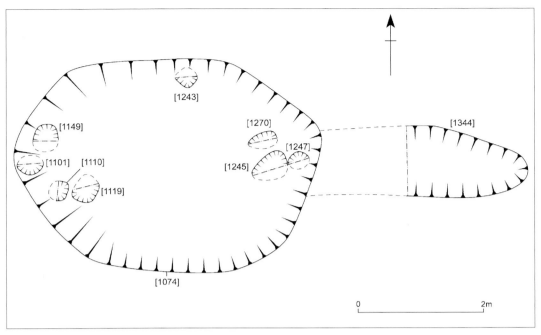

Figure 3.9 Sunken-featured building 1074.

Possible drainage feature 108 had been truncated by a large curvilinear ditch (group 107) which continued west to run parallel with ditches 1439 and 1502/1474. Ditch 107 which had steeply sloping sides and a 'U'-shaped profile may have also removed excess water into the palaeochannel (1584) to the north. The ditch contained frequent sherds of pottery (fills 1565, 1570 and 1399) which were spot-dated to between the late 12th and 14th century. Ditch 107 was truncated by a shallow north–south aligned ditch (1456) to the east of which was a spread/layer of silty sandy clay (1519/1390) which may have indicated a buried soil. A circular post-pit (1458) and a second circular unexcavated pit fill (1509) were situated within the corner of ditch 107, possibly indicating a structure in this location.

The large enclosure ditch 106 continued to the east of the site, parallel with ditch 107 and together they covered a distance of approximately 100m. The ditches had been heavily truncated by a number of later parallel gullies and ditches (1396 and 1445, Fig. 3.11) containing evidence relating to the late medieval and early post-medieval period (fills 1397, 1401 and 1444). The central portion of the two ditch groups (106 and 107) had unfortunately been obscured by later phase 7 activity. A third east–west aligned feature (1371) provided datable pottery (fill 1450) which indicated another contemporary drainage ditch. It had been cut through a very shallow undated north–south aligned gully (1369) which measured approximately 15m in length. The linear gully/ditch may have been related to a comparable east–west aligned feature (1233/1016/1235) seen to the south, which measured approximately 50m and was perhaps part of a further stock enclosure. A large irregularly-shaped pit (1028) which was situated immediately to the south of the gully had very gradually sloping uneven edges and may have been a watering hole.

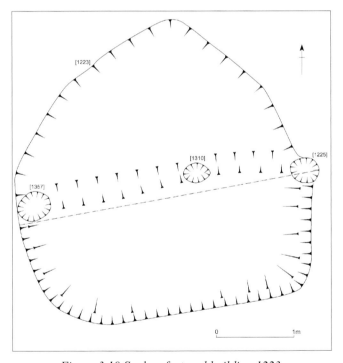

Figure 3.10 Sunken-featured building 1223.

The archaeological remains uncovered across the northwestern area of the site provided further evidence of a medieval pattern of field boundaries and drainage ditches. A number of northeast–southwest orientated ditches were exposed which may have represented the edge of an enclosure that extended beyond the northwestern edge of the excavated area. The largest of these features may represent an original field boundary ditch (1554) and measured in excess of 4.20m

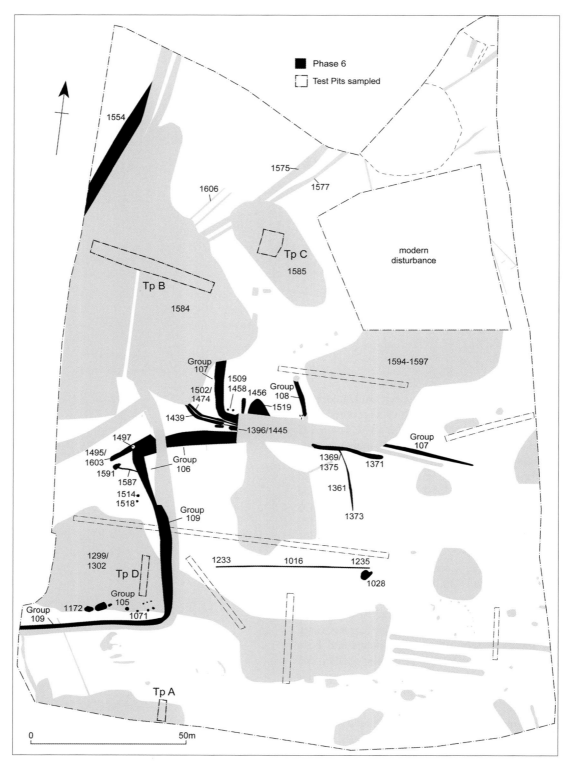

Figure 3.11 Areas of medieval period activity identified on site.

wide and 0.50m deep; animal bone and medieval pottery were recovered from fill 1552. This ditch was later truncated by a smaller ditch (1558), which was in turn truncated by the remains of a hedge line (1556), all following the same alignment. The area to the east of the field boundary ditches

was occupied by a large palaeochannel (1584). A number of parallel ditches and gullies (1575, 1577 and 1606), which were also aligned northeast–southwest, suggested a series of leats running between palaeochannel 1584 and a possible smaller palaeochannel/pond (1585).

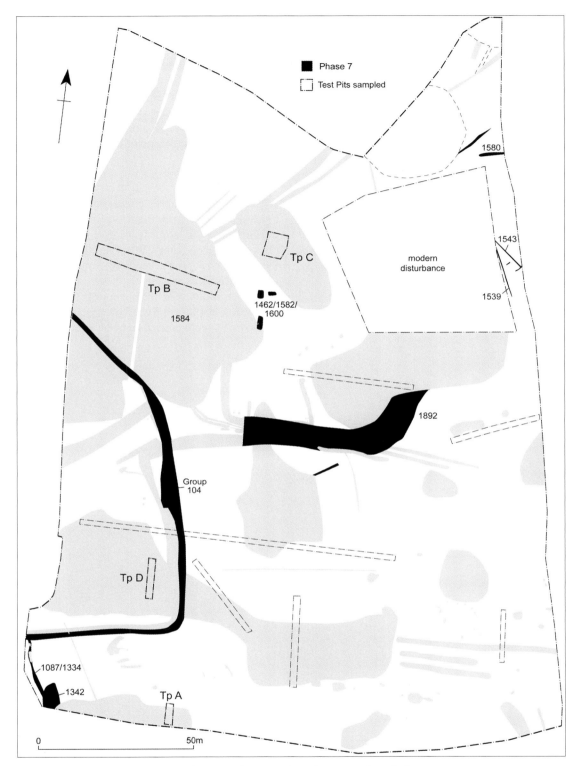

Figure 3.12 Areas of post-medieval activity identified on site.

3.3.7 Phase 7 – post-medieval (15th to 20th centuries AD)

The ditches which formed the southern and eastern sides of the large medieval enclosure group 106 in the southwestern area of the site had apparently silted up and been re-cut during the post-medieval period to create enclosure ditch group 104 (Fig. 3.12 and section 1178, Fig. 3.4). Enclosure ditch group 104 had a 'U'-shaped profile and measured 2.40m wide and 0.80m in depth. It contained pottery, tile and a substantial quantity of large snail shells (fill 1096). The enclosure was extended to the north beyond the original enclosure (109) where it truncates palaeochannel 1584, indicating that this feature had filled up by the post-medieval period (Chapter 9).

A large post-medieval ditch (1892) on an east–west alignment was located across the centre of the site cutting phase 6 ditches group 106, group 107, and 1371. It is possible that the phase 6 ditches were amalgamated during the post-medieval period into one substantial feature to improve the drainage in this location.

Further evidence of post-medieval activity was exposed in the northwestern area of the site as a number of horse burials were excavated (1462, 1582 and 1600). Two of the cuts (1462 and 1600) were aligned north–south the other was aligned east–west. The former had been cut through the upper fill of palaeochannel 1584, further indication that the palaeochannel was no longer a significant feature in the landscape. The initial evaluation of the site had highlighted the presence of the burials and provided a post-medieval date from analysis of the horse shoes. During excavation through palaeochannel 1584, the remains of a fourth horse skeleton was partially exposed.

The northeastern area of the site was only partially excavated as it became evident that it had been used for extensive dumping of building rubble. The evidence of activity in the extreme northeastern corner of the site was provided by a network of drains and narrow drainage ditches; a number of which were excavated (1543, 1539 and 1580) cut directly into the natural sandy soil and containing finds dated to the post-medieval period. In the extreme southwestern corner of the excavated area a large sub-circular cut (1342) contained a dump of 20th century building material and an undated northwest–southeast aligned ditch (1087/1334) terminated close to the southern edge of enclosure ditch 104.

3.4 Summary

Archaeological features and deposits recorded at the Mill Lane site ranged from the Mesolithic to the post-medieval periods, though some phases of activity were better represented than others. While some basic interpretation of the features has been given here, a more in-depth discussion of the periods of activity is given in Chapters 10 and 11. The discussions take into account the analysis of all the artefacts (Chapters 4–8) and palaeoenvironmental samples (Chapter 9) recovered during the excavations.

Chapter 4

Prehistoric lithics

Barry John Bishop

4.1 Introduction

The excavations conducted during 2008 and 2009 at the site resulted in the recovery of 1,027 pieces of struck flint and 2.5kg of burnt flint fragments (a full catalogue of the material by context is provided in Appendix 1). Approximately three-quarters of the struck flint, and nearly all of the burnt flint, was recovered from a variety of features and deposits that have been dated to the Neolithic or Bronze Age periods, with the remainder coming from later features where it had been residually deposited. Even with the material from the prehistoric deposits, it appears that a significant proportion had become incorporated from earlier activity and does not directly relate to the contexts from which it was recovered.

The assemblage may be regarded as moderately large given the size of the areas investigated. Retouched pieces account for 3.6% of the overall assemblage and cores 2.4%. It contained pieces representing all stages in the reduction sequence, from rejected 'tested' pieces and decortication flakes, to used and worn-out tools (see Table 4.1). It was evident that flint raw materials were procured and converted to tools and that those were being used and discarded at the site. Chronologically diagnostic pieces and the general technological character of the assemblage indicate that a significant proportion belongs to the Mesolithic and early Neolithic periods, although flintwork that both pre- and post-dates this is also present.

4.1.1 Raw materials

The raw materials used are dominated by good knapping-quality translucent black flint with occasional grey inclusions. Smaller quantities of opaque and translucent brown and grey flint are also present. Cortex is mostly rough but many pieces also retain thermal fracture scars and some rounded surfaces. Such material is typical of derived deposits, although it was evident that it had generally not been displaced from far, most likely from the Upper Chalk that outcrops a few kilometres to the south of the site. Some flint from glacial deposits may have been used, but the bulk of the material is likely to have been obtained from Quaternary alluvial deposits as are present along the Cam valley. The raw materials predominantly comprised thermally fractured nodular fragments that were mostly of small size, with the majority of flakes and blades measuring less than 50mm in maximum dimension. A few larger flakes and blades are present, however, and these suggest that the available raw materials were variable and larger pieces were occasionally obtained and used.

4.1.2 Condition

The condition of the assemblage is variable but pieces only exhibit minor chipping and abrasion. Much of it is likely to be residual or was found within reworked soil horizons.

Table 4.1 Quantification of lithic material.

	Decortication flake	Rejuvenation flake	Core	Conchoidal chunk	Micro-debitage	Micro-burin	Flake fragment	Flake	Blade	Blade fragment	Blade-like flake	Axe	Arrowhead	Burin	Scraper	Knife	Edge retouched/serrate	Microlith	Other retouched	Context total
No.	95	13	25	22	260	2	68	218	195	54	40	1	3	2	9	1	16	2	1	1027
%	9.3	1.3	2.4	2.1	25.3	0.2	6.6	21.2	19.0	5.3	3.9	0.1	0.3	0.2	0.9	0.1	1.6	0.2	0.1	100

However, the bulk of the assemblage was probably recovered from close to where it had been originally discarded. Recortication also varied, ranging from being absent to thick and heavy. There appears to be a chronological aspect to this, with earlier pieces often showing higher degrees of recortication, but this is far from exclusively so and localised soil conditions are also likely to have been important in determining the extent to which recortication occurred.

4.2 Late glacial flintworking

There is a small group of blades, comprising eleven pieces, that differ notably to the rest of the assemblage; they are significantly larger, are more heavily recorticated and often display signs of mineral staining. Five of the eleven pieces came from buried soil 1390/1519, located roughly in the centre of the site, with the others coming from features either cutting into it or located in its vicinity. This layer appears therefore to mark a focus for this phase of flintworking. The largest piece, a nearly complete crested blade, measures 112mm in length (Fig. 4.1.A) and others may have been comparably long but are now broken. A further blade shows evidence of cresting near its distal end and there is also a plunged blade struck to rejuvenate an opposed striking platform. Over half of the blades had been removed from opposed platformed cores and of the five pieces that still retain striking platforms, two had been ground, two are facetted and the remainder edge-trimmed. Retouched pieces include a short end-scraper made on a truncated blade that also has an inversely retouched bulbar end, possibly to accommodate hafting (Fig. 4.1.B), and a burin made by removing spalls longitudinally from a retouched bulbar end, and shows significant evidence of wear (Fig. 4.1.C). Although not retouched, one of the broken blades appears to have been deliberately snapped, the break having been initiated via a small notch cut into its side. This flintwork predominantly comprises useable blades and retouched implements suggesting that the flintwork, perhaps manufactured elsewhere, was employed in a variety of tasks conducted adjacent to the river.

The condition of this material sets it aside from the remainder of the assemblage and there are a number of technological features that suggest it significantly pre-dates the later Mesolithic flintwork also found at the site. These include the size of the blades, their condition and the techniques employed in making the assemblage. They have been struck from large, opposed platformed, blade cores that had complex striking platforms which includes the use of grinding and faceting. These traits, along with the presence of deliberately snapped blades, are most typical of assemblages manufactured during the late glacial or early post-glacial period, dating to *c.* 14,700–7,700BC.

4.3 Mesolithic and early Neolithic flintworking

Mesolithic and early Neolithic flintwork was found as residual material across much of the site but some concentrations recovered from within features and deposits, as described below, may reflect the locations of more intensive flintworking activities.

The presence of Mesolithic material is attested by the recovery of two microliths, two micro-burins and a transverse axe, all of which are diagnostic markers of the period. In addition, a large proportion of the flintwork recovered at the site is clearly blade-based, with 25% of the overall assemblage consisting of blades and a further 4% comprising blade-like flakes. Many of the cores recovered also display evidence of having produced blades and with these should be considered a number of core rejuvenation flakes, including core tablets, that reflect a concern with core maintenance. Most of the blades and associated blade manufacturing waste can only be confidently assigned to Mesolithic or early Neolithic industries. Nevertheless, the high proportion of prismatic blades, made with great skill and exhibiting parallel margins and dorsal scars, as well as the presence of numerous micro-blades, often associated with the manufacture of microlithic equipment, suggests that a significant proportion of the flintwork from the excavations belongs to the Mesolithic period.

Early Neolithic flintwork is evidenced by chronologically diagnostic pieces including leaf-shaped arrowheads. An unknown, but probably also significant, proportion of the overall assemblage is also likely to belong to this period. This includes a number of blades that in contrast to the prismatic types described above, are more casually produced and although of blade dimensions, have dorsal scars indicating that they were struck from multi-platformed cores that also produced flakes of a variety of shapes and sizes.

4.3.1 Mesolithic flintwork from ditches 1349/1351, 1082/1065 and 1078/1042/1008/1024

The most informative Mesolithic assemblage is perhaps that from the three Later Neolithic ditches found towards the southeast boundary of the site (ditches 1349/1351, 1082/1065 and 1078/1042/1008/1024) where it had presumably been residually incorporated. A breakdown of the material from these features is given in Table 4.2. This ditch complex produced an assemblage of 49 struck flints that are in a variable but frequently slightly chipped condition, consistent with it having been redeposited.

Although the presence of some material relating to the infilling of the ditches is likely, this assemblage was predominantly technologically homogeneous, being the product of a considered systematic reduction strategy. Diagnostic pieces, including a transverse axe, a micro-burin and a microlith, all indicate a Mesolithic date for their manufacture. This material was presumably present as a surface scatter that was disturbed by the cutting of the ditches and subsequently became incorporated into them.

Blades and blade fragments, most of which are prismatic and complete and include crested blades and micro-blades, contributed 34.6% of the assemblage. Also present is a skilfully worked, opposed-platformed micro-blade core,

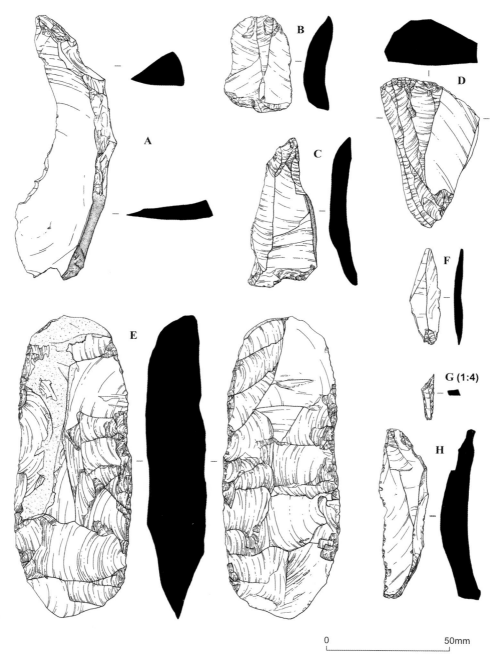

Figure 4.1 Lithic material recovered from the site (A–H).

Table 4.2 Composition of struck flint from ditch complex [1349/1351], [1082/1065], [1078/1042/1008/1024].

	Decortication Flake	Core	Micro-debitage	Micro-burin	Flake fragment	Flake	Blade	Blade fragment	Blade-like flake	Axe	Microlith	Context total
No.	2	3	5	1	6	11	11	6	2	1	1	49
%	4.1	6.1	10.2	2.0	12.2	22.4	22.4	12.2	4.1	2.0	2.0	100

capable of producing microlith blanks and typical of Mesolithic industries (Fig. 4.1.D).

The transverse axe (Fig. 4.2) displays fine bifacial working and is made from translucent black flint, retaining remnants of a weathered but rough yellow cortex around its butt and along part of one side (Fig. 4.1.E). It has the characteristic transverse sharpening blow and there are no traces of polishing. It is in a very sharp condition and its cutting edge shows no evidence of use. There is also no evident abrasion from around its butt that could indicate that it had been hafted. Although attempts at refitting were unsuccessful, a few of the flakes found in association are of the same colour and have similar cortex. Some of these are wide, thin and show a marked longitudinal curvature, being typical of those produced during biface manufacture, and potentially could have originated during the manufacture of the axe. If so, they would demonstrate that it was manufactured and discarded at this location. This would accord with the pristine freshness of the axe, which displays no evidence of wear or use, and its discard appears inexplicable unless it was intentionally discarded, perhaps as a votive deposit.

The microlith comprises a short obliquely truncated type measuring 17mm by 6mm and the micro-burin consists of a largely extant blade that has had its bulbar end removed using the micro-burin technique (Fig. 4.1.F). It shows no further modification and it is not clear why this too was not converted into a microlith. Interestingly, the microlith and micro-burin are made from the same opaque mottled brown flint and, although not from the same implement, may have been made using the same core. A further microlith, found in an Anglo-Saxon context a few metres to the south of the ditches, possibly also relates to this assemblage. It comprises a small but finely made scalene triangle type, measuring 10mm in length by 3mm in width (Fig. 4.1.G). Worked flint of probable Mesolithic date is also present in quantity amongst many of the other features in this area, and suggests that the southeastern part of the site may have been a focus for flintworking activities during this period.

Much of the flintwork from the site can be only broadly attributed to the Mesolithic or early Neolithic periods. This includes fairly substantial assemblages from the post-built structure (group 100) located immediately to the north of the ditch complex, which includes large quantities of micro-debitage indicative of flint knapping occurring in this area. Much of the assemblage recovered from the relict soil horizon (1210/1268) located immediately north of the post-built structure is also likely to belong to these periods. These assemblages are in a variable condition with many broken pieces present, consistent with them deriving from surface scatters incorporated into reworked soil horizons. They are chronologically mixed with pieces ranging in date from the Mesolithic through to the later Neolithic or Bronze Age, but with significant proportions belonging to the earlier periods; blades for example, contributed 28% of the assemblage excluding the micro-debitage. Implements belonging to these periods include serrated and edge-worn blades, and an unusual implement comprising a large and

Figure 4.2 ('E' in Figure 4.1) Transverse axe from 1041 (scale in cm).

relatively thick blade with a very worn and rounded distal end, comparable to the damage wear seen on fabricators (Fig. 4.1.H).

To the north of relict soil horizon 1210/1268, deposit 1459 produced a very dense concentration of flintwork that, again, is in a variable but often chipped and broken condition, typical of material recovered from soil horizons. It also appears to be chronologically mixed but contains a high proportion, at 29%, of blades and it also produced a broken but finely made and slender leaf-shaped arrowhead (Figs 4.3.I and 4.4). Also probably of early Neolithic or perhaps Mesolithic date is an unusual double-ended long-end scraper with a serrated lateral edge (Fig. 4.3.J), along with a number of other edge-trimmed and serrated flakes.

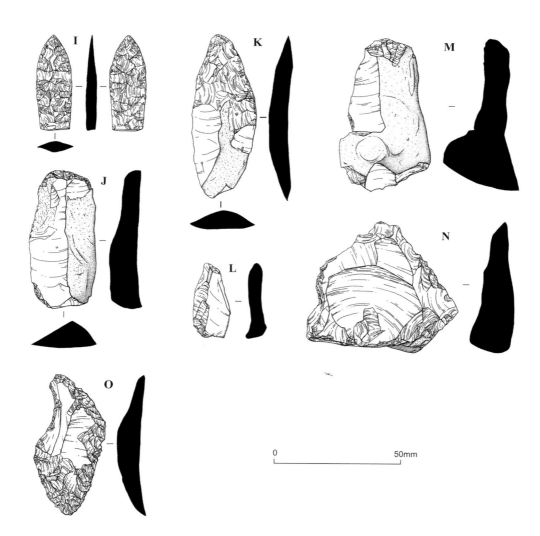

Figure 4.3 Lithic material recovered from the site (I–O).

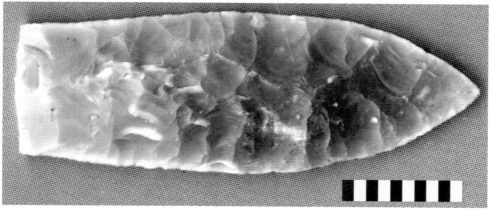

Figure 4.4 ('I' in Figure 4.3) Broken slender leaf-shaped arrowhead from 1459 (scale in mm).

4.3.2 Early Neolithic flintwork from post-built structure and spread 1066

The leaf-shaped arrowhead found in deposit 1459 demonstrates an early Neolithic presence at the site but the clearest evidence for flintworking during this period comes from deposit 1066 that appears to have accumulated around the post-built structure located in the southwest of the site (Table 4.3). None of the associated gullies and only one of the postholes forming the structure produced flintwork, this consisting of two blades recovered from posthole 1338. The overlying spread, however, contained a rich assemblage, comprising 195 pieces of struck flint and 0.25kg of unmodified burnt flint.

The paucity of flintwork recovered from the elements of the structure support the notion that it had been built prior to the deposit forming. The burnt flint from within this deposit had been variably heated as would be consistent with the incidental incorporation of natural pebbles within hearths and it is unlikely to have been deliberately produced. A high proportion of the struck material was also burnt and this suggests that flintworking was probably conducted whilst sitting around a hearth.

The struck flint represents a blade-based reduction strategy, with just under a quarter of the assemblage consisting of blades, although in contrast to the Mesolithic flintwork recorded from the ditch complex, many of these are not truly prismatic. Nevertheless, the presence of a distal micro-burin does indicate that some residual, Mesolithic, material has been incorporated into the spread. The assemblage is dominated by knapping waste, including decortication, trimming and rejuvenation flakes, cores and micro-debitage, along with unusable pieces, such as irregular and broken flakes. It may be regarded as waste from episodes of core reduction that culminated in blade manufacture, but contains few useful products or retouched implements, which are limited to five lightly edge-trimmed pieces.

Metrical analysis indicates that the flakes and blades, although variable, tend to be small, with the majority being less than 30mm in maximum dimension and only five just exceeding 50mm. The striking platforms are narrow, averaging 2mm, and all but the large primary core reduction flakes have their striking platform/core face angles trimmed.

Further evidence for the control and maintenance of platforms is provided by the core rejuvenation flakes, which include core tablets. The eight cores include 'tested' pieces, blade cores and flake cores, indicating that a range of flake shapes and sizes were being produced. They are mostly worked from only single striking platforms and show relatively minimal working; they range in weight from 25g to 43g. None showed any evidence of being shaped prior to flake production, possibly indicating that these had been largely rejected, with more-extensively worked examples removed for further reduction elsewhere.

Most pieces are in a sharp condition but there is a high degree of fragmentation amongst the assemblage and around a quarter of the struck pieces show evidence of having been burnt, this having occurred after manufacture but prior to incorporation into the spread. Refitting was attempted but due to the large numbers of small or broken pieces was largely unsuccessful. The wide range of colours and cortex types present within the assemblage does suggest it was formed from a number of knapping episodes.

4.3.3 Lithics from the early Neolithic curving feature 1254/1532/1547

A further group of early Neolithic flintwork was recovered from feature 1254/1532/1547, located on the eastern side of the site. This produced a total of 129 pieces of struck flint and the largest quantity of burnt flint from any feature excavated at the site (Table 4.4).

The flintwork is mostly in a good, although somewhat variable in condition with relatively few broken or burnt pieces present. A number of refitting sequences are evident, although the maximum number of refits from any individual sequence is only three, indicating that only small elements from any particular knapping episode are present, although this is difficult to qualify as only a small amount of the feature was excavated.

Blades contribute nearly 30% of this assemblage and it also contains two finely worked slender arrowheads of apparently very similar form, although one is broken and only its tip remains. The complete example would conform to Green's type 1C (table 11/18 in Green 1980) although it

Table 4.3 Composition of the lithic material from deposit [1066].

Context	Decortication flake	Rejuvenation flake	Core	Conchoidal chunk	Micro-debitage	Micro-burin	Flake fragment	Flake	Blade	Blade fragment	Blade-like flake	Axe	Arrowhead	Burin	Scraper	Knife	Edge retouched/serrate	Microlith	Other retouched	Context total
No.	17	5	8	7	35	1	23	40	35	12	7	0	0	0	0	0	5	0	0	195
%	8.7	2.6	4.1	3.6	17.9	0.5	11.8	20.5	17.9	6.2	3.6	0.0	0.0	0.0	0.0	0.0	2.6	0.0	0.0	100.0

Table 4.4 Composition of the lithic material from curving feature [1254/1532/1547].

	Decortication flake	Rejuvenation flake	Core	Conchoidal chunk	Micro-debitage	Flake fragment	Flake	Blade	Blade fragment	Blade-like flake	Arrowhead	Burin	Scraper	Edge retouched/serrate	Context total	Burnt flint	Burnt flint (wt g)
No.	12	2	6	1	11	6	38	30	7	6	2	1	3	4	129	197	1540
%	9.3	1.6	4.7	0.8	8.5	4.7	29.5	23.3	5.4	4.7	1.6	0.8	2.3	3.1	100		

is probably unfinished (Fig. 4.3.K). They have fine bifacial invasive flaking that concentrates around the tips and both are also very similar in form to the arrowhead found in deposit 1459, located close by to the south (see above). Other pieces of interest include a burin-like graving tool that consists of a short blade-like flake with numerous small flakes removed transversely across its distal end (Fig. 4.3.L). Three scrapers are also present. Two of these consist of cortical flakes with minimal convex retouch around their distal ends, whilst the other is notably different, consisting of a very thick flake that removed a large nodular protuberance and has a number of relatively large flakes removed from its distal end. It may even have functioned as a core, although wear around the working edge does indicate it was employed in working hard materials (Fig. 4.3.M). The remaining retouched implements all comprise serrated blades. The six cores recovered are mostly extensively reduced multi-platformed types and vary in weight from 31g to 147g with an average at 93g.

The burnt flint was all very intensively heated and the high quantities present suggest that it may have been deliberately produced, thus contrasting with the burnt flint from deposit 1066. The deliberate heating of flint is an often noted feature of many prehistoric sites and a number of possible uses for hot stones have been forwarded, although perhaps the most common explanation sees it as being generated during large-scale cooking activities (*e.g.* Hodder and Barfield 1991).

4.4 Late Neolithic and early Bronze Age flintworking

Later Neolithic/early Bronze Age material appears to be less well represented amongst the assemblage as a whole, although a few diagnostic pieces plus a number of competently made but unsystematically reduced flakes do indicate that flintworking continued at the site, albeit at a lesser scale than seen previously.

The assemblage from relict soil horizon 1210/1268, although containing a high proportion of Mesolithic or early Neolithic blades, also produced a number of unsystematic but competently produced large broad flakes. Many of these have facetted striking platforms and multi-directional dorsal scars, demonstrating that they were produced from cores that

have had flakes removed from a number of directions. This is reflected in some of the cores recovered from the deposit, which tend to be large and globular, with flakes removed from any appropriate surface. There is also a large thick flake (1268) that has had its edges trimmed and facetted along one margin, which was then used to remove a large flake from its dorsal surface. This is a comparable technique to that employed on 'Levallois' cores, which are typically later Neolithic in date (Fig. 4.3.N). Also of later Neolithic or early Bronze Age date is a broken narrow flake that exhibits invasive ripple flaking along both of its margins and which most closely resembles a plano-convex knife (Fig. 4.3.O).

No other diagnostic pieces of later Neolithic or early Bronze Age date were identified from the site but the flintwork recovered from ditch 1187/1189 may possibly belong to this phase of activity. This feature produced 27 pieces that, with the exception of a few pieces of translucent black flint and some burnt fragments whose colour could not be ascertained, were made from a semi-opaque grey speckled flint with a thin but rough cortex. Attempts at refitting proved unsuccessful but it is clear that these originate from the reduction of a single nodule. They comprise knapping waste and include many decortication flakes although no cores. There are also a few broken prismatic and non-prismatic blades present but no retouched pieces. Despite the lack of diagnostic pieces, the absence of evidence for sustained systematic reduction does differentiate it from the early Neolithic material discussed above, and suggests it may have been manufactured slightly later during the Neolithic. It all came from the same slot dug through the ditch and appears to be a discrete deposit of knapping waste, either dumped into the ditch or redeposited from a feature or surface scatter that the ditch truncated.

4.5 Discussion

The struck flint assemblage from Mill Lane may be regarded as relatively large and demonstrates that activity at the site started during the late glacial or early post-glacial period and continued until the later Neolithic or early Bronze Age. It was mostly recovered from cut features or preserved remnants of soil horizons where it was largely present as residual or as mixed, multi-period, assemblages. Given the removal of surface deposits and the limited excavation of some of the features and environmental deposits, it is likely that only a fraction of the material present at Mill Lane was actually recovered, further testifying to the intensive nature of occupation at the site during these periods.

This intensive use of the floodplain is evidenced elsewhere along the valley. This is perhaps best demonstrated *c.* 5km upstream at the Hinxton Genome Complex, where nearly three thousand struck flints dating to between the late glacial and Iron Age periods were recovered (Bishop forthcoming). The evidence from here is remarkably similar to that from Mill Lane, and is suggestive of fairly continuous activity occurring along the river margins over a very long period of time. Such intensive occupation was also identified at Hinxton Quarry around 3km upstream, where fieldwalking demonstrated that substantial quantities of struck flints were present within the ploughsoil (Evans 1993; Mortimer and Evans 1996; Austin and Sydes 1998; Pollard 1998a). The quantities recovered were described as "extraordinary" and attest to intensive activity along the riverine terraces of the Cam from the Mesolithic through to the Bronze Age (Evans 1993, 7, 10).

The assemblage recovered from the Hinxton Genome Complex was interpreted as largely representing a palimpsest of individual knapping episodes and it is likely that a similar origin for the Mill Lane material may apply. It is hard to be absolute when considering a largely residual and partially collected assemblage, but the impression given by the distribution of the struck flint is that it also represents a palimpsest involving numerous knapping and tool using events, suggestive of a succession of occupation episodes. This scenario would be typical for the Mesolithic and probably also for the great majority of early Neolithic occupation sites. It may be compared to the evidence recorded at Duxford Mill, located just to the north of the Hinxton Genome site, where both Mesolithic or early Neolithic surface scatters were preserved as discrete knapping events by later alluviation and peat formation (Schlee and Robinson 1995; Austin and Sydes 1998).

Of particular interest, given the rarity of material in Britain from these periods, is a small collection of flintwork that has late glacial or early post-glacial characteristics, although the lack of specific chronologically diagnostic implements means that their dating cannot be refined further (but see for example Barton 1991; Barton and Roberts 1996; Barton 1998; Conneller 2009; Cooper 2006; Jacobi 2004 for discussions of technological change and spatial relationships amongst late glacial/early post-glacial industries). Flintwork from these early periods is rare but find-spots do appear to largely focus along the tributaries and rivers of the major valleys, particularly those connecting the North Sea with the hinterland of southern and eastern Britain. This material is very similar in form and condition to a small collection of blades recovered at the Hinxton Genome Complex, and further late glacial flintwork has been recovered from beside a tributary to the river Cam at Great Wilbraham (Conneller 2009). Taken together, these sites suggest that the Cam

may also have witnessed relatively intense activity during this time.

A far more significant proportion of the assemblage is likely to belong to the Mesolithic, as testified by microliths, micro-burins and a transverse axe. This axe is very finely made if compared to most Mesolithic examples and exhibits no evidence of wear or use (Figs 4.1.E and 4.2). The lack of wear and the possibility that it was made and discarded in the vicinity may even suggest that it had been deliberately deposited, although as it was recovered from a later feature this remains difficult to qualify. It is well established, however, that during the Neolithic period axes were often deliberately discarded under what may be regarded as ceremonial or ritual circumstances in a variety of deposition contexts, including within rivers. There is also growing evidence that the intentional disposal of items and resources, often of high prestige value, into watery places may have a long pedigree and had started at least by the Mesolithic period (Bradley 1990; Pollard 2000; Chatterton 2006).

The microliths are narrow blade varieties of later Mesolithic date (Jacobi 1976; 1978). In addition to microlith use, the presence of micro-burins indicates that microliths were also being manufactured here. Additionally, many micro-blades and accompanying micro-blade cores were recovered and these may well reflect further manufacture of microlithic equipment. This was also occurring at the Hinxton Genome Complex although at both sites the numbers of microliths recorded is low compared to some Mesolithic 'hunting camp' sites and a more diverse range of activities might be represented. Nevertheless, microliths are usually associated with hunting equipment and it seems likely that one of the activities conducted at the site during the Mesolithic was hunting. The presence of the river and the mosaic of wetlands within which the site was situated would have provided a wealth of resources for hunter-gather communities, not limited to but certainly including ample hunting opportunities.

The quantity of struck flint and the probability that it survives as a series of palimpsests from discrete knapping episodes suggest that this site may have been a 'preferred location', one that was repeatedly returned to and which perhaps witnessed a variety of diverse activities. This is, however, a very similar scenario to that proposed for the Mesolithic occupation at the Hinxton Genome Complex and the many other scatters and finds of Mesolithic material suggest that rather than a preferred location, it was the valley floor of the river Cam that attracted occupation, wherever suitable dry and elevated ground could be found. Settlement during this period is likely, therefore, to have concentrated along this riverine corridor. Mesolithic flintwork has also been found in the surrounding landscape away from the rivers, such as at Bowers Terrace (Cambridgeshire HER MCB17619), Sawston Police Station (Mortimer 2006) and Bourn Bridge in Pampisford (Pollard 1998a). These do differ from the evidence collected from the Cam's valley floor, as they tend to be small and isolated scatters, perhaps indicating individual task-specific activities undertaken where and whenever circumstances required. The evidence is still meagre but it may be possible to see the valley floors and margins as corridors of movement and opportunity that formed the main focus for settlement and day-to-day routines, but which also provided the bases for exploring and operating within the wider landscape.

A concern with the manufacture of arrows continues into the early Neolithic period, as demonstrated by the recovery of three very similar long and slender examples, at least one of which may not have been finished. These represent a relatively high proportion of the retouched inventory and this is comparable to the quantities recovered from the Hinxton Genome Complex, where further evidence for their manufacture was identified. It is less easy to distinguish between most of the products of Mesolithic and early Neolithic industries but certainly by the latter period many simply-made and often serrated edge-retouched blades were being utilized, these accounting for nearly half of the entire retouched component. High proportions of these were yet again recovered at the Hinxton Genome Complex and they are also very comparable to the large collection of serrates recovered from the early Neolithic occupation sites at Parnwell or Stow-cum-Quy (Webley 2007; Drummond-Murray forthcoming). The type and range of the activities to which serrates were employed remains obscure; they have traditionally been regarded as composite sickles, essential elements in the Neolithic tool-kit and linked to harvesting silica-rich plants, particularly cereals. Experimental work involving micro-wear analysis suggests that serrated blades could have been used in cutting soft plant material (Avery 1982, 38; Grace 1992; Levi-Sala 1992; Bradley 1993; Donahue 2002). The harvesting of cereals certainly remains a possibility, but other candidates include rushes, also rich in silica, that would no doubt have been abundant in this riverine area.

Much of the early Neolithic flintwork was recovered, like the Mesolithic material, from later features and layers where it had been residually deposited, but there were two assemblage groups that might possibly shed light upon deposition practices during this period. The fragmented or burnt condition of much of the struck flint from spread 1066 and the presence of unworked burnt flint and reasonably substantial quantities of pottery suggests that it may represent a rubbish dump, or midden. It perhaps formed along the side of the post-built structure and had accumulated over time, allowing for the material to become differentially weathered. The presence of such middens has long been postulated and such features are often cited as the sources for the fillings of early Neolithic pits (*e.g.* Healy 1988; Pollard 1999; Thomas 1999; Garrow 2006; Lamdin-Whymark 2008). Due to preservational factors, however, surface deposited refuse accumulations are rarely encountered in Neolithic contexts. They only survive if protected from weathering and erosion, and are easily and rapidly transformed into formless scatters of predominantly lithic material through prolonged ploughing. This spread, although only small in size, is possibly a rare example of a feature type that may have been much more common on Neolithic settlements.

Although technologically similar, there are some notable differences in the typological make-up of the assemblage from feature 1254/1532/1547. It contains nearly three times as many, and a wider range of, retouched implements. The proportion of cores is similar but those from feature 1254/1532/1547 were nearly 50% heavier than those from deposit 1066, and they also tended to be more extensively worked, and utilized greater numbers of striking platforms. Feature 1254/1532/1547 also contained lower proportions of irregular conchoidally fractured chunks and had around two and a half times fewer pieces of micro-debitage.

It is clear that the material from feature 1254/1532/1547, which includes high proportions of tools as well as large quantities of knapping waste, represents all stages in the reduction sequence. It is comparable to the contents of some early Neolithic pits recorded at the Hinxton Genome Complex, which consisted of 'complete' assemblages, but stands in contrast to that from deposit 1066, which mainly consists of fragmented knapping waste and includes few tools, all of which are simple edge-retouched flakes. Many of the potentially useable products generated during knapping are missing, and this possibly includes any larger and more productive cores. Taken together, this suggests that the material from feature 1254/1532/1547 may have been selected to some degree, with larger, more complete and more recognisable pieces being chosen at the expense of smaller, broken or burnt fragments. It also contained relatively large quantities of intensively burnt flint, possibly the waste from cooking activities.

Although no re-fittable pieces were present between the two assemblages, and any direct associations may be unlikely, it is possible that they represent two aspects of a similar pattern of disposal that is often forwarded to explain artefact deposits at early Neolithic sites. At many early Neolithic sites the sole surviving evidence for occupation consists of pits that contain what may be regarded as occupation debris (*e.g.* Thomas 1999; Garrow 2006). This often includes pottery, burnt flint, bone and flintwork, but closer examination of the condition and make-up of the contents often suggests that they represent the selected residues taken from larger deposits of waste that had accumulated over some time, perhaps over the duration of the settlement. Such deposits are very comparable to the material recovered from feature 1254/1532/1547, which is perhaps more indicative of selected and deliberately deposited material. In contrast, the material from deposit 1066 may reflect a primary source, the 'pre-depositional context' in Garrow's (2006) terminology, from which such material may have been selected. In this light, it is interesting to note that some of the flint and pottery sherds from feature 1254/1532/1547 appeared to have been juxtaposed and show some evidence of deliberate placement. The reasons why such occupation debris may have been selected and formally redeposited are not clear but it is possible this occurred as part of ceremonial or commemorative practices, perhaps as an attempt at marking specific locations within the landscape.

The juxtaposition of diagnostic Mesolithic and early Neolithic material at Mill Lane invites some comments concerning the question of continuity across the transition. They certainly indicate continuity in the use of place and this is seen in assemblages from the Hinxton Genome Complex where, again, diagnostic pieces were recovered from the same scatters. This is a situation noted at many other places in East Anglia, particularly in the lower-lying areas such as the Fens and Fen-edge (Brown and Murphy 1997, 12). As demonstrated by the extensive work of the Fenland Survey, lithic scatters of later Mesolithic and early Neolithic date appear to be particularly prevalent around the Fen margins and its lower-lying feeder valleys, such as the Cam, where numerous, often superimposed, scatters have been recorded. Reynolds and Kaner (2000) argue that the fifth millennium BC may be marked by a transitional industry and that the frequent close association of lithic types from the Mesolithic and Neolithic, such as microliths, arrowheads and polished implements, may not merely represent the incidental mix of different industries, but possibly constitute a real phenomenon.

As the material from both periods at Mill Lane was largely residual and difficult to fully disentangle, it is impossible to say whether the juxtaposed material represents non-related and chronologically distinct knapping events, or a genuine transitional assemblage of the type suggested by Reynolds and Kaner (2000). What is more certain, however, is that both microliths and leaf-shaped arrowheads were being manufactured at the site, and it could be argued that these are mutually exclusive on a functional level. There also does seem to be some change in the techniques used to produce the two assemblages. Both are blade-based but the Mesolithic material most frequently employs pre-shaped and carefully maintained cores that were capable of repeatedly producing standardized prismatic blades, whilst the early Neolithic cores show less evidence of careful control, often using multiple and randomly aligned striking platforms that produced non-prismatic blades as well as a variety of other flake shapes. The evidence is far from conclusive, but it does hint that flintworking between the two periods is subtly different and although may easily reflect developments within a single cultural tradition, does not necessarily indicate direct association between the makers of the two assemblages.

The flintwork form Mill Lane provides evidence that that flintworking continued into the later Neolithic or early Bronze Age, but at a much-reduced scale compared to that seen earlier. Pieces belonging to these periods include a plano-convex knife and a Levallois style core and it is also likely that some of the competently but unsystematically made flakes could also belong here. A decline in the level of flintworking during the later Neolithic and early Bronze Age was also noted at the Hinxton Genome Complex and these sites may reflect a move away from settlement in close proximity to the river during this time, which may have only been visited sporadically or for specific purposes. The reasons for this shift in settlement foci are unclear and probably complex, although it does coincide with increased wetter conditions, which may have left the valley floor uninhabitable or only available on a seasonal basis.

CHAPTER 5

PREHISTORIC POTTERY

Ann Woodward

5.1 Introduction

The excavations produced a total of 457 sherds of prehistoric pottery, weighing a combined total of 1,729g. Most of the pottery was of earlier Neolithic date, but some pieces of later Neolithic and Beaker date were also identified. Virtually all of the pottery was found in sealed contexts, but the overall average sherd weight is fairly low at 3.8g. This demonstrates that the assemblage as a whole was highly fragmented. However, diagnostic rim sherds are fairly well represented, along with a few decorated items, and much of the pottery could be designated to period on the basis of distinctive fabric types.

5.2 Ceramic traditions – typologies, succession, and contextualisation

Much of the pottery came from a few well-defined locations, as summarised in Table 5.1. From these figures it can be deduced that some of the contexts were probably earlier Neolithic in origin. This applies to the curved shallow ditch 1254 and its associated contexts, the southwestern spread 1066 and the dark area (context 1510) east of spread 1459. The southeastern gully 1186 also contained earlier Neolithic pottery only, but in relatively small quantities. The old ground surface under the putative barrow or midden (1210/1268) contained a mixture of earlier and later Neolithic pottery together with Beaker sherds. This would indicate that the structure was not built until the Beaker period (late Neolithic/early Bronze Age) at the earliest. To the north of deposit 1210/1268, spread 1459 and its associated contexts contained a similar mixture of pottery, although rather more of it. Finally, a few sherds of later Neolithic and Beaker pottery were also found as residual items in the main ditches belonging to later periods on the site, and also within the sunken-featured buildings of Anglo-Saxon date.

5.2.1 Earlier Neolithic (c. 4000 to c. 2700 cal BC)

The most prolific category of pottery from the site was of distinctive fabric and belongs to the Bowl tradition. A minimum of *c.* 28 vessels was represented by different rim types and individual groups of sherds of similar fabric. Such vessels are round-bottomed, so no base angle sherds were found. The total absence of decorated sherds may indicate that the all the bowls represented were plain, but due to the fragmentary nature of the assemblage, the former occurrence of decoration cannot entirely be ruled out. A wide range of rim forms and vessel sizes are represented, as indicated in the items selected for illustration below.

Table 5.1 Prehistoric pottery: major context groups.

Context group	Contexts	Earlier Neo	Later Neo	Later Neo/EBA	Neo
Curved ditch 1254 *etc.*	1511, 1545, 1583	261 (1199g)			13 (3g)
SW spread	1066	40 (276g)			
?Old ground surface, barrow	1210, 1268	4 (11g)	9 (9g)	7 (8g) Beaker	2 (3g)
Spread N of barrow	1459	31 (23g)		8 (23g) Beaker	
Spread N of barrow	1465–1469	20 (50g)		3 (4g)	6 (14g)
Dark area E of 1459	1510	14 (2g)			
SE furrow	1081		3 (7g)		
SE gully	1186	7 (3g)			
Residual in later ditches and pit	1041, 1503, 1513			3 (2g) Beaker 6 (5g)	
Residual in Anglo-Saxon SFB features	1073, 1221, 1356		1 (33g)	3 (2g)	10 (7g)

Spread 1066 contained sherds from two vessels only, eleven from Vessel 1 and 29 from Vessel 2. Within the curved ditch there were three main vessels represented in context 1545: 38 from Vessel 1, 18 from Vessel 2 and 15 from Vessel 3 (wall sherds only). Also represented were a very thin-walled vessel (E and F below; ten sherds in total), several other fine burnished vessels (five sherds altogether) and various other vessels in coarse fabrics similar to those of Vessels 1 to 3. There were also many small fragments which could have derived from any of the coarser vessels from this context. In the same area, context 1583 contained nine sherds from one particular pot, Vessel 1, along with wall fragments from at least four further earlier Neolithic vessels. These sherds are presented in Figure 5.1 (labelled A–J).

Note: all the fabrics contain ill-sorted angular flint inclusions.

A. Thick outwardly rolled rim with a marked internal bevel, from a closed bowl; rim diameter *c.* 180mm, 18% surviving. Fabric 1LF and S; surfaces very abraded. Context 1066, Vessel 1. Petrology sample 1.
B. Thin rim sherd, the rim with marked external and internal expansion, from an open bowl; rim diameter *c.* 240mm, 11% represented. Fabric 2LF and S; surfaces very abraded. Context 1066, Vessel 2. Petrology sample 2.
C. Three joining rolled rim sherds from a necked neutral bowl; rim diameter *c.* 220mm, 13% surviving. Fabric 1LF and S: exterior surface burnished. Context 1545, Vessel 1.

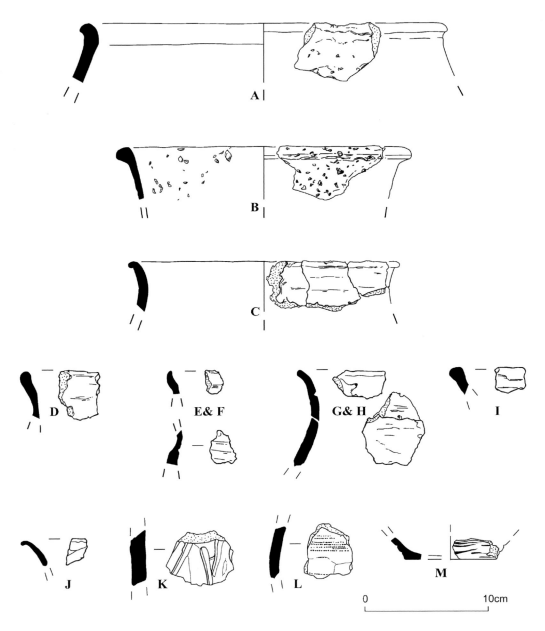

Figure 5.1 Prehistoric pottery from the site.

D. Gently expanded rim from a slightly open bowl. Fabric 1LF and S. Context 1545, Vessel 2.
E. Tapered incurving rim from a small bowl. Fabric 1LF and S. Context 1545. Petrology sample 3.
F. Concave neck fragment from a small bowl. Fabric 1LF and S; exterior surface burnished. Context 1545. Petrology sample 4.
G. Gently everted simple rim from an open bowl. Fabric 2LF and S. Context 1467, TP 25.
H. Gently concave neck fragment from the same bowl as G. Fabric 2LF and S. Context 1467, TP 25.
I. Expanded rim from an open bowl. Fabric 1LF and S; exterior surface well smoothed. Context 1583, Vessel 1. Petrology sample 8.
J. Very fine hook-shaped rim and upper neck from a wide open bowl. Fabric 1LF and S. Context 1510.

In general terms the petrological analysis confirmed the fabric descriptions that had been determined macroscopically. Samples from five illustrated vessels (sherds A, B, E, F and H above) plus two bowls not illustrated all contained crushed chert (flint), which had been deliberately added to the clay. In some samples, especially sherd I above, the chert inclusions may have been from a single flint. In three samples (sherds A, B and E above) a natural loose sand had also been added deliberately. However the other four samples lacked the coarse-grained sand component. It is interesting to note that all the Neolithic sherds tended to present a sandy texture, but the presence of deliberately added sand was not discernible to the naked eye. This aspect was only demonstrable by the petrological analysis. It was not possible to determine a precise provenance for the raw materials but all could have been local and certainly are regional in origin.

5.2.2 Later Neolithic

A small quantity of Peterborough Ware, of middle Neolithic date, was recovered. This comprised three sherds, all from a single vessel, from the southeastern furrow, 1081. The sherds were not decorated, and identification was based on the distinctive fabric type. The ill-sorted angular medium flint inclusions were held in a soft matrix which contrasted strongly with the hard sandy fabrics of the earlier Neolithic wares. Of late Neolithic date were nine sherds of soft undecorated ware containing grog and rare medium flint from the old ground surface beneath spreads 1210/1268. These probably belonged to the Grooved Ware tradition. And a decorated sherd of Grooved Ware dated *c*.3000 to *c*.2000 cal BC was found as a residual item in one of the sunken-floored buildings of Anglo-Saxon date (Fig. 5.1, sherd K):

K. Thick wall sherd decorated with uneven diagonal grooves forming a rough vertical chevron pattern. Fabric rare MF, soft and soapy. Context 1221 (residual).

5.2.3 Late Neolithic/early Bronze Age (c. 2400 to c. 1800 cal BC)

Thin sherds, often with distinctive reddish surfaces, and sometimes decorated, belong to the Beaker tradition of the late Neolithic and early Bronze Age. Such material was found in the old ground surface beneath the punitive barrow/midden (context 1268, seven sherds from a single vessel) and in the spread north of that feature (context 1459, eight sherds from at least two different vessels). Residual Beaker sherds were also found in later ditch fillings (contexts 1041 and 1513). The fabrics mainly displayed mixed recipes, containing various combinations of grog, sand and occasional flint and quartz. No thicker sherds in early Bronze Age grogged fabrics were identified. Petrological examination of one of the Beaker fabrics (vessel M below) showed that the inclusions, including chert (flint), were not deliberately added but were natural components of the clay. These sherds are represented in Figure 5.1 (labelled L and M):

L. Two joining wall sherds (modern break) with one horizontal zone of decoration and the upper edge of another; the decoration was executed by a fine toothed comb and comprises closely set horizontal lines, some of which overlap each other. Beaker. Fabric rare LQ and S and G. Context 1459.
M. Base angle and obtusely angled lower wall, decorated on the exterior with uneven incised horizontal strokes; base diameter *c*. 60mm, 18% represented. Beaker. Fabric G and S, plus occasional F. Context 1268. Petrology sample 3.

5.2.4 Abrasion and deposition

Although it proved possible to identify sherds belonging to just a few main vessels within each of the major earlier Neolithic contexts, each vessel was represented by relatively few sherds (see above for details). The degree of vessel representation is best illustrated by the percentages of rim surviving, which varied only between 11% and 18%. Most of the pottery was highly abraded, although the assessment of this characteristic was hampered somewhat by the presence of post-depositional encrustation. Where sherd conjoins could be identified the edges displayed ancient breaks. Also, in contexts 1066 and 1545, some of the pottery was classified as very abraded. All this indicates that the pottery deposited in these features was old and already broken when it was placed within the pits.

The Beaker material was very fragmentary and all was abraded. The occurrence of seven small sherds from a single vessel in context 1268 is of interest, but probably not sufficient to suggest that they derived from a whole vessel deposited with a burial. The residual Beaker items were, as one might expect, very abraded.

5.2.5 Vessel sizes

The earlier Neolithic assemblage is large enough to give some indication of the array of vessel sizes represented. The three measureable rim diameter (sherds A to C above: *c*. 180mm, *c*. 240mm, *c*. 220mm) show that large bowls were deposited, and indeed most of the pottery, both by sherd count and weight, did appear to derive from vessels in this size range. However, other rim types present do demonstrate that thinner walled vessels of medium size were also present.

Of particular interest is the significant presence of very small cups and bowls, represented by the illustrated sherds E, F and J above.

5.3 Discussion

The earlier Neolithic assemblages from Mill Lane appear to belong to a tradition of plain bowls. However, as mentioned above, the existence of decorated vessels cannot entirely be ruled out, as the sherds mainly derive from rims or lower wall areas. On the other hand, if any decorated vessels had been present it is likely that at least one decorated rim sherd would have survived in the context groups. The general lack of lower neck sherds may also account for the total absence of carinations, although the assemblage may have included gently S-profiled vessels only. The apparent absence of decoration means that the group is not comparable to the large decorated bowl assemblages of the Mildenhall Ware tradition from regional sites such as Hurst Fen, Suffolk (Clark *et al.* 1960) or the Etton causewayed enclosure in Cambridgeshire (Pryor 1998). It has far more similarities to the plain bowl tradition of Grimston Ware, which occurs throughout eastern England and Scotland. Within the region, this plain ware tradition is well represented at Padholme Road, Fengate, Cambridgeshire (Pryor 1974, fig. 6) and in abundance at Broome Heath, Norfolk (Wainwright 1972). The absence of carinations at Mill Lane is somewhat perplexing, but, as discussed above, may relate to the nature of the selection of sherds for deposition. Large bowls with strongly everted simple rims, as evident at Fengate (Pryor 1974, fig. 6), which are so characteristic of the Grimston tradition, are not represented at Mill Lane, although sherds G and H are similar. Gently expanded rims such as Mill Lane sherd D and the thin-walled hook-shaped rim, Mill Lane sherd J can also be matched at Fengate (*cf.* Pryor 1974, fig. 6, 10–11 and 6 respectively). Some Grimston Ware bowls possess fine fluting inside the rim, but this feature is not present at Mill Lane. The larger plain bowl assemblage from Broome Heath includes both carinated and S-profiled bowls, and according to the radiocarbon dates, both occurred together over a period of more than a thousand years. The Mill Lane profiles can be matched within the Broome Heath assemblage as follows: Mill Lane sherd A with Wainwright 1972, fig. 29, P293; no. 2 similar to fig. 28, P280; no. 4 with fig. 22, P203; nos. 7/8 with fig. 27, P273; and no. 10 with fig. 24, P236–242.

The pottery fabrics recorded at Mill Lane, with angular flint inclusions in a hard sandy matrix, are very similar to those defined for the plain ware assemblage from Broome Heath (Wainwright 1972, 23) and also to those of Mildenhall Ware assemblages from Spong Hill and Kilverstone, both in Norfolk (Healy 1988, 64; Garrow *et al.* 2006, 29). Both these recent detailed analyses noted a range of coarse and finer fabrics, but, as at Mill Lane, these appeared to form a continuum, although the finer fabrics do appear to be associated with smaller vessels. In contrast the Grimston Ware bowls from Fengate contained variable amounts of organic matter plus some sand, and the fabrics were soft

and flaky (Pryor 1974, 8), and the large Mildenhall Ware assemblage from Etton is characterised by a predominance of shelly wares (Pryor 1988, 161). These very different fabrics may represent a distinct regional variation in potting.

Moving closer geographically to the site at Mill Lane, it is instructive to consider the ceramic finds from the sites at Haddenham and Barleycroft Farm, Needingworth. Earlier Neolithic pottery from the causewayed enclosure at Haddenham mainly derived from secondary and tertiary ditch fillings. Most belonged to the Mildenhall Style, and the main fabric inclusions were flint (Gdaniec in Evans and Hodder 2006, 299–306). More rims were plain than were decorated, and some matches with the Mill Lane rim forms can be identified (Mill Lane sherd E *cf. ibid.*, fig. 5.32.2: small vessel with inturned simple rim, and sherd D *cf. ibid.*, fig. 5.32.1: simple expanded rim). At the Haddenham long barrow, vessels of Grimston Ware and Mildenhall Ware were found, again in sandy fabrics with poorly sorted flint and quartz inclusions (Knight in Evans and Hodder 2006, 158–161). The rolled rim of a fine plain bowl provides a match for Mill Lane sherd C (*ibid.* fig. 3.58, P4). The best-represented Grimston bowl, with internal fluting, was stratigraphically earlier than the Mildenhall Ware. This chronological pattern is repeated at Barleycroft Farm, Needingworth where fragments of Grimston-type bowls were found in tree-throws, which were dated by radiocarbon to an earlier phase than the Neolithic pits which contained decorated sherds of Mildenhall Ware (Evans *et al.* 1999, 244–247; Evans and Knight 1997). This area lies to the west of the River Ouse. To the east of the river, in the quarry areas near Over most Neolithic occupation was later, typified by Grooved Ware assemblages (Over Sites 3 and 4; Pollard 1998, 79–81), although within the low areas nearest to the river there was lithic evidence for later Mesolithic/earlier Neolithic usage scattered throughout this lower 'islanded' landscape (Evans and Webley 2003, 110). Ceramics relating to this activity comprised a significant element of sherds in earlier Neolithic flint fabrics from one of the 'islands', Godwin Ridge (Site 13) (Evans and Webley 2003, 87 and 104, table 21).

At Barleycroft Farm, two tree-throws contained substantial early Neolithic assemblages: F504 with a minimum of 157 sherds and F591 with 238. Mainly in fabrics containing dense flint and sand (Fabric 1) the vessels were characterised by simple and lightly rolled rims from plain open or neutral bowls, some of which possessed carinated and S-shaped profiles. There was a mixture of fine-ware bowls and heavier large vessels, while several sherds were wiped and slightly burnished (Evans and Knight 1997, 133–134, table 6.3). In all respects these assemblages appear to be extremely similar to the earlier Neolithic groups obtained at Mill Lane. It is also interesting to note that, within both the Mill Lane and Barleycroft Farm groups, the vessels are very partial and heavily worn. They appear to have been single dumped deposits, probably of occupation debris or midden material (*cf.* Evans and Knight 1997, 7). An early radiocarbon date of 3780–3650 cal BC (OxA-8110) relates to F591 and these features may have occurred as part of primary clearance and settlement in this location (Evans *et al.* 1999, 244–246).

The absence at Mill Lane of decorated bowl pottery of Mildenhall style is notable, and Middle Neolithic Peterborough Ware fabric is only represented by a few sherds from a residual context in a furrow. Chronologically the next meaningful group of pottery belongs to the late Neolithic to early Bronze Age period. This comprises a single sherd of decorated Grooved Ware, found residually in a later context, a group of sherds in possible Grooved Ware fabric from the old ground surface of the putative round barrow or midden, and a few groups of Beaker sherds. The decorated fragment of Grooved Ware (sherd K) is similar to a piece found at the Haddenham long barrow (Evans and Hodder 2006, fig. 5.32.10), but attribution to sub-style cannot be determined. The neatly zoned tooth-comb decoration on the Beaker wall sherds (sherd L) is typical of the decorative schemes that are found on earlier Beakers, such as those belonging to Needham's Low Carinated or Tall Mid-Carinated Beaker categories (Needham 2005, figs 5 and 6). The use of such Beakers overlapped, at least in part, with the later incidence of Grooved Ware (Needham 2005, fig. 13). The Beaker base fragments (sherd M), however, derive from a vessel with a bulbous rounded lower body. This profile type, in association with the roughly executed incised decoration, suggests that this vessel may have belonged to the later Beaker repertoire, perhaps a Long-Necked Beaker or one with an S-shaped profile (*cf.* Needham 2005, figs 9 and 10). This vessel base would date the areas beneath and around the putative round barrow into the early Bronze Age period, although no sherds of typical grog-tempered early Bronze Age ceramics, such as urns or accessory vessels, were identified.

CHAPTER 6

ROMAN PERIOD FINDS

6.1 Introduction

The vast majority of finds dating to the Roman period consisted of ceramic building materials, although a small quantity of Roman pottery was found in later features, in particular within the Anglo-Saxon sunken-featured buildings. A single Roman coin was also recovered. The Roman pottery assemblage was assessed as being of local significance only and full analysis was not recommended.

6.2 Roman ceramic building material
(by Sue Anderson)

6.2.1 Forms and fabric

A total of 76 fragments of Roman tile were identified weighing 8,408g. Table 6.1 shows their distribution by fabric and form.

A variety of fabrics is present, suggesting that the ceramic building material (CBM) used at the site was from more than one source. The fine and medium sandy fabrics with few inclusions were the most common types in this group, and the fine soft clay pellet fabric was also relatively frequent. Other Roman tile assemblages in the area have similar ranges of fabrics. For example, sites on the A428 Caxton Common to Hardwick Improvement Scheme produced small quantities of Roman tile in mainly sandy or micaceous sandy fabrics,

Table 6.1 Roman tile by fabric and form (see chapter 2 for a key to fabric codes).

Fabric	Roman tile	Flanged tegula	Imbrex	Box flue
fs	19			2
fsc	4	1		
fscp	6	1	1	10
fsm	1			1
ms	14	5	2	1
mscp	2			
msf	1	1		
msfe	1			
msffe				2
msv	1			

although this area also produced a small group of shelly fabrics (Wells 2007). Clay pellets are a common 'inclusion' in Roman tile fabrics across a wide area of East Anglia, occurring on sites in Norfolk, Suffolk and Essex.

Eight fragments of six flanged *tegulae* (FLT) were identified. Flange widths and heights were recorded where possible, and tile thicknesses measured. Four flange widths measured 25–34mm, four flange heights measured 36–44mm, and six tile thicknesses 21–26mm. Flanges were generally knife-trimmed close to the base. Two examples of underside cut-aways were observed, both in the form of vertical cuts (*cf.* Brodribb 1987, Type 4, fig. 7.4). Four flanges were complete enough to identify the form in cross-section; one had a gently curving convex slope from the top (*cf.* Brodribb 1987, fig. 6 top left) and three were rectangular (*cf.* Brodribb 1987, fig. 6 top right). One flanged *tegula* from the fill of a sunken-featured building (1067) had a circular nail hole – Brodribb suggests that *tegulae* with nail holes were probably used in the lowest, overhanging, course of the roof (Brodribb 1987, 11). Two tiles showed signs of burning, one from 1221 being fully reduced.

Three fragments of two *imbrices* (IMB) were present. One was thicker than 11mm, and the other was 16mm thick. Both were heavily abraded.

Sixteen pieces of twelve box flue tiles (BOX) were present. All were measurable and varied in thickness between 15–22mm. Of these, nine fragments were combed, generally in straight vertical or diagonal lines. The combs had variable numbers of teeth, with examples of 4, 5+, 5–8 and 8–10 teeth being recorded on individual fragments, and both shallow and deep combing were present. In one case the tile may have been scored, rather than combed, with a lattice pattern. One fragment from 1133 had *opus signinum* adhering to the surface, and four pieces showed signs of burning.

Forty-nine fragments of 39 tiles were of uncertain type (RBT). Thicknesses of otherwise unidentifiable tiles may provide a clue to the original function. In this group they varied between 14–44mm. Table 6.2 shows the numbers of measurable tiles in ranges of thicknesses, and suggestions of types. The quantities form a skewed distribution, with the majority being thicker types which may have been used in walling.

None of the very large, thick tiles used to span the *pilae* in hypocaust systems were present here. One tile in pit fill 1073, however, did have a coating of *opus signinum* on the

Table 6.2 Thicknesses of RBT and possible types.

Thickness (mm)	No.	Possible type
14–19	3	Imbrex, box flue or flanged *tegula*
20–24	3	Flanged *tegula* or box flue
25–29	2	Flanged *tegula*?
30–34	2	Floor/wall brick
35–39	9	Floor/wall brick
40–44	4	Floor/wall brick

underside; it was only 14mm thick which would be unusually thin for a floor tile in a bath house, so it may have been a fragment of box flue tile.

Seventeen fragments showed signs of abrasion, but several of these were in soft, fine fabrics which tend to be more susceptible to erosion. Twenty-six fragments showed signs of burning, including several of the box flue fragments. Whilst this may be related to use in a hypocaust system, surface reduction may also occur during firing, or may be related to the use of Roman tile in either contemporary or Anglo-Saxon hearths. One box flue tile in pit fill 1088 had a rubbed edge and worn surface, possibly suggesting re-use as a floor tile. The presence of white lime mortar on two fragments (pit fills 1088 and 1221) may also indicate re-use in a later period.

6.2.2 Discussion

Only three fragments of Roman tile were recovered from a context assigned to the Roman period. The majority of stratified CBM from this site was collected from SFB fills (36 fragments) and ditch/gully fills (32 fragments). General layers contained 15 fragments, with pits containing the same amount (15 fragments). Nineteen fragments came from subsoil, other layers and drains. None of this material was recovered from buildings which would have incorporated the material in their superstructure, and the assemblage

therefore represents demolition rubble and hardcore, whether intentionally or unintentionally used. It can, however, provide some clues to buildings and structures which once stood on or near the site.

The Roman tile in this assemblage included fragments of roofing, floor and/or walling and hypocaust system tiles. Potentially this suggests that there may have been a bath house or other substantial structure somewhere in the area. No structures of this period have been identified within the confines of the excavated area. The presence of a variety of fabrics amongst the Roman tiles suggests that more than one kiln produced the material, and therefore it may have come from more than one structure or more than one phase of building. However, the assemblage is small and interpretation is limited as a result.

6.3 The coin
(by Roger White)

One clipped Roman coin was recovered from the fill of pit 1088 (Fig. 6.1). The coin is a silver *siliqua* of Valentinian II, minted 375–378. Without the mint mark it is not possible to say where it was minted. Coins were no longer imported to Britain after *c.* AD 409 and thus the clipping (and imitation) of *siliquae* must have started at around this time and continued for some period after this date. Recent analysis of metal-detected late Roman coins by Sam Moorhead of the British Museum demonstrates that these coins could have been circulating as late as the mid-5th century within a tri-metallic coinage (S. Moorhead, pers. comm. ARA villas conference July 2009). The implications of this for the Sawston find are that rather than a *terminus post quem* of AD 375, which this coin would normally have, the pit fill which contained this coin must date to sometime after the first decade of the 5th century. It should be noted too that stratified site finds of clipped *siliquae*, as compared to hoard finds and metal-detected finds, are rare. The occurrence of a clipped *siliquae* on a rural site of this type is most unusual and suggests occupation here well into the fifth century.

Figure 6.1 Clipped Roman coin from 1088 (scale in mm).

6.4 The Roman pottery
(by R. Perrin)

Some 58 sherds of Roman pottery, weighing 725g, were recovered from the excavations (Table A4.1, Appendix 4). All bar one sherd of Lower Nene Valley colour-coated ware (LNVCC) were reduced (grey and dark grey) or oxidised (reddish-yellow and cream) wares (Table A4.2, Appendix 4); there was no samian ware or amphora. The LNVCC sherd, from a dish or bowl, was the only obvious regional import, though the reddish-yellow oxidised wares included a probable Colchester mortarium and the complete base of a possible candlestick which may have been produced in the kilns at Hadham. Two other mortarium sherds were made at either the Oxfordshire kilns or, more probably, at Harston, near Cambridge, which produced similar vessels (Pullinger and Young 1982). Another reddish-yellow oxidised ware sherd had a grey core and traces of a red-colour coat and was, again, a product of kilns either in Oxfordshire or Harston. The single cream oxidised ware sherd was part of a flagon base. Apart from the regional wares, the rest of the pottery is likely to have been produced locally. The 'War Ditches' kilns in Cambridge (Hughes 1902a and b; Lethbridge 1948) produced a range of oxidised wares and

grey wares were made at various kilns such as Horningsea (Evans 1991), Teversham (Pullinger and White 1991) and Cherry Hinton (Evans 1990). In addition to the vessel forms already noted, the assemblage included various types of jars, bowls and dishes.

Though their presence indicates some form of Roman activity in the vicinity, none of the features and deposits from which they derived have been attributed to the Roman period and most of the pottery is therefore likely to be residual in later contexts (Fig. 6.2). It is notable that a significant proportion of the Roman pottery came from layers associated with Anglo-Saxon sunken-featured buildings (group 101), including two of the mortaria, the candlestick and the sherd of LNVCC. It is just possible that this is another example of the 'collection' of certain types of Roman pottery fabrics in the Anglo-Saxon period which has been noted elsewhere (*e.g.* Orton Hall Farm: Perrin 1996, 182, 189–190). Another explanation may be similar to that noted at Fordham in Cambridgeshire, where it was suggested that Roman tile found in the fill of a sunken-featured building had been contained in turf which had been used in its construction and had been sourced somewhere close to a Roman bath building (Evans forthcoming).

Figure 6.2 Residual Roman pottery from 1067 (scale in cm).

CHAPTER 7

EARLY ANGLO-SAXON FINDS

7.1 Introduction

Finds dating to the early Anglo-Saxon period comprised pottery, ceramic building material, bone and antler artefacts, animal bone and two small blue glass beads. The majority of these finds relate to the Anglo-Saxon sunken-featured buildings (SFBs) (1170, 1132, 1074, 1018, 1223 and 1381) and were recovered from the fills of the structures as well as the associated early Anglo-Saxon pits and postholes (Fig. 3.6).

7.2 Early Anglo-Saxon pottery
(by Sue Anderson)

Table 7.1 shows the quantification of handmade Anglo-Saxon pottery by fabric group. At this site, the quartz-tempered fabrics dominated, but there were also fairly high proportions of granitic and calcareous fabrics. All other fabric types produced less than ten sherds each.

The estimated vessel equivalent (EVE) of 2.15 is based on 24 measurable rims, but there were a further three rims which could not be measured. Measurements of handmade vessels are always approximate unless a large proportion of the rim is present. For this reason, the minimum number of vessels (MNV), based on sherd families, was estimated for each context, producing a total MNV of 179 vessels.

7.2.1 Fabrics

Fifteen basic fabric groups were distinguished on the basis of major inclusions (ESHW was used for sherds too small to be assigned to the major categories). However, it should be noted that, as with all handmade pottery, fabrics were extremely variable even within single vessels and categorisation was often difficult. Background scatters of calcareous material, unburnt flint, grog, white mica and other less common inclusions, such as feldspar and ferrous pieces, were present in many of the fabrics. All Anglo-Saxon wares were handmade, and colours varied throughout from black through grey, buff and brown to red, often within single vessels. General fabric descriptions are listed below.

Organic tempered

ESO1   Heavily grass tempered with few other inclusions.
ESO2   Grass tempered but containing a much greater proportion of sand than ESO1.
ESOM   Abundant organic tempering in association with granitic inclusions.

Table 7.1 Early Anglo-Saxon pottery.

Description	Fabric	Code	No.	Wt (g)	eve	MNV
Early Saxon grass-tempered	ESO1	2.01	1	10		1
Early Saxon grass and sand-tempered	ESO2	2.02	3	45		3
Early Saxon grass and granitic	ESOM	2.11	4	44		3
Early Saxon coarse quartz	ESCQ	2.03	165	1410	0.51	27
Early Saxon medium sandy	ESMS	2.22	120	1623	0.63	60
Early Saxon fine sand	ESFS	2.04	32	433	0.12	25
Early Saxon fine sand and mica	ESSM	2.08	1	8		1
Early Saxon fine abundant quartz	ESFQ	2.24	9	75	0.07	3
Early Saxon sparse shelly	ESSS	2.07	2	21		1
Early Saxon sparse limestone	ESSL	2.14	4	198		3
Early Saxon coarse limestone	ESCL	2.13	1	16	0.05	1
Early Saxon sparse chalk	ESSC	2.141	32	764	0.07	17
Early Saxon granitic	ESCF	2.10	28	367	0.55	22
Early Saxon granitic and calcareous	ESCM	2.21	13	222	0.15	7
Early Saxon ferrous oxide	ESFE	2.20	1	82		1
Early Saxon handmade wares	ESHW	2.00	4	1		4
Total Early Anglo-Saxon			420	5319	2.15	179

Quartz tempered

ESCQ Coarse quartz tempering; generally moderate or abundant large grains of sub-rounded quartz in a finer sandy matrix, often poorly sorted.

ESMS Medium sand tempering with few other inclusions, sand grains generally well-sorted.

ESFS Fine sand tempering with few other inclusions.

ESSM Very fine sand and abundant white mica.

ESFQ Fine abundant 'sparkly' quartz (greensand?).

Calcareous tempered

ESSS Sparse to moderate fine shell and sand tempering, shell generally leached out.

ESSL Sparse limestone inclusions in medium sandy matrix.

ESCL Sparse to moderate coarse limestone fragments.

ESSC Sparse, rounded chalk in a fine to medium sandy matrix, sometimes leached out.

Granitic tempered

ESCF 'Charnwood Forest' type, containing granitic tempering (dark mica, feldspar).

ESCM Mixed calcareous and granitic inclusions, calcareous fragments generally sparse.

Ferrous oxide

ESFE Medium sandy with abundant rounded ferrous oxide fragments and sparse chalk.

Many sites in East Anglia and the East Midlands have produced similar fabric groups, although they occur in different proportions. The differences are partly related to local geology and period of use, but neither fully explains the wide variety of fabrics in use at different Anglo-Saxon sites. In general, fine, medium and coarse quartz-tempered pottery tend to be the most common fabric groups at sites in the region, although in the later early Anglo-Saxon period these appear to have been replaced to some extent by grass-tempered pottery. Organic-tempering is thought to have developed in the later part of the early Anglo-Saxon period in Essex (Hamerow 1993, 31) and Suffolk (K. Wade, pers. comm.).

A comparison with other early Anglo-Saxon assemblages from Cambridgeshire recorded by the author (Anderson 1998; 2000; Anderson and Tester 2000; 2001) shows that there is little consistency in the proportions of fabrics, even at sites within a few miles of Sawston (Fig. 7.1). The proportion of sand tempering is relatively high at most of the sites, with the noticeable exception of Hinxton, the closest site to Mill Lane both geographically and temporally.

Slightly further to the south, at Great Chesterford, Essex, the fabrics of pottery from the early Anglo-Saxon cemetery were analysed (Williams 1994), and in that group sandstone was by far the most frequent fabric with much smaller proportions of the granitic, limestone and sand-tempered groups. Williams concludes that most of the pottery was probably made locally to the site, although he suggests that the granitic and oolitic limestone vessels could have been imported from further west and north.

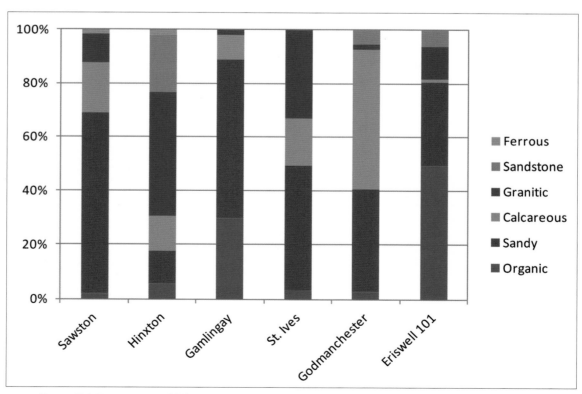

Figure 7.1 Proportions of fabrics at Early Anglo-Saxon sites in Cambridgeshire (based on weight).

7.2.2 Forms

Rim and base types were classified following Hamerow (1993, fig. 26). Eight vessels had flaring rims, fourteen vessels had vertical ('upright') rims, and five had incurving rims. Eight vessels had flat-rounded bases, seven had rounded or saggy bases, and five were flat-angled.

Rim diameters of vessels were measured where possible. In this group, both bowls and jars were fairly evenly dispersed between 80–230mm with a very slight peak between 180–200mm. In general, bowl rim sizes give a rough idea of the overall size of the bowl and the measurements show that both small and relatively large bowls were present in this group. For jars however, even quite large carinated vessels can have narrow necks and small rim diameters, so the measurement does not provide a good indicator of vessel size when only fragments survive. Nevertheless at least two jars had rim diameters of 200mm or more, suggesting that some vessels were relatively large. A broad range is expected for a settlement site, but contrasts with the generally small range and 'personal' size of vessels which often occur in inhumation cemetery assemblages. For example, most of the inhumed vessels at Flixton, Suffolk (Anderson forthcoming a) were in the range 110–160mm, whilst those at the settlement site at Flixton were between 50–200mm and at Bloodmoor Hill, Carlton Colville, Suffolk (Tipper 2009, 217) rim sizes ranged between 35–280mm.

No vessels were complete in profile, but it was sometimes possible to suggest the vessel type on the basis of rim or base form, where enough of the body was present. It was also possible to get an idea of shape from some of the larger body sherds, and carinated vessels were especially identifiable from even small pieces. Eleven vessels were identified as bowls, one as a possible lamp, and fifteen as jars. Those for which more detailed shape descriptions could be applied are shown in Table 7.2.

Some vessels had evidence for surface treatment. Table 7.3 shows the main types found. Although most may originally have been smoothed, sometimes this surface had worn away through use, and there were many sherds in this group for which it was clear that the surface had never been smoothed. Few decorative elements were identified other than those normally intended as rustication, and no stamps were present. Applied decoration in the form of small solid bosses (or possibly unpierced lugs) and cordons were present in a few cases, and there were some examples of diagonal incised lines or grooves.

Whilst many pots showed signs of sooting and/or burnt food residues, there was no evidence that any of the vessels had been used for industrial processes. However, the presence of a lamp may be indicative of craft activities which required an internal light source being carried out.

7.2.3 Dating

This assemblage shows elements which place it largely in the first half of the early Anglo-Saxon period (5th–6th centuries). Very little organic-tempered pottery is present and there are no 'baggy' vessels typical of the later part of the period;

5th-century characteristics such as *Schlickung* and carinated vessels are present, but no stamped decorative schemes more typical of the 6th century were found. Calcareous-tempered wares, and possibly also granite-tempering, are more characteristic of 6th-century groups, however, so there is some material of this date. The globular vessels and hemispherical bowls might also belong to that century. Unfortunately very few of the forms could be defined in detail and this makes any close dating of the assemblage difficult.

7.2.4 Distribution

The majority of the early Anglo-Saxon group came from SFBs in the south of the site (G101) and associated pits (G103). Small quantities of sherds came from pit 1307 in G102, possible sunken-featured building (SFB) 1381 near the middle of the eastern edge of the site and possible SFB 1018 in the southeast corner. A few sherds were residual in later features including drainage gully 1016 and ditch 1098

Table 7.2 Identifiable forms/shapes of Anglo-Saxon vessels.

Form	MNV
sub-biconical?	1
carinated	1
short rim, sloping/concave neck	2
shouldered	2
offset-shouldered globular	1
round-bellied (globular)	3
hemispherical bowl	2
incurving bowl	2
straight-sided bowl	1
lugged hanging bowl?	1
flaring-sided lamp/small bowl	1

Table 7.3 Surface treatment and decoration of Anglo-Saxon pottery.

Surface treatment	with decoration	MNV
Burnishing	None	10
	Notched cordon	1
Smoothing	None	18
	Incised lines	1
	Bossed	2
Grass wiping	None	2
Roughened	None	1
Schlickung	None	1
None	Finger-pinched rustication	6
	Finger-nail rustication	1
	Fine combed rustication	2
	Incised line rustication?	3

(G104), or were from unphased layers 1064, 1264 and 1359. Groups of pottery from the sunken-featured buildings are described below.

Sunken-featured building 1018

Eleven body sherds of a single ESMS vessel were found in the fill of this pit, and a sherd from an ESCQ vessel with internal sooting was recovered from a bulk sample.

Sunken-featured building 1074 (including postholes 1247 and 1270, gully 1344 and pit 1238)

Seventy-six sherds from 39 vessels were recovered from this feature. These included fragments of seven jars with flaring or upright rims and a bowl with a small applied boss. Decorated vessels included three with finger-pinched rustication and two with incised lines. The linear gully 1344 associated with this structure contained ten sherds from eight vessels, one of which was decorated with fine combed rustication.

The pit 1238 to the northeast of SFB 1074 could be associated with its use (as opposed to the pottery from its backfill which probably accumulated largely following its demolition). This contained 65 sherds, of which 37 were from a jar with an upright rim. Another jar and two bowls were also present.

Sunken-featured building 1132 (including postholes 1250, 1293 and 1383, and cut 1304)

Eighty-seven sherds from 46 vessels were found in SFB 1132 and associated features. Identifiable vessels comprised three bowls and two jars with flaring and upright rims. One bowl was straight-sided, one was hemispherical and the third was a small shouldered globular vessel with a pointed circular boss or lug (Fig. 7.2.A). Sherds with surface treatment included one with a roughly grooved surface, one with *Schlickung*, and one with finger-pinched rustication.

Sunken-featured building 1170 (including postholes 1208, 1289, and 1291)

Forty-three sherds from 39 vessels were collected from SFB 1170 and its postholes. Identifiable vessels comprised an inturned-rim bowl, three jars with upright or flaring rims, and a lamp with a flaring rim. One body sherd had finger-pinched rustication.

Sunken-featured building 1223 (including postholes 1225 and 1357)

This SFB contained 96 sherds from 16 vessels. Nineteen sherds were from an inturned-rim bowl with a flat-rounded base (Fig. 7.2.B). Sixty sherds were from a hemispherical bowl. Two other bowls and a jar with a short flat-topped upright rim and sloping neck were also identified. Surface treatment included finger-pinched and fingernail rustication (Fig. 7.2.C), surface roughening and burnishing, and one vessel had a large cordon with notching (Fig. 7.2.D).

Possible sunken-featured building 1381

Twelve sherds from three vessels were recovered from this feature, including six sherds of a bowl with an inturned rim, possibly a hanging vessel. A large body sherd from the same vessel was found in posthole 1383 in SFB 1132.

Fabric distribution in the sunken-featured buildings

Figure 7.3 shows the distribution of the main fabric groups in the four main sunken-featured buildings. The two smaller possible sunken-featured buildings contained only quartz-tempered sherds. SFBs 1074 and 1223 show similar proportions of the main fabrics. SFB 1074 produced one

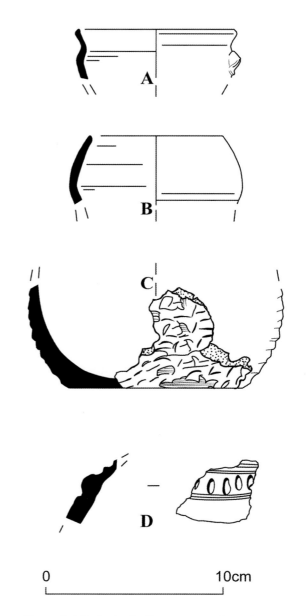

Figure 7.2 Early Anglo-Saxon pottery from the site.

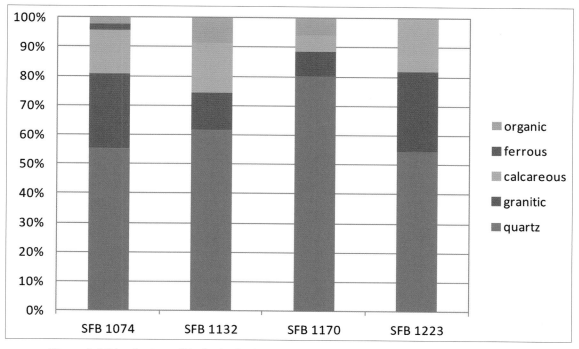

Figure 7.3 Distribution of Early Anglo-Saxon fabrics in the sunken-featured buildings (MNV).

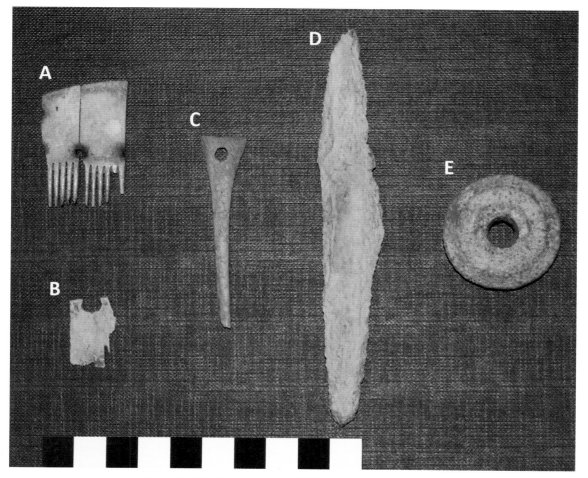

Figure 7.4 Worked bone from 1073 and 1088 (scale in cm).

organic-tempered vessel, but this was from the gully 1344 rather than from the structure itself. The higher quantities of organic pottery and reduced amounts of granitic and calcareous wares from SFBs 1132 and 1170 may indicate that they were backfilled slightly later than the other two.

The pit 1238 to the northeast of SFB 1074 contained almost entirely quartz-tempered wares with a single rimsherd of a granitic ware. This is in contrast to the broader range from the SFB itself and may be further evidence that the pit was contemporary with the use of the structure, whilst the fill of the SFB pit (which includes 6th-century elements) was later.

Four of the vessels were illustrated (Fig. 7.2):

A. ESCF bowl?, flaring rim, pointed circular boss or lug. SFB 1132, fill 1088, Phase 5.
B. ESMS bowl, inturned rim. SFB 1223, fill 1221, Phase 5.
C. ESSL, fingernail rustication. SFB 1223, fill 1221, Phase 5.
D. ESSC, burnished, large cordon with notches. SFB 1223, fill 1221.

7.3 Ceramic building material
(by Sue Anderson)

The 51 fragments of CBM recovered from Anglo-Saxon features were all of Roman date (see Chapter 6). Most were found in four sunken-featured buildings in Group 101. Several pieces showed signs of burning, suggesting that they may have been scavenged for use in hearths or ovens during the Anglo-Saxon period.

Ungrouped	Pit 1018 produced one fragment of FLT.
G101	Roman tile was recovered from four SFBs in this group, 1074, 1132, 1170 and 1223. Ten fragments of RBT and a piece of BOX came from 1074, with five fragments showing signs of burning. SFB 1132 contained six fragments of RBT, four fragments of BOX and two pieces of an IMB; four were burnt. Posthole 1134 contained one burnt piece of BOX with *opus signinum*. SFB 1170 contained ten fragments of RBT, two pieces of FLT and a BOX fragment; four pieces were burnt. The fills of 1223 contained seven fragments of RBT, four fragments of FLT and a piece of BOX. Five fragments were burnt. One piece of RBT had white lime mortar along one edge.
G103	Pit 1238 produced two fragments of RBT.

The Roman tile recovered from the site was largely found discarded in features of Anglo-Saxon and later date. Roman tile was sometimes recycled in the early Anglo-Saxon period as lining material for hearths or ovens, and signs of burning on many fragments suggest that this may be the case here. Other Anglo-Saxon settlements in the region have produced Roman tile from SFBs, for example Bloodmoor Hill, Carlton Colville, Suffolk (Anderson 2009, 34) where 28 individual SFB pits produced between one and 35 fragments each.

7.4 Bone and antler artefacts
(by Penelope Walton Rogers and D. James Rackham)

Bone and antler objects (Fig. 7.4) were recovered from the fills of SFB 1074 and SFB 1132 and, as such, they are most likely to represent waste material dumped at the end of the hut's life (Tipper 2004, 184–185). They cannot be closely dated, but they are typical of finds from Anglo-Saxon settlements and some can be confidently associated with the activities of women.

From context 1073 in SFB 1074, there were two antler tooth-plates (sf 7, Fig. 7.4.A) and the heavily eroded remains of a third (sf 9, Fig. 7.4.B), which together represent the remains of at least one, possibly two, single-sided composite hair-combs. The connecting plates which would have held the tooth-plates together are absent, but their presence is indicated in sf 7 (Fig. 7.4.A) by a pale, unstained area running across the plates and the remains of iron riveting on the edges. The plates of sf 7 have a gently sloping back, but sf 9 has a curved shape cut into its back, which represents ornament at the comb end (MacGregor *et al* 1999, 1926-32; Riddler and Trzaska-Nartowski 2013, 107-45). Single-sided composite antler combs were in use in Britain from the late Roman to the late medieval periods (Ashby 2007). It is impossible to date them from the tooth-plates alone, although the dimensions and shape of these examples make an origin in the Roman period unlikely. Hair combs appear in both male and female burials (including cremation burials) of the early Anglo-Saxon period, although they have a slight bias towards women (Williams 2003, 114–115; Stoodley 1999, 31, 38; Riddler and Trzaska-Nartowski 2013, 143–144).

A near-complete garment pin made from a young pig fibula, sf 8 (Fig. 7.4.C) came from the same fill as the comb tooth-plates, context 1073. Pig fibulae have a naturally flared flat distal end which can be easily pierced. In this example, the head has been trimmed, the shank pared down, the 'eye' cut or gouged and there is evidence for wear on the mid shaft. There is a persistent confusion in the archaeological literature between these objects and needles, although their shape is unsuited to sewing and they lack the wear pattern of genuine bone needles (Walton Rogers 1997, 1783). In costume terms, they belong to the broad class of perforated and ring-headed pins which were fastened with a loop made of a leather thong or cord. They typically have most polish on the tip and shank and an example with remains of a thong slotted through the 'eye' was found crossways at the throat in Grave 137, a female burial, at Castledyke, Lincolnshire (Walton Rogers 1998, 276). Pig-fibula pins were in use throughout the Anglo-Saxon period. Pins in general are mostly found in adult women's graves, although they were occasionally used for purposes other than garment fastening in adult male and child burials (Stoodley 1999, 32, 41; Walton Rogers 2007, 178).

A fractured piece of animal long bone (Fig. 7.4.D), from the same fill, 1073, has an eroded surface which makes it impossible to judge whether it represents debris from food production or an object in the early stages of manufacture. However, a similar but better-preserved example from 9th-century Coppergate, York, had cut marks which identified it as a rough-out for a double-ended pin-beater (Walton Rogers

1997, 1755–1756). This was a weavers' hand-tool, used with the warp-weighted loom until the 10th or 11th century (Walton Rogers 1997, 1753, 1755; 2001, 162).

A single antler spindle whorl (sf10, Fig. 7.4.E), was recovered from the fill, 1088, of SFB 1132. It is plano-convex (Walton Rogers Form A) and its regular appearance and faceted profile suggest that it has been lathe-turned. Antler whorls were at their most common in eastern England in the 5th and 6th centuries, but the 5th-century examples were mostly cylindrical (Form B) and the plano-convex whorl did not come into use, in bone, stone and clay as well as antler, until the 6th and 7th centuries (Walton Rogers 1997, 1736; 2007, 24–25; Riddler and Trzaska-Nartowski 2013, 145–148). Spindle whorls were used for drop-spindle spinning, which was a woman's craft. The drop-spindle was easily portable and a single whorl is merely an indication that an Anglo-Saxon woman was in the vicinity at some stage, not that yarn was necessarily spun in that particular building (Walton Rogers 2007, 46).

Catalogue of bone artefacts (Figure 7.4)

A. 1073 SF 7

Two near-complete antler tooth-plates from a comb, 7a and 7b. Both plates have sloping backs and appear to have been contiguous. The teeth are 13mm long and they have transverse cuts, deeper on one face than the other. Both plates have a pale clean zone where they will have been covered by the comb connecting plates. Rivets are represented by semicircular indentations surrounded by iron corrosion on the edges of the plates, and a single cylindrical iron rivet remains *in situ*.

7a. Five surviving teeth. Two rivet holes on one edge and an intact iron rivet on the other.
Plate including teeth: 39 × 12 × 3mm. Rivet L.8, D.2mm.

7b. Originally seven teeth: five are in position, one is detached but present and one is absent. Rivet holes on both edges, one engaging with the intact rivet on fragment 7a.
Plate including teeth: 42 × 15 × 3mm.
Species not identifiable, but probably red deer.

B. 1073 SF9

Fragment of flat antler plate, surface eroded. Probably an end tooth-plate from a comb. Tapering section, large, rounded indentation on spine of plate and remains of tooth at tapered end. Species not identified, but likely to be red deer. 23 × 15 × 2.5mm.

C. 1073 SF8

Incomplete bone pin with flat, pierced triangular head; tip missing. The naturally flared head has been trimmed, the 'eye' gouged or cut, and the shank and tip shaped with a blade or file. Some polish mid-shaft. Made from distal shaft of juvenile pig fibula, epiphysis unfused. L.63mm, W. head 15mm; W. shank 3.5–4.5mm; D. perforation 4mm.

D. 1073 no SF

Fractured piece of animal long bone, possibly a rough-out for a weaver's pin-beater; surface eroded. Species not identifiable, but size and shape suggest horse or cattle. 128 × 19 × 11mm.

E. 1088 [1132]

Complete antler spindle whorl, surface eroded. Plano-convex with prominent ridge around circumference; faceted in profile; probably lathe-turned. Hour-glass spindle hole. Most probably made from burr; species not identifiable but likely to be red deer. Walton Rogers Form A1. D.32mm, Ht.15mm, spindle hole 10mm–8mm-9.5mm.

7.5 The Anglo-Saxon animal bone
(by Matilda Holmes)

Bones were in poor to fair condition, with a moderate amount of fresh breakage and refitted fragments (Appendix 3, Table A3.2), which suggest that burial conditions were not conducive to good preservation. The assemblage was highly fragmented (Fig. 7.5), the majority of bones were represented by four zones or less (after Serjeantson 1996), indicating that they were subject to heavy breakages through butchery or trampling prior to deposition.

The high incidence of gnawed bones indicates that much of the assemblage was not buried immediately after disposal, rather, it was exposed for dogs and rodents to chew on. This is also implied by the ratio of loose molars to those remaining in the jaw – teeth are hard to separate from the mandible when fresh, but once the soft tissue has degraded they more likely easily fall out and become detached.

The large numbers of gnawed bones probably affected the proportion of butchery marks visible, which was fairly low. There were also few burnt bones, suggesting that bones were not exposed to fire as part of processing or disposal.

7.5.1 Species representation and diet

Although both the early Anglo-Saxon and less closely dated general Anglo-Saxon features may have been contemporary, the differences in species proportions between the two assemblages makes it unreliable to interpret them together (Appendix 3, Table A3.3). The high proportion of pig bones in the Anglo-Saxon sample is unusual from low status sites, as are the relatively high numbers of deer and domestic birds (domestic fowl and geese) from both the early Anglo-Saxon and Anglo-Saxon assemblages, although deer were represented by antler fragments, except for one red deer radius from an Anglo-Saxon context. High proportions of cattle such as those represented in the early Anglo-Saxon sample are also recorded from contemporary high status sites such as Yeavering, Northumbria (Higgs 1977) and Cadbury Congresbury, Somerset (Noddle 1970, 1992). As there was little monetary wealth, the possession of goods was

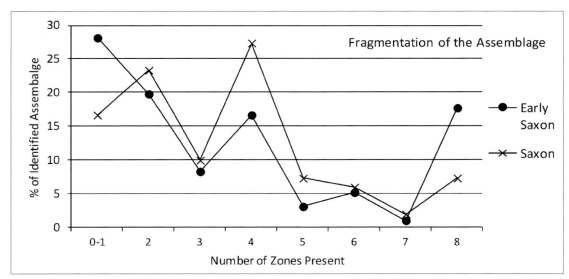

Figure 7.5 Fragmentation of the Assemblage. To illustrate the degree of fragmentation of bones, the number of zones recorded for each fragment is plotted (using zones as described in Serjeantson, 1996).

probably the best indicator of status in this phase (Holmes 2011, ch.7). However, the samples are not large enough to be more forthcoming as to the status of the settlement.

The sieved samples contained a number of background species, including frog and mouse (Appendix 3, Table A3.4), which would be common, naturally occurring species. There were no large samples of bird or fish bones recorded however, indicating a real dearth of such animals from the assemblage, which is not uncommon on Anglo-Saxon sites.

Both fusion and tooth wear indicate that animals were culled at prime meat ages, with none of the limb bones of cattle, sheep or pigs coming from animals older than three years of age, although cattle vertebrae indicated the presence of older animals, presumably breeding stock. This is a common husbandry strategy in the early Anglo-Saxon phase, reflecting the widespread subsistence economy of the majority of the population.

7.5.2 Carcass representation and butchery

Although the sample sizes of body parts represented are small (Appendix 3, Table A3.5), there is a notable absence of elements from the upper hind leg (pelvis, femur and tibia). Carcass parts indicative of primary butchery waste are abundant (head, vertebrae and lower legs – metapodia and phalanges), as well as elements from the upper fore legs (scapua, humerus, radius and ulna). There is also a lack of horn cores, and if the sample were larger, such a pattern would point to the redistribution of particular parts of the carcass. However, the low quantity of bones makes trends unreliable. As noted above, the prevalence of canid gnawing has most likely destroyed much of the observable butchery marks, although chop marks were recorded on cattle bones (cervical vertebra, first phalange, radius, scapula and humerus).

Figure 7.6 Anglo-Saxon glass beads from 1381 (scale in mm).

7.5.3 Summary of the early Anglo-Saxon animal bone

This small assemblage of early Anglo-Saxon animal bones is typical of the type of husbandry observed from contemporary self-sufficient settlements in England, where cattle, sheep and pigs were raised for meat rather than secondary products. The diet of the population is towards the more privileged end of the scale, with high numbers of cattle, as well as domestic fowl and goose.

7.6 The glass beads
(by Cecily Cropper)

Two glass beads were recovered from an early Anglo-Saxon context, the fill of a possible sunken-featured building (1381) along with a relatively significant amount of early Anglo-Saxon pottery. Both are annular and of a royal blue colour (Fig. 7.6), common within Anglo-Saxon settlement areas (Guido, 1999, 48), but of a colour and type that is so ubiquitous that close dating is inhibited without associated

Figure 7.7 Buckle loop from 1067 (scale in mm).

finds. Anglo-Saxon beads tend to be discussed primarily as grave goods within datable burials (see in particular Brugmann 2004). Guido does not even provide schedules for monochrome blue beads.

7.7 The buckle loop
(by Penelope Walton Rogers)

Sf 22 from context 1067 is the loop from a small copper-alloy buckle, without its tongue (Fig. 7.7). It is oval-to-circular, but wider and thicker on one side. Buckles with a swollen tongue-rest are found in Marzinzik's Type I.11 (oval loops) and I.12 (round loops). They are usually made of iron, but often occur in East Anglia and the East Midlands, (Marzinzik 2003, 189–190, 195), and this Cambridgeshire example is probably just a copper-alloy variant of the same. Small buckles, 20mm or narrower across the loop, are most common from the mid 6th century onwards (Marzinzik 2003, 34).

A plied linen cord, approximately 2mm thick, runs across the band in two places and there appears to be the imprint of a knot on one side (Fig. 7.7 insert). This can be interpreted as a suspension cord. A buckle loop without its tongue, in a cluster of rings of different sizes, in a baby-size grave at Dover Buckland II G377 (Walton Rogers 2007, 217) suggests that such objects could be used to entertain children. Metal rings are also thought to have had a use in pagan healing practice (Meaney 1981, 12–13, 170–178). In either case, this will have been the secondary use of the buckle.

Catalogue *(Figure 7.7)*

Cast copper-alloy buckle loop. Almost circular, with one side wider and thicker than the other. Cross-section of band is rounded rectangular. Loop 21 × 20mm; band 4–5.5mm wide × 3–4mm thick. A multi-ply cord runs across the band in two places and the imprint of a tangle of threads on the outer face suggests a knot. The cord is S-plied (2.0mm thick) from Z-spun (0.8mm) yarns. The fibre is flax or hemp (identified with a polarising transmitted-light microscope at ×400 magnification). Sf 22, context 1067.

Chapter 8

Late Anglo-Saxon, medieval and post-medieval finds

8.1 Introduction

Finds dating to the later Anglo-Saxon and subsequent medieval and post-medieval periods consisted of pottery, ceramic building materials, and horse burials. These finds were retrieved from a variety of contexts including enclosure and field boundaries located within the centre of the site (Fig. 3.11).

8.2 Late Anglo-Saxon and medieval pottery
(by Sue Anderson)

8.2.1 Late Anglo-Saxon and early medieval

A total of 853 sherds weighing 9108g were collected during the excavations at Mill Lane, Sawston. Table 8.1 shows the quantities of 11th–14th-century pottery in this assemblage.

Distribution

Medieval pottery was recovered from 58 features or layers. The majority was found in ditch fills, particularly those in the central part of the site. The largest single group was from ditch 1566 (G107), which contained 65 sherds from 25 vessels including several jars with late 12th-/13th-century rim forms. Gully 1439 produced 64 sherds, but

these were from a single vessel, a Hedingham Ware jug. Thirty-six sherds from seven vessels were found in ditch 1571 and there were 25 sherds from 17 vessels in ditch 1603. Pit 1591 contained 22 sherds from six vessels. All other features produced less than 20 sherds each, suggesting broad dispersal of this material across the site with few concentrations of rubbish disposal.

Figure 8.1 provides illustrations of nine of the vessels:

A. MCWG jar, rim B4. Ditch fill 1565, Phase 6.
B. HCW jar, rim C1? Ditch fill 1440, Phase 6.
C. HCW jar, rim C1. Ditch fill 1565, Phase 6.
D. MCW jar?, rim B2. Applied thumbed strip or possibly handle attachment? Subsoil 1001.
E. MCW jar, rim C1. Ditch fill1602, Phase 6.
F. MCW jar, rim H2. Ditch fill 1440, Phase 6.
G. HCWF bowl?, upright plain rim. Pit fill 1561, Phase 6.
H. MCW spouted pitcher, rim C1? Combed wavy line decoration. Ditch fill 1565, Phase 6.
I. HFW1 jug, flaring rim. Peat 811, Phase 6.

Coarsewares

The only late Anglo-Saxon or Saxo-Norman fabric in this group was St Neot's Ware (STNE), which is described by

Table 8.1 Late Anglo-Saxon to medieval pottery (11th–14th c.) – the key to the fabric codes is provided in Chapter 2.

Description	Fabric	Code	No.	Wt (g)	eve	MNV
St Neot's Ware	STNE	2.70	3	19	0.05	3
Early medieval ware	EMW	3.10	54	210		16
Early medieval ware gritty	EMWG	3.11	13	125		2
Early medieval ware shelly	EMWS	3.14	7	48		1
Early medieval sparse shelly ware	EMWSS	3.19	15	28		1
Medieval coarseware	MCW	3.20	163	1770	1.58	89
Medieval coarseware gritty	MCWG	3.21	10	182	0.27	5
Hedingham coarseware	HCW	3.43	29	394	0.33	17
Hedingham coarseware (fine variant)	HCWF	3.431	39	237	0.15	5
Medieval shelly wares	MSHW	3.50	1	2		1
Unprovenanced glazed	UPG	4.00	1	3		1
Hedingham Ware	HFW1	4.23	81	300	0.25	8
Total Late Anglo-Saxon and medieval			416	3318	2.70	149

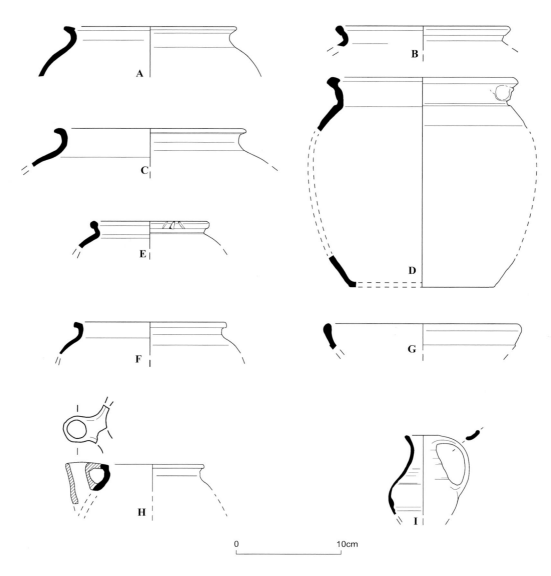

0   10cm

Figure 8.1 Medieval pottery from the site.

Hurst (1956), and Baker *et al.* (1979). A small quantity was recovered from three contexts, two of them in association with later material. Two bowl rims were present, and the third sherd was a small body fragment. It is likely that these sherds were contemporary with the earliest medieval activity on the site, in the 11th century.

Early medieval wares are generally defined as handmade wares which first appeared in the 11th century and continued to be made into the 13th century in rural parts of East Anglia. Sometimes pots were finished on a wheel and many have wheelmade rims luted onto handmade bodies; rim forms suggest that this technique probably started towards the middle of the period in most areas. The following fabrics were present:

EMW   Handmade, medium sandy with few other inclusions, generally thin-walled. Hard. Dark grey-black, occasional oxidised patches.

EMWG   Generic fabric group for handmade wares with common to abundant sand greater than 1mm in diameter.

EMWS   Generic fabric group for handmade wares with common to abundant coarse shell tempering.

EMWSS   Handmade, fine to medium sandy, usually oxidised on one or both surfaces, sparse shell inclusions. Hard.

The early medieval period was represented by 89 sherds, indicating no more than 20 vessels, in medium and coarse sandy and shelly handmade fabrics typical of the area. The majority were oxidised with reduced cores, although a few finer black examples similar to those more typical of Norfolk were also present. Only one rim was present, but the form was not identifiable due to damage and abrasion.

Medieval coarsewares are generally wheelmade wares which have an overall date range spanning the 12th–14th centuries. Most are well-fired and fully reduced to pale to dark greys, although oxidised wares are also found. Several coarsewares were identifiable, although it was clear that most contained a similar range of inclusions. Hedingham wares (HCW, HCWF) are defined by Cotter (2000, 75–91) and Walker (2012). The fabrics listed below are of uncertain provenance and were distinguished largely on the basis of coarseness and abundance of inclusions.

MCW   Wheelmade, fine to medium sandy with few other inclusions. Hard. Pale to dark grey. Generic fabric group for coarsewares made at currently unidentified production sites.

MCWG   'Gritty' version of MCW, with moderate to common coarse quartz sand and few other inclusions.

MSHW   Generic fabric for wheelmade medieval shelly wares – usually containing abundant shell and few other inclusions.

Medieval coarsewares made up the bulk of this group. Many were in soft fabrics similar to pottery produced at Sible Hedingham, although only a few were positively identified as this ware. Forms and fabrics were generally similar to Essex wares, and one jar with a Suffolk-type square-beaded rim was also present. Based on dating for the Essex ware forms (Drury 1993a), the majority of these wares were 12th–13th-century types, with none of the later, acutely everted, rims present in the assemblage.

Identifiable vessels included 22 jars (Fig. 8.1, A–F), three bowls (Fig. 8.1.G), a spouted pitcher (Fig. 8.1.H), and a shallow dish or dripping dish. A body sherd with a handle attachment was probably from a jug or spouted pitcher. Table 8.2 shows the distribution of rim forms and vessel forms.

Glazed wares

The glazed wares made up 7% of the high medieval assemblage by MNV, which is within normal limits for a rural assemblage. For example a contemporary group from Cedar's Park, Stowmarket, produced 9% (Anderson forthcoming b), but the Mill Lane figure is lower than the 14% proportion found in the large assemblage at Longstanton (Anderson 2010a).

The glazed wares at Mill Lane were dominated by Hedingham Ware (HFW1; Cotter 2000, 75–91; Walker 2012) and the majority of these vessels were jugs but only two rims were present. One jug had an upright thickened rim, a wide strap handle and a sagging base, and was decorated with brown slip lines under a light green glaze. Another was a small? globular jug with a flaring rim and green glaze (Fig.

8.1.I). Other vessels had orange or green glaze. One other glazed ware was present, a small sherd in a soft orange fabric which was not micaceous; it is likely to be another Essex or South Cambridgeshire ware ('sandy orange ware').

8.2.2 Later wares

Very little pottery could be dated later than the 14th century. Table 8.3 shows the quantities of these later wares.

Distribution

All material of this period was from phase 7 ditch fills. As the quantity was small, there was no particular clustering and the later pottery was probably dispersed across the site during agricultural activity.

Fabrics

Sherds identified as 'LMTE' are of similar type to late medieval wares manufactured elsewhere in East Anglia (Jennings 1981; Anderson *et al.* 1996) but the fabrics are closer to Hedingham wares. PMRW is a generic fabric used for unglazed red earthenwares of the post-medieval period. REFW covers all factory-made fine white earthenwares made from the late 18th century onwards. YELW is a buff-bodied, yellow-glazed version of industrial slipware and includes mixing bowls and mocha-decorated wares (Slesin *et al.* 1997).

Table 8.2 Identifiable rims and vessel forms (MNV).

Rim	Jar	Pitcher	Bowl	Dripping dish
Essex type B2	1			
Essex type B4	4			
Essex type C1	5	1		
Essex type H1	3			
Essex type H2	3			
Suffolk square bead	1			
Upright beaded	1			
Beaded			1	1
Inturned			1	
Upright			1	

Table 8.3 Medieval and later pottery.

Description	Fabric	Code	No.	Wt (g)	EVE	MNV
Late Essex-type wares	LMTE	5.60	2	15		1
Post-medieval redwares	PMRW	6.10	7	258		1
Refined white earthenwares	REFW	8.03	6	192		3
Yellow Ware	YELW	8.13	1	5		1
Total late medieval to modern			16	470	0	6

Forms

Seven fragments of a later medieval or post-medieval redware pipkin or chamber pot (sooting on the handle suggests the former function) were recovered from ditch fill 1397; this was probably a local product as the rim form was a development of medieval type C1 (Drury 1993a). Two sherds of probable late medieval date were found in ditch fill 1401. Modern wares comprised a small fragment of yellow-glazed refined ware, and two base sherds of whiteware plates or saucers, one with blue transfer printing. A further four sherds in refined whiteware were collected from upper ditch fill 1578; these were part of a transfer-printed toilet bowl of the early cone-shaped form.

8.2.3 Pottery by site phase: medieval

A summary of the pottery by site phase is provided in Table 8.4. The largest groups were from phase 5 (Anglo-Saxon) and phase 6 (medieval). Some post-Roman sherds were intrusive in earlier features. Unphased material will not be discussed further.

Pottery was recovered from 39 features assigned to this phase. Most contained less than 10 sherds each. The largest single groups were from ditch 1565 (G107), ditch 1570, ditch 1602 and pit 1590. Only small quantities of residual pottery were present, suggesting that the medieval features did not disturb earlier features to any great extent, and there were no intrusive sherds. The identified vessels from this phase included nineteen jars, three bowls, three jugs, a dripping dish and a spouted pitcher.

Peat 811   Nine sherds of a small globular HFW1 jug (93g) were found. 12th–13th century.

Ditch 708   Fill 709 contained eleven sherds (76g) of an EMWG vessel. 11th–13th century.

Ditch 803   Eighteen sherds (2 EMW, 7 EMWS, 1 MCW, 8 MCWG) from six vessels including two jars (rims B4 and H1) were recovered from the fills of this ditch. The lowest fill 804 contained the H1 jar rim. M.–L. 13th century.

Table 8.4 Pottery types present by phase (sherd count). Shading indicates residual material.

Pot period	Phase 3	Phase 4	Phase 5	Phase 6	Phase 7	Un
ESax			408	3	1	8
LSax		1		1		1
EMed				89		
Med	2	1	1	296	3	21
LMed					2	
PMed					7	
Modern					7	
Uncertain			1			
Total	2	2	410	389	20	30

Ditch 806   One abrade MCW sherd (5g) was found in fill 807. Med+.

Ditch 903   Three sherds of MCW (22g) were recovered from the upper and lower ditch fills. Two sherds cross-matched with sherds in ditches 906 and 911. 12th–14th century.

Ditch 906   The upper fill 907 contained two sherds of EMWG and two sherds of MCW. One of the latter was from a vessel also found in ditch 903. 11th–13th century?

Ditch 909   Fill 910 contained seven sherds of an EMW vessel and six sherds of MCW including two jar rims (H2). E.–M. 13th century.

Ditch 911   Three sherds of MCW were found in the lower fill. One base fragment was from a vessel also found in ditch 903. 12th–14th century.

Ditch 913   A base fragment of MCW (42g) was collected from the lower fill. 12th–14th century.

Gully 1016   Three sherds of ESCQ (4g) were residual in this context. ESax.

Gully 1233   One sherd (3g) of MCW was found. 12th–14th century.

Gully 1235   One sherd (4g) of MCW was found. 12th–14th century.

Gully 1439   This feature contained 64 sherds (146g) of an HFW1 jug with upright thickened rim and wide strap handle.

Ditch 1451   A MCW jar rim (H1), a small UPG body sherd and two fragments of HFW1 were recovered from the fill. M.–L. 13th century.

Linear 1456   One sherd of EMW was found in the fill. 11th–13th century.

Pit 1497   Eighteen sherds of two HCWF vessels and a base fragment of HCW were found. One of the HCWF vessels had a cross-link with a sherd in G106 ditch 1500. 12th–13th century.

PH 1509   A base sherd of MCW was recovered from this unexcavated feature. 12th–14th century.

Pit 1514   A small sherd (1g) of MCW was collected. 12th–14th century.

Ditch 1549   One sherd of HCW (22g) was found. 12th–13th century.

Pit 1562   The lower fill contained an HCWF bowl rim, two fragments of HCW handle and six sherds of an MCW vessel. 12th–13th century.

Ditch 1571   Five sherds of two HCW vessels and 31 sherds of five MCW vessels including a jug were recovered from the fill. 13th century.

Pit 1591   Seventeen sherds of an EMW vessel, two HCW sherds including a ?C1 jar rim, and three sherds of MCW including two ?jar rims (one B2?) were found. L. 12th–13th century.

Ditch 1603   Twenty-six sherds were recovered, including a residual rim of a STNE bowl, eleven sherds of EMW, eleven sherds of MCW including two jar rims (C1 and square bead), one sherd of MCWG and two fragments of HCWF. 13th century.

Group 104   Ditch 1279 upper fill produced three sherds of MCW. 12th–13th century.

Group 105   Pit 1071 contained a sherd of MCW. A jar rim (H1) was found in the base of pit 1172. Feature 1256 contained six sherds of an MCW vessel. M.–L. 13th century.

Group 106   Ditch 1441 contained three sherds of EMW, nine sherds of MCW including a bowl and a jar (rim H2), a jar rim sherd of HCW (C1?), and a decorated body sherd of HFW1. Upper fill of ditch 1489 contained two sherds of an HCWF jar. Two fills of ditch 1500 contained a sherd of MCW and fragments of body and base of an HCWF vessel. The latter was also found in pit 1497. 13th century.

Group 107   Ditch 1398 contained twelve sherds of three EMW vessels and seven fragments of four MCW vessels. Ditch 1406 contained two small sherds of MCW. Ditch 1566 contained 15 sherds of an EMWSS vessel with beaded rim, 15 sherds of HCW including two jar rims (B4, C1), 33 sherds of MCW including two jars (B4, C1), a spouted pitcher (C1) and a dripping dish, a jar rim of MCWG (B4) and one sherd of MSHW. 13th century.

Group 108   Ditch 1392 contained four sherds of MCW. One sherd of EMW was collected from ditch 1422, and two tiny sherds of HFW1 came from ditch recut 1420. 12th–13th century.

8.2.4 Pottery by phase: post-medieval

Sixteen of the 20 sherds found in features of this phase were of post-medieval or modern date, with residual sherds comprising early Anglo-Saxon and medieval fragments. Eight features, all ditches, produced pottery. The forms identified are as described in the section on post-medieval and modern pottery (above), as none of this material was intrusive in earlier features.

Ditch 808   A base fragment of REFW saucer with transfer-printed decoration was found. 19th–20th century.

Ditch 1396   Seven sherds of a PMRW pipkin with a strap handle and thickened everted rim were found. 16th–18th century.

Ditch 1400   Two sherds of LMTE were found, with two residual sherds of HFW1 including a jug handle. 15th–16th century.

Ditch 1445   A base fragment of REFW was found. L.18th–20th century.

Ditch 1580   Four sherds of a blue floral transfer-printed toilet bowl were collected. 19th century.

Group 104   Ditch 1098 contained a residual fragment of ESFQ. Ditch 1143 contained a small fragment of YELW. A tiny sherd of MCW came from ditch 1508. 19th–20th century.

8.2.5 Discussion of late Anglo-Saxon, medieval and post-medieval pottery

There is a gap of some 400 years in the ceramic record following the early Anglo-Saxon period (see Chapter 7). The earliest pottery in the medieval group is of Saxo-Norman (11th-century) date and whilst some of the early medieval wares may be contemporary, the very small quantity of St Neot's Ware suggests that activity was not intensive much before the 12th century. Most of the forms amongst the medieval wares could be dated to the 12th–13th centuries, suggesting that occupation of this period was also relatively short-lived.

Most of the medieval pottery was scattered in the fills of enclosure and boundary ditches, but there were no real concentrations suggestive of nearby occupation. Most sherds were fragments of single vessels which had probably been dispersed through manuring, although a few vessels, such as the Hedingham Ware jug in gully 1439, were more complete and may represent rubbish disposal which remained in situ. Very little of the medieval assemblage was residual in later contexts.

The forms and fabrics are largely comparable with Essex types. Similar (unsourced) forms were present in Cambridge in the 13th century (*e.g.* Edwards and Hall 1997, figs 2.12 and 2.32; both comparable with Essex form B4 illustrated by Drury 1993a, fig. 39). These wares probably represent a continuum of local potteries which spread across northwest Essex and southern Cambridgeshire, although a few vessels (such as the Suffolk-type square bead rim) seem to have come from further afield. The glazed wares at this site were certainly from Essex, however, comprising largely Hedingham Ware. No coarsewares from Ely were present in this group, and they were certainly present in Cambridge before this site was abandoned. If the market in Cambridge had been the main source of ceramic vessels for Mill Lane, some Ely Ware would surely have reached the site as it travelled widely across the region. It has been noted previously that Ely Ware was not common in villages south of Cambridge and did not occur in the 10th–13th-century assemblage from Hinxton Hall (Spoerry 2008, 72), with Essex micaceous wares and Hertfordshire greywares forming the dominant groups in this area. A similar pattern with regard to Essex wares has been identified in south Suffolk by the present author (*e.g.* at Preston St Mary, Anderson 2010b), and it seems that production sites in north Essex were the dominant sources, or at least had a strong influence on the forms being made at many more local (but currently undiscovered) potteries which were operating in south Suffolk and Cambridgeshire at the time. It seems that, unlike their Anglo-Saxon predecessors, the medieval population looked to the south and east for its pottery.

8.2.6 Late Anglo-Saxon, medieval and post-medieval pottery: conclusions

The medieval period is represented by pottery of 11th–13th-century date. Whilst the early Anglo-Saxon pottery is concentrated in a few largely structural features of this date, the medieval wares were dispersed across a wider area and were manly recovered from ditch fills apparently unrelated to settlement. The pottery types in use in both main periods of activity were generally locally made and were typical of rural sites in the region, being largely utilitarian with few examples of highly decorated wares. No imported wares were present in the high medieval period, and very little pottery was sourced from more than 20 miles away.

8.3 Medieval ceramic building material
(by Sue Anderson)

One piece of medieval estuarine roof tile and 14 fragments of post-medieval roof tile (RT) were recovered, the majority from ditch fill (1507). Most of the post-medieval tiles were in red-firing fabrics, but there were also three fragments of white tiles. Of the 15 fragments of plain tile, only one had a peg hole (round). No nib, hip, or pantile fragments were present. Table 8.5 shows the quantities of post-Roman material by fabric and form.

Six heavily abraded fragments, representing two bricks, were in a fine estuarine silty clay fabric typical of 'early' bricks (EB). This type of brick was produced between the 13th–15th centuries in the east of England (Drury 1993b). All fragments were from ditch fill (1507), and were found in association with the small fragment of medieval roof tile, as well as post-medieval fragments.

Fragments of post-medieval 'late' brick (LB) were also collected from ditch fill (1507) and from subsoil (1001). The latter was 63mm thick, suggesting a 17th-/18th-century date. A fragment of a white-firing air brick (AB) was found in upper ditch fill (1578) and measured 70mm thick, suggesting a 19th-century date.

Table 8.5 Post-Roman CBM by fabric and form. (Key: RT – plain roof tile; EB – early brick; LB – late brick; AB – air brick).

Fabric	RT	EB	LB	AB
EST	1	6		
FS	3			
FSG	1			
FSF			1	
MS	1			
MSF	1		4	
MSFFE	5			
WFS	2			
WMS	1			1

8.3.1 Ceramic building material by phase: medieval

Features of this phase produced only three pieces of tile, all Roman. They were recovered from ditch 1571, and north–south ditch 1422 in group 108. Presumably the fragments were re-deposited from disturbed Anglo-Saxon features.

Ungrouped   Ditch 1571 produced a large fragment of RBT measuring over 140mm wide and 36mm thick.

G108   Ditch 1422 contained one piece of RBT (36mm thick) and a fragment of burnt FLT.

8.3.2 Ceramic building material by phase: post-medieval

The small quantity of medieval CBM in the assemblage was recovered from features of this phase, perhaps suggesting that it represented demolition rubble from an earlier structure which was pulled down in the early post-medieval period. There were a few residual pieces of Roman tile in the Phase 7 group as well, but the majority of material from this phase was post-medieval and comprised largely plain roof tile with occasional fragments of brick.

Ungrouped   One fragment of heavily abraded IMB was recovered from linear feature 1400.
Ditch 1445 contained a small fragment of possible RBT and a piece of BOX.
Ditch 1472 produced a fragment of post-medieval roof tile.
The upper fill of ditch 1580 contained a fragment of 19th-century air brick.

G104   Ditches 1504, 1508, 1526 and drain 1127 produced 26 fragments of CBM including medieval roof tile and early brick, post-medieval roof tile, late brick and small fragments of RBT.

8.3.3 Discussion

Only two medieval bricks and a fragment of medieval roof tile were recovered. These were in estuarine clay fabrics typical of eastern England in the 13th–15th centuries. These abraded fragments, all found in the large post-medieval ditch Group 104, were probably deposited in agricultural fields through manuring, before ending up in the ditch fill.

The post-medieval assemblage comprised a small quantity of plain roof tiles, some 17th- to 19th-century bricks and an air brick, in fabrics which are comparable with other assemblages from the region. Most of this material occurred in features assigned to Phase 7. Like the medieval material, it may have reached the site through manuring, although sometimes tile and brick fragments were deliberately imported to fields to provide metalling or hardcore for commonly-used thoroughfares such as gateways.

Figure 8.2 Horse burial 1462 in plan facing west.

8.4 Animal burials
(by Matilda Holmes)

A total of five horse skeletons, one dog and a partial cattle skeleton were recovered from post-medieval contexts 1462, 1582 and 1600 (Fig. 3.12) and from the upper fills of palaeochannel 1584. Two of the cuts (1462 and 1600) were aligned north–south the other was aligned east–west. The burial of largely intact animals with little sign of butchery suggests that they were not eaten; rather it was a convenient form of disposal of working animals. No further work was undertaken on this assemblage (Fig. 8.2).

CHAPTER 9

PALAEOENVIRONMENTAL ANALYSES

B. Gearey, E.-J. Hopla, K. Krawiec, E. Reilly and R. McKenna,
with a contribution by V. Fryer (charred plant remains and molluscs)

9.1 Introduction

Within the study area a series of features were identified as palaeochannels of the River Cam. It should be noted that the site plans (see Chapters 1 and 3) represent the extent of these features as they were apparent on the ground, but the exact planforms of the channels could not be accurately plotted due to the presence of significant depths of colluvial-alluvial deposits which blanketed the area and sealed the channel fills.

Palaeoenvironmental analyses focused on the two trenches excavated through a palaeochannel feature on the west side of the site (1584 and 1299/1302, Fig. 9.1). Test Pit B was excavated through a large palaeochannel (1584) in the northwestern part of the site, just to the west of some of the medieval archaeological features. Three bulk samples from this palaeochannel were submitted for coleoptera (beetle) and plant macrofossil assessment and subsequent full analysis: 0.0–0.25m (top sample); 0.25–0.41m (middle sample); and 0.41–0.61m (bottom sample). Samples were also collected using monolith tins from which four sub-samples (0m, 0.24m, 0.40m and 0.64m) were taken for pollen assessment.

Test Pit D was excavated through an east–west oriented palaeochannel feature (1299-1302) in the southwestern part of the site, adjacent to both Anglo-Saxon and later medieval features (Chapter 3). Four bulk samples for coleoptera (beetle) and plant macrofossil assessment were recovered: 0.5–0.7m, 0.7–0.9m, 1.0–1.2m and 1.2–1.4m (bottom sample). Samples were also collected using monolith tins from which four sub-samples (0.50m, 0.66m, 0.88m and 1.22m) were taken for pollen assessment (Fig. 9.2).

Two other test pits (A and C) were excavated for palaeoenvironmental sampling: Test Pit A contained no deposits of palaeoenvironmental potential but four bulk samples (0–0.25m, 0.25–0.50m, 0.50–0.75m and 0.75–1.00m) were recovered for coleoptera (beetle) and plant macrofossil assessments from Test Pit C. Samples were also collected using monolith tins from which ten sub-samples (0m, 0.16m, 0.32m, 0.48m, 0.62m, 0.80m, 0.96m, 1.12m, 1.28m and 1.43m) were taken for pollen assessment. Four sub-samples (sub-fossil wood fragments) from Test Pit B

and two from Test Pit D were submitted to Beta Analytic, Florida for dating using the AMS method (Table A2.8, Appendix 2).

Samples for the assessment of the plant macrofossil assemblage, mollusc shells and other remains were taken from a variety of archaeological features of prehistoric to post-medieval date, and 62 were submitted for analysis (Fryer 2009). Although plant remains and mollusc shells were present within all of the assemblages studied, a considerable issue of context disturbance and macrofossil intrusivity was recorded and further quantification was not recommended. A summary of the assessment results by phase is included towards the end of this chapter in section 9.4.

9.2 Results

9.2.1 Test Pit B (palaeochannel 1584)

The stratigraphy of this section was recorded as grey silt clay with occasional coarse flints and gravels (0–0.25m), overlying brown well humified peat with occasional sub-fossil wood fragments and gravels (0.25–0.41m) with a basal deposit of grey-green silt with molluscs, coarse sands and gravels (0.41–0.61m). The results of the coleopteran analyses are provided in Tables A2.1 and A2.2 and the results of the analysis of the plant macrofossils from Test Pit B are presented in Table A2.3 and the remaining components of the samples and habitats of taxa recorded in Tables A2.4 and A2.5 (all in Appendix 2). Remains of plant macrofossils were present in all the samples examined and there were sizeable assemblages of identifiable remains of interpretative value, but the quality of preservation varied amongst the samples. The major component of the samples was herbaceous detritus, which was generally very poorly preserved, although it was possible to recognise buds, bud-scales, moss stem fragments and leaves. Some fragments (up to 2cm) of sub-fossil wood fragments were also recorded in the samples; however, these were too small and poorly preserved to enable identification to species. Molluscs were present in the samples in small numbers, although no

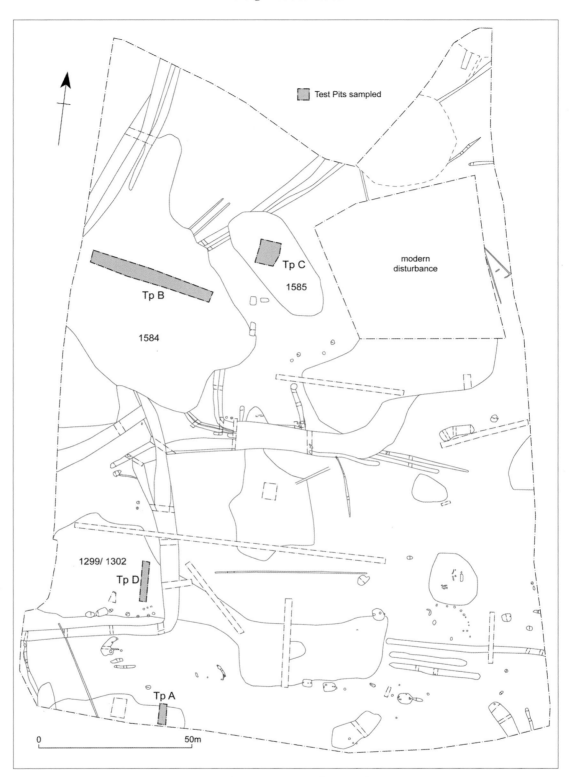

Figure 9.1 Palaeoenvironmental test pit locations.

further analyses were carried out of this material. Pollen concentrations were generally very low and full analyses were not carried out on any of the sequences, but the results of the assessments provide some supplementary data.

SAMPLE 0.61–0.41M DEPTH

Radiocarbon dates: 0.58–0.63m: 3570±40 BP (Beta-260586; 1920–1730/1720–1690 cal BC) to 0.38m: 3390±40 BP (Beta-260585; 1690–1500 cal BC).

Figure 9.2 Taking monolith samples in Test Pit D.

Coleoptera

The radiocarbon dates indicate that these deposits accumulated wholly in the early–middle Bronze Age and therefore pre-date the main archaeological features in the northwest of the site. The index of diversity for this assemblage is extremely high (73) and the sample is dominated by aquatic/wetland and plant feeding species (Table A2.2, Appendix 2); the stratigraphy of the deposits (grey-green silts) also implies deposition in shallow open water. Figure 9.3 illustrates the habitat groups present in this deposit. Within the plant-feeding group, wetland plant feeders are dominant including species such as *Plateumaris discolor* (sedges, cotton-grass), *P. affinis* (sedges, marsh marigold), *Prasocuris junci* (brooklime), *Notaris acridulus* (sedges, rushes) and *Pelenomus comari* (marsh cinquefoil, purple loosestrife) (Table A2.1, Appendix 2). Plant macrofossils from this deposit also suggest that wetland plants were present, probably growing within the channel itself (McKenna 2010). Aquatic and wetland beetles suggest a standing body of water with muddy fringes, illustrated by the presence of species such as *Octhebius bicolon*, *Limnebius truncatellus* and *Platystethus cornutus/degener*.

Dung/foul species and beetles that live in decaying vegetation are also well-represented at this level (Table A2.1, Appendix 2). Indeed, many of the beetles in these categories could be represented in both. In particular, damp-loving Staphylinidae such as species of *Anotylus*, *Oxytelus* and *Platysthetus* are equally likely to occur in wet decaying plant matter and animal dung. However, the presence of dung beetles such as *Aphodius erraticus* and *Aphodius contaminatus*, amongst others, indicates that animal dung was also accumulating within or in very close

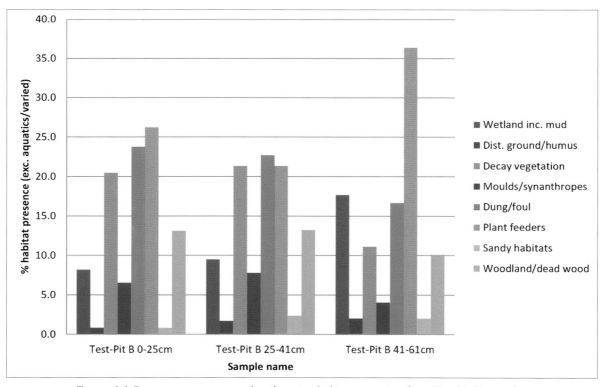

Figure 9.3 Percentage presence of each major habitat grouping from Test Pit B samples.

proximity to the open channel. In addition, carrion beetles such as *Ptomophagus*, *Choleva* and *Catops* spp. suggests that animal matter (corpses, bones or skins) was also present in the channel.

A moderate woodland/dead wood associated fauna was also recorded at this level. It includes species found under bark or in dead wood, such as *Anobium punctatum*, *Phloeonomus pusillus* and *Colon* sp. *P. pusillus* generally occurs in conifers and is the first indication from these assemblages of the presence of conifers either growing in the landscape surrounding the channel or as timber on the nearby site (Alexander 2002). Woodland associates comprise species found generally alighting on trees/shrubs such as the Elaterids *Agriotes pallidulus*, *A. acuminatus* and *Adrastus pallens*, as well as leaf defoliating species like *Phyllobius* spp. and *Rhynchaenus alni*. The latter is found on elm (Bullock 1993).

Three other habitat groupings emerge from this assemblage. A small number of species associated with heath/sandy habitats are present, including *Bledius* sp., *Stenus biggutatus* and *Hoplia philanthus*. The ground beetles *Anchomenus dorsalis* and *Agonum muelleri* are indicative of disturbed/arable ground/humus layer, although the former is more common in dry habitats, while the latter favours damper ground (Luff 2007). All these species may suggest the presence of exposed/disturbed ground in close proximity to the channel, either as a result of human activity or naturally occurring open ground. Many of the plant feeding beetles recorded occur on weeds and ruderal plants, including *Brachypterus urticae* and *Nedyus quadrimaculatus* (on nettles), *Gastrophysa viridula* and *Pelenomus quadrituberculatus* (on dock and knotweed), *Ceutorhynchus contractus* and *C. ersymi* (on various Cabbage family plants). Of course, the presence of seemingly divergent habitat preferences within the assemblage may be the result of local flooding episodes, with runoff accumulating in the channel bringing with it a very diverse insect assemblage from further afield.

The final habitat group comprises species that live on moulds (on decaying plants, wood, stored food products etc) and are generally considered 'synanthropic' during later periods *i.e.* the Anglo-Saxon and medieval periods (Kenward and Allison 1994). Species such as *Lathridius minutus* (grp), *Cryptophagus* spp., *Mycetaea subterranea*, *Typhaea stercorea* fall into this category. Given the early date for this deposit, it is not possible to say definitively if these species are associated with human habitation and ejected occupation debris or simply reflect accumulating dry plant/leaf litter from the nearby woodland. The archaeological remains in close proximity to this channel do not date from the Bronze Age but there are earlier archaeological features further south that could be the source of synanthropic species.

Cumulatively, this assemblage suggests that the channel at this time, while still an open body of water, was steadily accumulating decaying and rotting organic matter. Open ground, possibly with grazing animals, was also present and there is a suggestion of woodland or a woodland edge environment. Grazing animals may account for the disturbed

ground elements of the fauna as animals churned up ground around the channel to access it for drinking water. However, human activity or episodes of flooding transporting fauna from further afield may also account for some of these species.

Plant macrofossils

The preservation of the plant remains was very good and the majority of the macrofossils such as *Ranunculus flammula* (lesser spearwort), *Persicaria hydropiper* (water pepper), *Lycopus europaeus* (gypsywort), *Sagittaria latifolia* (broadleaf arrowhead), *Alisma* (water plantain), Lemnoideae (duckweeds), *Cladium mariscus* (great fen sedge) are indicative of damp and/or open water environments. Moss fragments were identified as *Sphagnum* (bog moss). Bud scales were identified as *Populus* (poplar). Open grassland is also represented by the remains of *Polygonum* (knotgrass), *Knautia arvensis* (field scabious) and *Lapsana communis* (nipplewort). Hedgerow/scrub is represented by *Betula* (birch), *Populus*, and perhaps also *Sambucus nigra* (elder). Waste ground may also be implied through *Urtica* (nettles) and *Capsella bursa-pastoris* (shepherds purse).

SAMPLE 0.41–0.25M DEPTH

Radiocarbon dates: 0.38m: 3390±40 BP (Beta-260585; 1690–1500 cal. BC) to 0.25–0.27m: 2590±40 BP (Beta-280639; 810–760/680–670 cal. BC).

Coleoptera

The base of this deposit dates to the middle Bronze Age and the top of the sample to the later Bronze Age/early Iron Age. The character of the assemblage overall does not change dramatically although the overall aquatic element of the fauna (as a proportion of the entire assemblage) drops from 16% to 11%. The overall wetland fauna also drops from 17.7% to 9%, which suggests that the channel was gradually in-filling, and dung/foul and decaying vegetation species becoming more dominant (as a proportion of the entire fauna exc. aquatics/varied; Fig. 9.3).

Another notable element of this assemblage is the dramatic fall in the index of diversity score, from 76 to 29. While the MNI for this deposit is higher than the bottom deposit (364 compared to 246 individuals), it is dominated by larger numbers of individual species. This suggests highly conducive breeding conditions for particular species *e.g. Carpelimus bilineatus*, which occurs in damp decaying vegetation, *Anotylus rugosus*, which occurs in dung or foul decaying matter and *Octhebius* spp. (possibly *O. bicolon*), which occurs in aquatic habitats and mud beside water.

Two other significant elements of this fauna are the higher percentage presence of woodland/dead wood species and mould/synanthropes. The former group, in particular, contains a diverse range of leaf defoliators and general woodland dwellers as well as a significant dead wood element. Three of these species are generally found on pine (*Dryophilus pusillus*, *Ernobius mollis* and *Hylastes angustatus*), while three others are generally found in ash (*Hylesinus oleiperda*,

Lepersinus fraxini and *Ptelobius vittatus*) with the latter also found in elm (Alexander 2002). This is a clear indication of the presence of pine, ash and possibly elm either in the surrounding environment or the timber from these trees being used in structures on the adjacent site. However, the earlier dated remains further to the south could be the source of structural wood debris, which perhaps ended up in the channel. The mix of ash, elm and pine in woodland terms would be unusual; however, elements of this fauna may be coming from further away through flooding episodes.

The same mix of possibly 'synanthropic' insects occurs at this level as at the previous level but in markedly higher numbers (almost 8% overall). However, it is still not possible to determine if these species are occurring within dry mouldy decaying plant matter in local woodland stands or from dumped occupation debris.

The plant-feeding group of species sees a significant drop in numbers in this deposit, especially among the wetland indicators. However, general ruderal indicators are still present. One interesting finding is *Bruchidius villosus*, which occurs on broom, gorse and occasionally birch. It suggests, again, the presence of scrub or perhaps woodland edge/ pasture woodland in the locality (Cox 2001). Overall, the insect assemblage indicates that the channel still contained standing water; however, the accumulating plant and other waste material, both from plants growing within the channel and possibly from activity in the surrounding landscape, had markedly increased.

Plant macrofossils

The preservation of the organic material was again very good. Moss fragments, identified as *Sphagnum* moss and bud scales identified as *Populus* were both recorded. Waste ground was represented by the remains of *Sambucus nigra* and *Urtica*. However, the most abundant remains *Sambucus nigra*, *Populus*, *Corylus avellana* and *Betula* probably indicate hedgerows/scrubland. Damp habitats are represented through *Ranunculus flammula*, *Persicaria hydropiper* and *Eleocharis palustris* (spike rush).

Sample 0.25–0.0m depth

Radiocarbon dates: 0.25–0.27m: 2590±40 BP (Beta-280639; 810–760/680–670 cal BC) to 0.03–0.05m: 260±40 BP (Beta-280638; 1520–1590 and 1620–1670 cal AD /1770–1800 and 1940–1950 cal AD).

Coleoptera

The radiocarbon determinations indicate either a very slow rate of accumulation for the upper part of the sequence, or the presence of a hiatus in the sequence. The latter is most likely given the change in stratigraphy from an organic peat to a silt-clay at 0.25m. It is also possible that one or both of the determinations is inaccurate. However, there is some evidence in the coleopteran record to confirm that this deposit incorporates material from a later Holocene, post-Roman context (see below).

The top of this section is the least rich in numerical terms (MNI 142), although the index of diversity has increased to 59. This suggests a great admixture of habitat sources for the assemblage. An initial view of Figure 9.3 suggests greater affinity with the middle of the section (0.41–0.25m) than the bottom (0.61–0.41m). There is a continued decline in the wetland/muddy water's edge/aquatic element of the fauna although both are still represented by species like *Platystethus cornutus/degener*, *Anacaena globosus* and *Heleophorus* spp. The presence of species of *Heleophorus* and another beetle, *Agabus nebulosus*, suggests that the channel was now only filled with water on a temporary basis, perhaps seasonally, as both can be indicative of recently formed ponds, puddles and other temporary water bodies (Merritt 2006).

Dung/foul and decaying vegetation indicators form the bulk of the assemblage, while plant-feeding species show a slight increase on the middle sample. This is due to an overall increased presence of both generalist grassland/ pasture indicators and species suggestive of scrub/woodland margin *e.g. Sitona striatellus* (on gorse) and *S. hispidulus* (clover). The woodland/dead wood element is not as diverse as the middle sample but is still notable. It included leaf miners such as *Rhynchaenus quercus*, the elm bark beetle, *Scolytus scolytus*, the pine timber beetle *Dryophilus pusillus* and *Lissodema denticolle* (also in sample 0.41–0.25m), which occurs under the bark of dead wood. *Siagonium quadricorne* is a small Staphylinid, which occurs under the bark of elm, oak and occasionally pine. Its only occurrence in these samples is at this level. *Phyllotreta undulata*, which is ubiquitous in all three deposits, occurs on oak and lime but is also known from various Brassica (Cabbage) species so its exact source in this context is unclear.

While the insects still suggest a continued presence of at least temporary water in the channel, it is dominated by decaying vegetation, both from the living plant communities within/fringing the channel and from further afield. Dung beetles suggest the presence of grazing animals and many of the plant feeders suggest disturbed (perhaps arable?) ground. The source of the woodland/dead wood beetles in open to speculation; they may reflect actual living woodland in close proximity but they may also have resulted from discarded wood-working waste. The synanthropic element of the assemblage is notable here. It contains two species, *Oryzaephilus surinamensis* and *Typhaea stercorea*, which are known pests of stored foodstuffs and grain, in particular. While the latter occurred in earlier deposits (0.61–0.41m), the former is believed to have only arrived in Britain during Roman times (Buckland 1981; 1982). While occasionally found in outdoor situations in Britain today, under bark of dead wood, it is generally considered highly synanthropic, generally occurring in grain stores, stables, warehouses etc in stored grain and residues (Halstead 1993; Koch 1989). It is difficult to know whether it is related to the archaeological structures that existed on the nearby site or came from naturally occurring dead wood but it is certainly more likely, coupled with other synanthropic indicators, to have come from the former. The presence of this likely post-Roman synanthrope would seem to confirm the uppermost radiocarbon dates, which suggests that the top of the deposit at this location dates to the later Holocene.

Plant macrofossils

The preservation of the organic material was very good. Numerous bud scales were present in the sample, and the majority was well preserved, but identification was not possible. *Sphagnum* mosses were present. Waste ground is represented by the remains of *Urtica*, *Rubus*-type (bramble), *Sambucus nigra*, and *Knautia arvensis* hints at grassland. Damp ground was represented by a single seed of *Eleocharis palustris*.

TEST PIT B POLLEN ASSESSMENT

Pollen preservation was very poor, with only the basal (0.64m) and top (0m) samples sufficient for an assessment. The basal spectrum was dominated by *Pinus sylvestris* (Scots pine) (89%) with Cyperaceae (sedges) (5%) the next most abundant. The top sample (0m) contained Cyperaceae (71%), Poaceae (wild grasses) (14%) and Lactuceae (dandelions etc.) (9%). The absence of reliable data from the middle section of both sequences hinders interpretation and no further palynological work was carried out. The available pollen data indicates a transition from Scots pine dominated woodland during the initial stages of peat formation to open sedge and grassland by the close of peat accumulation, but further meaningful comment is not possible.

9.2.2 Test Pit D (palaeochannel 1299–1302)

The stratigraphy of this section was recorded as coarse, grey silty clay with rootlets and flint nodules (0–0.50m) overlying dark brown organic sediment which was increasingly silty towards the base at 1.40m. Two radiocarbon dates were obtained from this palaeochannel; 0.64m: 3400±40 BP (Beta-260583; 1750–1590/1590–1530 cal BC) and 1.17m: 4480±40 BP (Beta-260584; 3320–3220/3180–3160/3120–2920 cal BC). These determinations indicate that the associated palaeoenvironmental sequence is at least partly contemporary with the earlier Bronze Age/Neolithic archaeology on the site, but not with the remainder of the largely Anglo-Saxon and medieval archaeology in close proximity Test Pit D.

SAMPLES 1.4–1.2M AND 1.2–1.0M DEPTH

Radiocarbon dates: 0.91m: 4480±40 BP (Beta-260584; 3320–3220/3180–3160/3120–2920 cal BC).

Coleoptera

Preservation conditions for insects in deposits from the southwestern palaeochannel were very poor compared to the northwestern channel (1584) with generally very low MNI and low indices of diversity (Tables A2.1 and A2.2, Appendix 2). The basal two samples were particularly poor with very fragmented and indeterminate insect remains making up the bulk of the assemblage. Figure 9.4 illustrates the habitat profile for the small assemblages recovered from the bottom two samples. Muddy damp ground conditions clearly

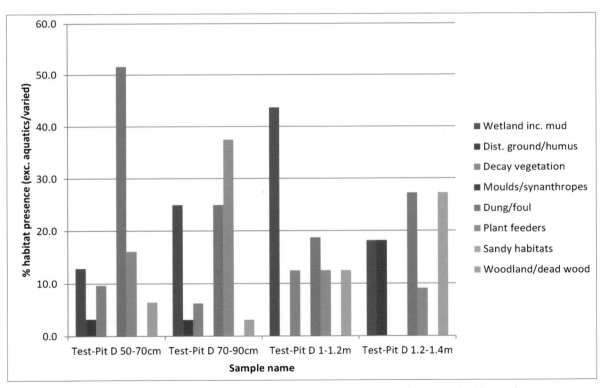

Figure 9.4 Percentage presence of each major habitat grouping from Test Pit D samples.

prevailed and the channel was, at least, temporarily filled with water, indicated by species such as *Anacaena globosus*, *Platystethus cornutus/degener*, *Ochthebius* spp. and *Cyphon* sp. No wetland plant feeders were identified suggesting that, unlike the northwestern channel, this feature did not support a significant wetland plant community, implying that the site was perhaps only seasonally waterlogged. This may explain the poor preservation of insect remains.

A very small number of non-specific woodland/scrub indicators also occur at these levels. However, one significant find was the Scolytid, *Ernoporicus caucasicus*. This beetle feeds exclusively on lime and is nationally scarce in Britain today, being found mainly in areas of old parkland (Alexander 2002). It has been recorded from a number of floodplain sites, generally in palaeochannels, in the Midlands, including Bole Ings (Notts.), Croft (Leics.), Runnymede (Surrey) and Langford Quarry (Notts.) (Brayshay and Dinnin 1999; Greenwood and Smith 2005; Howard *et al.* 1999; Robinson 1991; Smith *et al.* 2005). What is perhaps surprising is that it does not occur in samples from the northwestern palaeochannel (Test Pit D) and there are no other lime-specific beetles in those assemblages. Its occurrence, however, would suggest the presence of lime in the locality at this earlier time. In general, little can be discerned about the surrounding environment of the palaeochannel at this time, as the assemblages are so poorly preserved in comparison to palaeochannel 1584.

Plant macrofossils

1.20–1.40m

The preservation of the plant macrofossil material was poor, with only single seeds of *Potentilla* (cinquefoils/tormentils) and cf. *Ranunculus* (buttercup). Both of these were very badly preserved and lacking in most morphological characteristics, and were only identifiable from their general shape.

1.00–1.20m

Preservation of the plant macrofossil remains was very poor with a few seeds of *Sambucus nigra* recorded, mostly fragments, which probably only survived due to their robust seed casings, indicating that the sample has been affected by differential preservation.

Sample 0.9–0.7m depth

Coleoptera

While preservation was slightly better at this level, the assemblage was still very poor in numerical terms. It was moderately diverse in species terms (Table A2.2, Appendix 2). Figure 9.4 presents the habitat profile and it differs somewhat from the lower part of the section. Wetland/muddy ground indicators are proportionally reduced but this may simply be as a result of differential preservation. Those wetland species that occur still indicate largely muddy ground/damp decaying vegetation conditions, rather than open water, and include

Cercyon marinus, *Carpelimus bilineatus* and *Dryops* sp. However, the plant-feeding beetles present mainly indicate a living wetland plant community and include species such as *Notaris acridulus* and *Limnobaris dolorosa/t-album* (both on sedges, rushes), *Prasocuris phelandrii* and *Plateumaris/Donacia* spp. (various wetland plants) (Bullock 1993). *Phyllopertha horticola* also occurs and is generally found at the roots of grassland and in meadows, often close to water.

These data might point to a temporary expansion of the channel at this time, perhaps a more permanent body of water, which could support a living wetland plant community. It is notable that there is no other clear signature of the wider landscape in this assemblage and the woodland element is negligible.

Plant macrofossils

Preservation of the plant macrofossils was again poor; although there were numerous whole and fragmentary plant macrofossils, these were too decayed and lacking in morphological characteristics for reliable identification. Those seeds which could be identified were taxa with robust seed casing such as *Potentilla*, *Rubus* and *Betula* (Table A2.6, Appendix 2).

Sample 0.7–0.5m depth

Radiocarbon date: 0.64m: 3400±40 BP (Beta-260583; 1750–1590/1590–1530 cal BC).

Coleoptera

The top sample of this sequence has a similar MNI to the preceding sample but a very different profile. The radiocarbon date from close to the top of this sample (0.64m) of 3400±40 BP (Beta-260583; 1750–1590/1590–1530 cal BC) indicates that this section of channel had almost completely infilled during the middle Bronze Age, with the overlying unit of coarse clay and flint suggesting that sometime after this point, the channel deposits were sealed beneath a layer of colluvial material, probably washed down from the adjacent dryland slopes. A small aquatic/wetland element is present with species indicative of pools or stagnating water recorded e.g. *Haliplus* sp., *Coleostoma orbiculare, Cyphon* spp., *Dryops* sp. and *Hydrobius fuscipes*. However, the dominant habitat group is dung/foul, represented by a number of examples of the dung beetle genus, *Aphodius*, and other species such as *Saprinus* sp., *Megasternum obscurum* and *Cercyon* sp. Dung from locally grazing animals and/or putrifying plant matter within the channel would account for most of these species. There is no synanthropic element to the fauna and, again, the woodland element is small. It is notable that disturbed ground/waste ground elements of all the assemblages from this palaeochannel are negligible.

Therefore, with the exception of *Ernoporicus caucasicus* at 1.2–1.0m and the presence of dung beetles in the top sample (0.7–0.5m), few indications of the surrounding environment of the southwestern palaeochannel can be derived from these assemblages. There is a suggestion that from 0.9–0.7m, the palaeochannel was temporarily wetter than preceding or subsequent periods. This may be related to wider environmental or hydrological changes but it is difficult to draw robust conclusions from such small, poorly preserved assemblages.

Plant macrofossils

Preservation of the plant macrofossil was relatively poor. Once again, those plant macrofossils recorded belonged to taxa with robust seed casings, such as *Sambucus nigra* and *Potentilla* which will survive well in waterlogged deposits. The remains of *Carex* (sedges) and *Eleocharis palustris* more delicate specimens were poorly preserved (Table A2.6, Appendix 2).

TEST PIT D POLLEN ASSESSMENT

Pollen concentrations were very low and the samples from 0.7–0.9m and 1.0–1.2m did not yield sufficient counts for an assessment. The basal sample (1.46m) was dominated by *Pinus sylvestris* (Scots pine) (82%) with *Corylus avellana*-type (most probably hazel rather than sweetgale) (10%) the next most abundant, and the top sample (0.74m) characterised by Cyperaceae (64%) and Poaceae (21%).

9.2.3 Assessments of Test Pit C

COLEOPTERA AND PLANT MACROFOSSILS

Preservation was very poor and concentration was extremely low in all four samples (0–0.25m, 0.25–0.50m, 0.50–0.75m and 0.75–1.00m) and full analyses were not possible.

POLLEN

The top and bottom samples yielded low concentrations of poorly preserved pollen and an assessment count was not possible for samples 0.00m, 0.16m, 0.96m, 1.28m and 1.43m. Samples 1.12m, 0.80m and 0.62m were dominated by *Pinus sylvestris* (Scots pine) up to 99%. The two samples which produced reliable counts (0.32m and 0.48m) were dominated by *Corylus avellana*-type (between 30% and 59%) with *Pinus sylvestris*, *Betula* (birch) and *Tilia* (lime) the next most abundant. The pollen data from Test Pit C are thus also relatively sparse, but reflect Scots pine-dominated woodland during the initial stages of channel infill. Pine then decreased as hazel became the dominant woodland species locally with lime also present, prior to a transition to a more open landscape.

9.3 Discussion

9.3.1 Comparison with previous evaluation: chronology

A radiocarbon date of 9690±100 BP (Beta-157529, 9290–8770 cal BC) was previously obtained from the base (2.25–2.35m) of the peat deposits in Trench 8 (JSAC 2001).

Two other dates are also available from the base of peat deposits (Trench 6, 2.3–2.4m, 9590±50 BP (Beta-157532, 9160–8730 cal BC)) and two inconsistent determinations from the top of the peat deposits (Trench 6, 1.0–1.10m, 2130±40 BP, Beta-157531, 350–300 and 220–50 cal. BC; 1290±40 BP, (duplicate), AD 660–790 cal BC). These data suggest that the palaeochannel started to infill during the Mesolithic, hence earlier than the dates reported above. This can be attributed to the fact that the evaluation radiocarbon dates (JSAC 2001) were from deeper deposits compared to Test Pit D (basal date at 0.91m depth) and Test Pit B (basal date at 0.58–0.63m depth). The variation in dates for the top of the organic deposits perhaps indicates variable later truncation of the sequences and also lack of sediment homogeneity. This latter factor may be related to evidence in the insect samples for human disturbance to the deposits. The presence of a 0.50m thick colluvial deposit in the Test Pit D sequence suggests the erosion and re-deposition of material from adjacent slopes, probably in the late or post-Bronze Age and maybe confirming the insect evidence for local anthropogenic disturbance to the dryland soils.

9.3.2 Palaeoenvironments at Mill Lane

While the assemblages from Test Pit D (southwestern palaeochannel) produced poor and relatively uninformative assemblages from all three proxies, Test Pit B (northwestern palaeochannel) assemblages were extremely rich and diverse in beetles and plant macrofossils. Pollen preservation was generally poor overall, although these data provide some supplementary information. Palaeochannels tend to have extremely diverse assemblages of beetle fauna as they reflect both the living insect communities of the channel itself and the habitats that may surround them (Robinson 1991). This means that 'teasing out' or disentangling the various pathways by which insect death assemblages accumulate in such deposits can be difficult. However, three broad habitat types emerge at Mill Lane: wetlands, woodlands and waste/disturbed/arable environments.

WETLANDS

The abundant evidence for wetland environments is almost entirely a reflection of the environment of the sampling site itself; waterlogged, boggy ground with areas of open water, fringed with a rich variety of wetland plants including aquatic plants, rushes, sedges and reedmace indicated by the insect and plant macrofossil assemblages (Table A2.3, Appendix 2). Open water in close proximity to the dryland edge may have served as a convenient water source for grazing animals, as evidenced by the variety of dung beetles in the samples. The channel itself was undoubtedly part of an earlier course of the River Cam, which currently flows to the west, probably incised during the earlier Holocene and taking permanent flow until the later Bronze Age. At this point, it appears to have been cut off from the main fluvial system, presumably as the river meandered back west across its floodplain. The southwestern channel, 1299–1302, was clearly cut-off earlier than 1584. The channels may have subsequently taken occasional flow during flood events. Indeed, 1584 has one flowing water beetle species, *Elmis aenea*, occurring in both the bottom and middle samples of the section. This evidence has disappeared by the upper sample and it is tempting to suggest that it was also completely cut off from any significant flowing water supply by this point. The exact pattern and timing of channel aggradation cannot be easily established from the current data, as the study area is located at the very edge of the floodplain.

WOODLAND

The insects (Table A2.3, Appendix 2) from Test Pit B in particular indicate that woodland and possibly wood pasture existed within the surrounding environment during the Bronze Age. A diverse woodland and woodland edge fauna is recorded in the samples from this northwestern palaeochannel. Elm, ash, oak, willow and birch are all indicated, while three pine-dependents are also recorded. Pine pollen percentages are particularly high in the basal samples from both the southwestern (Test Pit D) and northwestern palaeochannels, apparently confirming the dominance of this tree in the early Holocene landscape. Lime is also represented by one insect species from the Neolithic-dated samples of the southwestern palaeochannel (Test Pit D) but as noted above, no lime obligates occur in the northwestern palaeochannel (Test Pit B). This may be due to taphonomic factors or possibly reflects some spatial variation in woodland cover, as the upper part of the southwestern palaeochannel and the lower two samples from the northwestern palaeochannel are broadly contemporary. The pollen data are too sparse to permit much comment, but lime was not recorded in the basal samples from Test Pit B or D, but was present in that of Test Pit C. Lime pollen grains are large and poorly dispersed (Greig 1982) and this tree is often under-represented in pollen diagram (Birks and Birks 1980). These differences may indicate spatial and temporal variation in the abundance of lime trees during the Neolithic– Bronze Age at Mill Lane. Woodland of a similar composition is suggested by the pollen samples taken from the undated sequence through the northeastern palaeochannel (Test Pit C). Pollen concentration and preservation varies throughout the sequence but it is evident that there was a shift from pine dominated woodland to mixed hazel woodland, but there are no radiocarbon dates to provide an absolute chronology for this process. The plant macrofossil samples provide less evidence of the surrounding woodland and appear to be dominated by remains of the local, peat forming vegetation. Occasional records of *Corylus avellana*, *Populus* and *Betula* are present and abundant, with unidentifiable woody detritus recorded in most of the samples.

The presence of Pine obligates in the insect record suggests the significance of Scots pine in the woodland at Mill Lane, probably related to the dominance of this species on the exposed sands and gravels at the floodplain edge. Palaeoecological study of peat sequences from Thorne Moors, South Yorkshire, indicate that Scots pine

was an important component of native birch-oak-pine mire woodlands in more southerly parts of Britain until at least the middle Bronze Age (Whitehouse 2006). Other eastern midlands floodplains sites have produced few pine-dependent insect species, so this is a notable element of the Mill Lane fauna (Smith and Whitehouse 2005).

All three insect species recorded here are often regarded as 'recent' introductions but *Hylastes angustatus* has been identified in early Holocene levels at Strangford Lough, Co. Down, Northern Ireland (Whitehouse 2006). Some pine-dependents may have died out and been re-introduced to England in the last hundred years or so with the widespread commercial planting of pine. It is, therefore, perfectly possible that all three species found here are native to eastern England up to the early–middle Bronze Age. There is one further possible explanation for the presence of pine-dependents in this channel and this will be discussed further below.

WASTE GROUND/DISTURBED/ARABLE GROUND

A significant number of beetles recorded from the deposits at Mill Lane suggest the presence of disturbed ground in the vicinity of the palaeochannels (Table A2.9, Appendix 2). Weeds and other herbs of waste/disturbed ground including nettles, docks, plantain, thistles and brambles are all indicated by the insects. Nettles and brambles are also present in the plant macrofossils in varying quantities throughout Test Pit B. The role of prehistoric humans in directly creating and maintaining the open, disturbed conditions at Mill Lane is uncertain and the spread of plants such as docks and nettles might equally have been encouraged by concentrations of grazing of wild and/or domestic animals at the ecotone between dryland and wetland. The plentiful dung beetles in most of the samples certainly suggest the presence of such animals. It is possible that naturally more open conditions might have been attractive in a variety of ways to human communities, providing access to water and other resources. The close association of the Neolithic features with the palaeochannel may certainly be interpreted in this way; it could even be postulated that the evidence for carrion might reflect the discarded remains of animals butchered by the Neolithic peoples, although there is no faunal evidence of such activity. However, it should also be stressed that occasional flooding episodes could have resulted in the incorporation of sub-fossil material from a relatively wide area.

Some indicators of grassland/meadow or fallow ground plants, especially clover and daisy, are also present in the insect assemblages, particularly from the middle sample of the northwestern channel onwards (Test Pit B, 0.41m to the top), and imply a more open, cultivated landscape from the later Bronze Age into the Iron Age. The subsequent spread of grassland environments are suggested by the pollen data, with grasses and dandelions recorded in the top samples from the southwestern and the northwestern channels. The available palaeoenvironmental data are insufficient to reconstruct the precise pattern and process of vegetation change and the chronology from the upper part of Test Pit B is inadequate to relate the evidence very closely to the archaeology.

9.3.3 Comparisons with other sites

The results of these analyses can be compared to those from study of the lower Welland valley, north of Peterborough (French and Pryor 2005; Pryor 1998), which imply a similar sequence of environmental change on the floodplain. Investigation of a series of interconnected alluvial belts in the Maxey-Etton area indicates that a low sinuosity, braided river channel system during the late glacial/early Holocene was subsequently replaced by a higher sinuosity meandering river. By the Neolithic, the impact of rising base levels (sea levels) and the effect of anthropogenic disturbance to the catchment resulted in further change to the river system and the development of an anastomosed system. Whilst the investigation of the palaeochannels at Sawston have focused on a relatively small area of the distal edge of the floodplain of the River Cam, the general character and timing of events indicates a broadly similar pattern of development.

The palaeoentomological data can also be compared to the results of other studies: a small but significant group of palaeochannel sites has been examined for insects in the midlands of England. Two of these are in close proximity to archaeological sites, Mingies Ditch and Runnymede Bridge (Robinson 1991; 1993). At Runnymede, changes from a largely wooded to a largely agricultural landscape were reflected in the diverse, rich insect faunas from a former channel of the River Thames. The late Neolithic deposits contained a strong *Urwald* ('old woodland') element. A late Mesolithic–early Neolithic deposit at Mingies produced a rich woodland fauna, including the presence of the lime feeder, *Ernoporius caucasicus* (Robinson 1993). By the time of occupation of the Iron Age hillfort at Mingies, the landscape was largely agricultural and pastoral in character. The Mesolithic through to Bronze Age landscape traced through the examination of multiple bore hole samples from the river Trent floodplain at Bole Ings, suggests that willow swamp was gradually replace by alder carr on the floodplain itself. The adjacent slopes, which were dominated by oak, beech and lime from the very early Neolithic onwards, were eventually affected by anthropogenic clearance after the middle Bronze Age (Brayshay and Dinnin 1999).

9.4 Conclusions

The insect, plant macrofossil and pollen analyses of the palaeochannel deposits have produced some detailed if occasionally slightly enigmatic evidence for Holocene palaeoenvironments at Mill Lane. During the earlier Holocene, it would appear that the palaeo River Cam incised a channel or channels into the western edge of the study area. Whilst there is no direct evidence of the wider environment at this time, the Mesolithic activity recorded on the site (see Chapter 4) was thus taking place adjacent to active river channels, within a landscape that was probably dominated by Scots pine

woodland. The subsequent accumulation of organic deposits in the channels reflects the abandonment of these features as the fluvial regime shifted from erosion to aggradation, in response to rising relative sea level and perhaps increased sediment supply resulting from human impact on the catchment, and the earlier courses of the river became cut-off from permanent flow. The earliest evidence for this is the southwestern part of the site, where accumulation in Test Pit D began at a date of *c.* 4480±40 BP (Beta-260584; 3320–3220/3180–3160/3120–2920 cal BC), and at a later date of 3570±40 BP (Beta-260586; 1920–1730/1720–1690 cal BC) in the northwestern palaeochannel. Previous assessment work (JSAC 2001) indicates that channel aggradation might have begun during the 10th millennium BC.

The evidence therefore suggests that the environmental context for the extensive Neolithic activity on the site was one of some channels still carrying flowing freshwater and other previously active channels, probably apparent as sinuous depressions, which still contained areas of open water but were being colonized by sedges, rushes and other wetland vegetation. The precise structure of the vegetation beyond the floodplain edge during this period is somewhat unclear, although it was probably dominated by woodland including Scots pine and Lime. This was apparently not an entirely closed canopy, with evidence for more open, somewhat disturbed soils on which plants such as nettles, knotweed and docks were growing. Neolithic activity at Mill Lane was thus taking place within this mosaic of habitats including woodland, scrub, areas of flowing and still water, and grassy clearings. The palaeoenvironmental record may indicate naturally more unstable habitats associated with the dynamic environments of floodplain edges, but perhaps also created in part and maintained by wild grazing animals. The possible role of human communities in manipulating the local vegetation cannot be clearly determined.

During the Bronze Age and into the Iron Age, by 2590±40 BP (Beta-280639, 810–760/680–670 cal BC), areas of flowing water were probably much restricted as the palaeochannels gradually infilled with decaying plant matter. There is evidence for mixed deciduous woodland during this period, with dead wood from pine, ash and elm falling or being washed into the channels. Evidence for the continued presence of grazing animals is also recorded. Accumulation of peat continued, although in drier conditions, presumably related to autogenic processes as sediment accumulation raised the surface above the water table. The precise nature of later changes and specifically the opening up of the woodland and spread of grassland and pastoral habitats is unclear, but the general impression from Test Pit B is of an expansion of such environments through the later prehistoric period. However, the archaeological remains on the site date predominantly from the Anglo-Saxon to medieval periods and it seems likely that the insect date in particular records direct evidence of this activity. The presence of stored product pests (especially *Oryzaephilus surinamensis* and *Typhaea stercorea*) in the uppermost sample from Test Pit B, probably demonstrates the deposition of human occupation debris in the channel. This may represent the deliberate disposal of waste food material on the damper, more marginal soils, and hence away from habitation, or perhaps the effect of slope wash processes depositing material from occupation areas up-slope. However, there is also the possibility that some of the wood indicators derived from structural wood used on site and discarded in the upper part of the channel. Indeed, much of the upper part of the channel may have been directly disturbed by human activity, causing an even greater 'mixing' of habitat sources. Certainly, the Anglo-Saxon sunken-featured buildings would have been constructed largely of wood and some of this wood may even have been imported or reused. This might provide another explanation for the presence of pine-dependent beetles in the deposits.

9.5 Charred plant remains and molluscs
(by V. Fryer)

The results of the assessment of the charred plant macrofossils, mollusc shells and other remains are summarised below by phase.

9.5.1 *Neolithic and Bronze Age*

At the eastern side of the excavation, a possible area of prehistoric settlement was defined by a series of postholes and small postpits (group 100). Of the seven samples taken from this group three contain cereals, seeds and nutshell fragments. However, the density of material recovered is only consistent with small quantities of scattered or wind-blown detritus, much of which was probably accidentally incorporated within the feature fills along with the charcoal/charred wood. Shells of open country molluscs are common throughout, with specimens of *Pupilla muscorum* and *Vallonia costata* predominant, both of which are common in areas of short-turfed grassland.

The three contemporary ditch assemblages and the sample from layer 1066 are similarly composed, although in these instances charcoal is generally very scarce. The mollusc assemblages appear to indicate that the ditches were dry with grassy sides and bases.

9.5.2 *Early Anglo-Saxon pit fills*

Four assemblages are from pit fills of early Anglo-Saxon date (groups 101 and 103). All are small and relatively sparse, containing only occasional cereal grains and charcoal/charred wood fragments, and it would appear very unlikely that any are the result of the deliberate deposition of material within the pit fills. As with the prehistoric deposits, the mollusc assemblages are again indicative of predominantly dry, short-turfed grassland conditions. Fragments of black porous material are common within samples 103 (pit 1385) and 104 (pit 1304), but as both assemblages also contain moderate densities of coal, it is assumed that much of this material is intrusive within the pit fills.

9.5.3 *The early Anglo-Saxon sunken-featured buildings*

Five possible sub-rectangular sunken-featured buildings were recorded within the southeastern sector of the excavated area (group 101). Samples were taken from the main pits and postholes within buildings 1074, 1132, 1170 and 1223. The assemblages from structures 1074 and 1170 are very sparse, and as materials commonly identified as components of domestic refuse are so rare, it could be tentatively suggested that these structures may have served as stores or workshops.

Although still quite scarce, cereals and weed seeds do occur within the structure 1132 features. Three of the four assemblages also contain bone fragments and it would therefore appear more likely that this structure served as a domestic dwelling, with the recovered material being derived from detritus which fell through the floor into the underlying pit and structural features. It is possibly of note that one sample contains charred sedge fruits and another sample contains shells of *Succinea* sp., a mollusc commonly found on marginal wetland plants. Both could be indicative of materials used within the building as litter or thatch.

With the exception of charcoal/charred wood fragments, plant remains are again scarce within the structure 1223 features. However, all four assemblages contain shells of woodland/shade loving molluscs, possibly indicating that the building had lain derelict for some considerable period.

9.5.4 *The other early Anglo-Saxon features*

Three assemblages are from other features of early Anglo-Saxon date. Although all are sparse, sample 3 (pit 1018) does contain a moderate density of cereal grains and may be indicative of a small deposit of hearth waste or similar domestic refuse. The remaining assemblages contain an insufficient density of material for accurate interpretation.

9.5.5 *Medieval features*

During the medieval period, the northern and western areas of the site appear to have been partitioned by the construction of enclosure and field drainage ditches, many of the latter apparently emptying towards the area of a large palaeochannel. Sixteen assemblages from features of probable medieval (11th to 14th century) date were studied. Although plant macrofossils are generally extremely scarce, possibly suggesting that these features were well removed from any main centre of occupation or industrial/agricultural activity, a sample from ditch 1603 may contain a small deposit of cereal processing waste, comprising a number of severely puffed and distorted grains, a moderate density of bread wheat type rachis nodes and a limited range of segetal weed seeds. The few de-watered seeds noted within the medieval assemblages are mostly of ruderal weeds and/or woody shrubs, possibly indicating that parts of the site were poorly maintained and at least partially overgrown.

Although the mollusc assemblages are largely dominated by shells of open country species, a range of shade loving, marsh and freshwater obligate taxa are also now present, most notably within the ditch deposits, and it would appear most likely that many of the ditches were muddy and at least seasonally waterfilled.

The single assemblage from post-medieval ditch 1539 closely parallels the material from the medieval ditch fills, containing a large number of mollusc shells indicative of a wet, partially shaded ditch situated within an open grassland landscape.

9.5.6 Conclusions from the analysis of charred plant remains and molluscs

During the medieval and post-medieval periods the focus of activity on the site appears to have shifted slightly to the partition, drainage and utilisation of the wet grassland areas to the west, with the whole area being sub-divided by an extensive series of drainage ditches. These ditches drained into the palaeochannel features and with the exception of a single assemblage of possible charred cereal processing waste from ditch 1603, there is nothing to indicate the presence of any nearby arable activity during these periods.

CHAPTER 10

PREHISTORIC AND ROMAN ACTIVITY

10.1 Introduction

The nature of human activity at the Mill Lane site during the prehistoric and Roman periods varied considerably; the archaeological evidence indicates the importance of the location to those who visited it, either as a local to hunt and gather food, a place of seasonal occupation, or even as a site for votive deposition.

The earliest use of the site of Mill Lane dates to the late glacial period evidenced by a small and uncommon collection of flint of that date. There is considerable evidence for activity through the Mesolithic and Neolithic periods, however, though from the Bronze Age onwards, the intensity of human activity had reduced. Whilst there is no direct evidence of Iron Age occupation, the site's proximity to the fort of Borough Hill indicates local activity at this time. Similarly, there is very little evidence of Roman impact on site, although Roman period artefacts recovered from Anglo-Saxon contexts indicate settlement within the vicinity. The following chapter discusses the archaeological remains alongside the artefact evidence and attempts to chart the changing activities and attitudes at this marginal location.

10.2 The first settlers: a sedentary population or seasonal use of a preferred place? Mesolithic to Bronze Age activity

10.2.1 Mesolithic activity

The large quantities of residual Mesolithic flint recovered at Mill Lane indicate the site held some significance to early populations, being returned to on numerous occasions throughout the period. As with the majority of Mesolithic flint working sites no evidence for settlement was identified during the excavation, although the concentrations of flint recovered from the central area of the site, and that found within later features in the southeast and central portions, indicate that these areas may have been foci for flintworking activities (Chapter 4). The presence of microliths and hunting tools suggests that this river and wetland location within an otherwise pine dominated landscape would have provided a wealth of resources for small Mesolithic hunting camps. Associations between lithic scatters and rivers have been noted elsewhere for the Mesolithic period, such as across the Humberhead Levels in Yorkshire (Van de Noort 2004).

The importance of the site at Mill Lane to these early populations seems to have been highlighted by the likelihood that the fine Mesolithic axe may have been manufactured and discarded at the site, without ever being used, perhaps as a votive offering. It was found, along with a large collection of Mesolithic flint incorporated within a later Neolithic feature. One explanation for this residual material is that the feature may have been cut through the location of an earlier flintworking surface scatter adjacent to palaeochannel 1299/1302. This re-use of Mesolithic flintworking areas by the Neolithic inhabitants may not have been an accidental occurrence, but a deliberate attempt to re-establish a place in the landscape. It is also possible that the action of marking out of this area as a preferred place continued into the Neolithic through the deliberate incorporation of surface or midden material into Neolithic pits (see below).

Elsewhere within the broader region Mesolithic flintwork has been interpreted as representing short term occupation (Pollard 1998, 10, 40 and 83). As at Mill Lane, Mesolithic flintworking at the sites of Over and Fordham Moor was identified upon raised areas within landscapes dominated by palaeochannels indicating a consistency in choice over occupation sites (Evans and Webley 2003, 85 and 87; Gdaniec et al. 2007, 61).

It is also noteworthy that a small collection of earlier, late glacial blades was recovered from the centre of the site near to the palaeochannel. While the assemblage suggests that the tools were manufactured elsewhere and brought to the riverside location to take advantage of the hunting and gathering opportunities it afforded, one of the blades appears to have been deliberately snapped (Chapter 4) and left at the site.

10.2.2 Early Neolithic activity

The early Neolithic features and artefact assemblage from Mill Lane suggests several episodes of settlement activity. By the this period, the palaeoenvironmental evidence indicates that the channels still held running water, but that flow was retarded by the deposition of organic material. The wetland edge would have become dominated by wetland plants including sedges and rushes, but with pine and lime dominated woodland locally. There is some evidence for disturbed soil and perhaps grassy clearings (see Chapter 9). The presence of relatively large flint and pottery assemblages accumulating at this time within spreads or layers, together with evidence for postholes and other ephemeral features, may indicate a relatively sustained period of occupation or reflect the residues of repeated occupation activity.

The most significant occupational evidence from this phase was in the southwestern corner of the site where deposit 1066 and the associated postholes (1103, 1327, 1329 and 1338) produced a sizeable collection of early Neolithic pottery and flint (Fig. 3.2). It is highly likely that the postholes indicate the presence of a temporary structure, perhaps a small workshop, and the fact that so few artefacts were recovered from the postholes supports the theory that the structure was built before deposit 1066 formed. The flint assemblage, including a large proportion of burnt flint recovered from deposit 1066, indicates that several knapping episodes occurred within the structure, probably whilst the toolmakers were sitting round a hearth (Fig. 10.1). Whether these episodes occurred within one season or over several is impossible to clarify (Chapter 4). Several sherds from two vessels were incorporated into deposit 1066 and the artefact collection does appear to be a primary deposition of material (Chapter 4), which is a relatively rare occurrence on early Neolithic sites. Such midden deposits have been speculated as the source for the contents of the pits regularly found on early Neolithic sites, appearing to contain deliberate and structured deposits derived from elsewhere (Garrow 2006). This midden deposit, associated with a small structure, may thus be considered to represent a more common feature of early Neolithic activity than current evidence suggests, as they can easily be transformed into formless scatters and reincorporated into later features, either intentionally orunintentionally.

An exceptionally large assemblage, including early Neolithic pottery, struck flint and burnt lithics, was recovered from curving ditch 1254/1532/1547 (see Fig. 3.2). The flint assemblage appears to have been specifically selected rather than an accidental accumulation. Furthermore, the pottery is highly abraded, suggesting that it was broken a significant time before it ended up in the ditch. It may also be notable that pottery appeared placed directly over flints, indicating that this might have been structurally deposited. This suggests that the residues of settlement were not necessarily casually discarded, but intentionally deposited as a symbolic process. At the Over site, carefully stacked or bundled collections of pottery, bone and flint were found within several pits (Pollard 1998) which were thought to relate to concerns over process, transformation and regeneration.

The quantities of burnt flint recovered from ditch 1254 may have been used for heating water within a settlement context, on a smaller scale perhaps than later burnt mounds of the Bronze Age regularly recorded in central England and western Britain (Darvill 1987). This implies that cooking activities were taking place alongside the manufacture of hunting tools, indicating that the Mill Lane site was being used a base for hunting and foraging during the early Neolithic, and that the structured deposits may have been an attempt to mark the location within the broader landscape. The archaeological features are, nevertheless, ephemeral and there is no evidence for any form of substantial settlement architecture, suggesting that activity here may have been in the form of short-lived episodes.

Figure 10.1 Reconstruction of an early Neolithic workshop next to the river, from the flint working and midden deposits in the southwest corner of the site, facing northwest.

A number of other sites in the region have recorded evidence for early Neolithic activity in association with palaeochannels and alluvial environments. At Barleycroft Paddocks, Over, Cambridgeshire, Neolithic pit clusters have been identified on the River Ouse floodplain (Evans and Knight 1997). Pottery and flintwork within tree-'throw' features (Evans and Knight 1997, 30) may relate to an early phase of settlement and tree clearance, with the features possibly having been used as expedient shelters (Evans and Knight 1997, 69). In a similar way to that at Mill Lane, careful placement of pottery, flintwork and burnt flint was recorded in certain pit features which formed distinctive deposits (Evans and Knight 1997, 17), with others being characterised by less structured dumping of material (Evans and Knight 1997, 22). It is likely that artefacts were deliberately re-deposited into pits from midden material associated with episodes of settlement (Evans and Knight 1997, 23) although unlike the Mill Lane site no evidence for the original middens was recovered. Possible ephemeral sub-circular and sub-rectangular stake-built structures were also identified (Evans and Knight 1997, 27), suggesting a degree of sustained occupation.

Early Neolithic activity has also been recorded in association with a palaeochannel at the River Snail in Fordham Moor, Cambridgeshire (Gdaniec *et al.* 2007). Field-walking and test-pitting identified early Neolithic flintwork and occasional pottery scatters in the vicinity of the palaeochannel. Spatial patterning in the data was used to suggest clusters of activity in the area *(Gdaniec et al.* 2007, 53 and 61). Excavation identified early Neolithic flintwork and pottery together with animal and human bone alongside a miniature pottery vessel from palaeochannel sediments that were dated to the late fourth and early third millennia BC (Gdaniec *et al.* 2007, 54). Should the human bone be contemporary with this activity (Gdaniec *et al.* 2007, 54), it could indicate that depositional practices existed which had a ritual and social significance alongside other settlement activities.

Further afield at Hurst Fen, Mildenhall, Suffolk, a significant pit group with substantial quantities of pottery and flintwork was excavated in the 1950s (Clarke 1960). Despite a significant artefact assemblage little evidence for substantial structures was identified on the site apart from a row of stake-holes. Sites such as this may represent more sustained levels of occupancy than that represented by the more ephemeral evidence from Mill Lane, which may suggest diversity in the mode of occupation at larger regional scales. However, the lack of substantial domestic architecture does, as with Mill Lane, suggest that occupation may have been episodic rather than permanent.

10.2.3 Late Neolithic to early Bronze Age

Evidence for human activity during the late Neolithic was present in the southeastern corner of the site where heavily truncated postholes, ditches, and possible midden deposits were recorded. The shallow remains of the three east–west aligned ditches (1078/1042, 1082/1065 and 1349/1351, Fig. 3.3) contained large quantities of flint and pottery with the majority of the finds deriving from the earlier phases of activity on the site. It was noted during excavation that artefacts appeared to have been intentionally placed into the ditches during specific dumping episodes. This suggests that evidence for the earlier occupation of the site, such as surface scatters and/or midden deposits, was collected and intentionally placed into these ditches along with contemporary material. Given the residual nature of much of the material found within these features, it could be surmised that the late Neolithic/early Bronze Age populations at the site specifically undertook the collection of these artefacts, although it is unknown whether they took them from primary or secondary depositional sources. As noted for earlier periods, the collecting of this material may have been a symbolic act marking the place in the landscape, or even a new boundary in the form of the parallel ditches. This would attribute the elaborate discarding of 'rubbish' to the period of occupation at the site. Alternatively, the deposition may have occurred before a period of residence, clearing the ground of previous traces of occupation. If so, then surface scatters and middens may have been specifically left as markers in the landscape, detailing activities and maybe even interactions that had taken place there during previous seasons. Unfortunately, it is not possible to ascertain if it was the same group returning to these known locations seasonally, or new people occupying a location which had been marked as a good 'base of operation'.

Two possible middens were recorded to the north of the parallel ditches. Deposits 1459 and 1210/1268 (see Fig. 3.3) contained large quantities of early and late Neolithic pottery along with Beaker sherds indicating that they did not form until the earlier Bronze Age. Much of this pottery was heavily abraded suggesting that the sherds were old and already broken before they arrived within these deposits. Similarly, the flint recovered from these features is chronologically mixed with many broken pieces present suggesting that the material may have been collected from surface scatters around the site to intentionally build these features, perhaps creating what could have been visible as mounds during the late Neolithic/early Bronze Age. An early indication that deposit 1210/1268 may represent the remains of a possible barrow seems unlikely since no typical funerary ceramics or artefacts were identified (Chapter 5).

Positioned between the potential midden deposit 1210/1268 and the east–west aligned ditches was a collection of heavily truncated features that might once have been structural. The arc of shallow postholes (Group 100, Fig. 3.3) may indicate the presence of a roundhouse with the western postholes having been lost to later ploughing along with any potential internal features. This would indicate a more significant habitation of the site than seen in previous phases, although this remains speculative. It is also possible that the parallel ditches (1078/1042, 1082/1065 and 1349/1351) represent a site boundary demarking the southern extent of the late Neolithic occupation. No specific occupational evidence was recorded to the south of these ditches, although this may be coincidental as they lie close to the southern extent of the excavation area and it is possible that such remains do exist beyond.

How the structure and settlement activity at Mill Lane relates to potentially contemporary ditch features on the site is therefore uncertain. Field boundary ditches have been argued to date from the early Bronze Age at Flag Fen (Pryor 2001, 409), although ditches have been demonstrated to post-date early Bronze Age monuments within other areas of the Flag Fen basin (Pryor 2001, 411). Field systems and enclosed settlements are also frequently considered to date more generally from the middle Bronze Age across southern England (*e.g.* Barrett *et al.* 1991; McOmish *et al.* 2002; Brück 1999b). The potential for residuality within the east-west ditch features must be considered, as must the presence of a sherd of medieval pottery from ditch 1078/ 1042.

In the Over landscape, late Neolithic occupation, characterised by pits and artefact scatters, has been recorded on the subtly higher ground within a landscape also consisting of palaeochannels (Pollard 1998; Evans and Webley 2003). A Grooved Ware associated rectilinear structure has been recorded along with Grooved Ware associated pits in the vicinity of a former river channel (Pollard 1998). The size of the rectilinear structure at Over has been given to suggest that it did not function as a dwelling and may have had some other and possibly ritual function (Pollard 1998, 42). The structured deposition of pottery, bone, flint and human bone has been suggested at the site, and planned symmetrical arrangements of pits have been recorded along with more amorphous pit groups. Spreads of 'dirty soil' in the vicinity of certain pit groups have been interpreted as possible evidence of midden areas (Pollard 1998, 21–25) and may bear comparison with the layers recorded at Mill Lane. The site is, nevertheless, interpreted in terms of transitory settlement patterns without significant accumulation of domestic materials, although activity may at the same time be emphasising the significance of 'place' in the landscape (Pollard 1998, 42–44). Elsewhere in this landscape a very small 'hengiform' structure has been recorded associated with Grooved Ware and a 'midden' deposit (Evans and Webley 2003, 73).

Whilst there is evidence for occupation at Mill Lane in this period, the site does not appear to have had the same structured focus as some of the Over sites, which may suggest it represents several short-lived phases of occupation. Long term continuity with earlier Neolithic settlement could, however, suggest that this location was regarded as significant, whether environmentally or socially, by successive generations. Though whether such significance was consciously maintained across such large time-scales is debateable.

Elsewhere, substantial pits associated with animal bone have been recorded for the early Bronze Age at Isleham, Cambridgeshire, together with an ephemeral structure (Gdaniec *et al.* 2007, 27–37). Notably, the structure is semi-circular and can be compared with that recorded at Mill Lane, although it is not well dated. Pits located a certain distance from the structure have been dated to the early Bronze Age, and have clear evidence for structured deposition in the form of deliberately arranged animal skulls and a miniature bow carved from antler (Gdaniec *et al.* 2007, 35–36). The relationship between the pits and the possible roundhouse is,

however, uncertain. Nevertheless, as with the late Neolithic pit digging activity at Over (Pollard 1998), the evidence from Isleham suggests that occupation may have been interspersed with activities that were not simply domestic or practical and that 'occupation' may have encompassed a range of practices. By analogy with these sites, activity at Mill Lane in this period may not necessarily have been associated with an economically driven, permanent or well defined settlement site, as may be expected for later periods of prehistory and history.

10.3 Abandonment? Iron Age and Roman evidence

10.3.1 *Later prehistoric activity*

By the later prehistoric period, the palaeoenvironmental evidence indicates that flow within the palaeochannels had become restricted as they infilled with organic sediment. At this time, the wider landscape was one of mixed deciduous woodland with grazing animals, perhaps with increased localised clearance. Although flintworking continued into the early Bronze Age period at the Mill Lane site, activity was at a much reduced scale compared to previous phases (Bishop, Chapter 4). Therefore, artefact evidence suggests that the use of the site during the prehistoric periods may have been considerably less intensive during the Bronze Age and, despite the presence of a significant lowland fort, Borough Hill, dating to the early, middle and late Iron Age directly to the south of the excavation area (JSAC 2003), no features or artefacts dating to the Iron Age were recorded at Mill Lane. The fort may not, therefore, have been surrounded by contemporary occupation, at least in the area of the current site.

The evaluation of Borough Hill's defences in 2005 revealed a sequence of three large ditches (Poppy *et al.* 2006), commencing with the middle ditch. Although the ditches had begun to silt up during the Iron Age, the upper parts remained open until the medieval or post-medieval periods. Evidence for domestic activities were recovered from within the enclosed area in the form of animal bones and pottery, indicating that the hillfort was occupied for at least a short period.

Hillforts such as the Borough Hill site have generally been seen as a specialised form of settlement, their size and complexity suggesting they represent the communal effort of a large sector of a social group under the coercive power of the leadership (Cunliffe 2005). While a large number of hill forts have been investigated, the excavations have largely involved sections through the ramparts and gates (Cunliffe 2005). In several cases the portions of the forts interiors have been investigated (for example at Winklebury, Danebury and Maiden Castle) but very little emphasis has been placed on what lies within the immediate environs of the fort. This has been identified as an important research focus within the British Iron Age research agenda (Haselgrove *et al.* 2001) as it is currently not known whether the lack of Iron Age features in an area so close to a contemporary earthwork is exceptional, or 'the norm'. Regionally, very little work has been undertaken on hillforts, though trial excavations at the Iron Age ringwork at Arbury Camp, Cambridgeshire, suggested a lack of activity beyond the confines of the Iron Age fort (Evans and Knight 2002, 44). The snail and soil reports from the excavation of the Iron Age and Roman enclosure at Werrington, also in Cambridgeshire, suggest that the earthwork lay within undisturbed grassland (MacKreth *et al.* 1988). As with Arbury Camp, no settlement evidence was recorded outside the enclosed area at Werrington, which may suggest the fort at Sawston is not unusual in this respect.

A sub-rectangular enclosure to the immediate northwest of Borough Hill was recorded through geophysical survey and sample excavated as part of the earlier evaluation (see Fig. 1.3). The feature may have been Iron Age in date (JSAC 2003), although its relationship with the fort remains unclear. Whatever the function of this enclosure, contemporary activity does not appear to have extended further to the north. However, Iron Age activity taking place to the east, west or south of the fort cannot be ruled out.

So why was the location of the Mill Lane site, which seems to have been of such importance to the seasonal visitors in earlier pre-history, no longer seen as a preferable place to settle, neither seasonally or long term? Seeing that the palaeochannel still offered an open body of water during the Bronze Age that was close to both open ground and woodland, it may be assumed that grazing animals were drawn to the channel for drinking water. Towards the end of the Bronze Age the channel was gradually filling in. Later (undated) deposits indicate that by the close of the prehistoric period the channel was only filled with water on a temporary basis, perhaps seasonally. This seems to be an environment that would have provided a plethora of hunting and gathering opportunities and it is therefore likely that the inhabitants of Borough Hill would have visited the area of the Mill Lane site to take advantage of these. Due to the heavy truncation at the site it may be that all evidence for these possible visits has been lost, or that the activities undertaken, such as gathering wetland plants or hunting animals, did not leave any form of physical trace; activity without an archaeological signature. Rather than the site being abandoned during late prehistory, it seem more likely that the types of activity taking place were refocused away from those which would leave archaeological evidence.

10.3.2 *Were there Romans nearby?*

Evidence dating to the Roman period was extremely limited at the Mill Lane site. The ceramic building material recovered during the excavations does not seem to represent any built structures on site, but does indicate the potential for Roman period buildings nearby. Equally, the residual sherds of Roman pottery from features at the current site may indicate nearby settlement, perhaps in the form of ditched field systems and the agricultural manuring of fields. The large

ditch (1485, see Fig. 3.5) on the western edge of the site may indicate the presence of a Roman field system beyond that edge of the excavation, and a spread of material towards the centre of the site (1390) also contained several sherds of Roman pottery.

It is notable that Roman pottery sherds were recorded during the evaluation of the fort to the south (JSAC 2001), which also indicate settlement in the vicinity in this period, though it is not possible on current evidence to suggest that the earlier ringwork necessarily formed a focus for settlement at this time. The late Roman coin also indicates occupation into the 5th century, although the lack of Romano-British structural remains suggests that the focus of occupation in this period lay elsewhere.

10.4 Conclusions

Throughout prehistory and into the Roman period, the landscape at Mill Lane changed dramatically from a riverside, pine dominated landscape during the Mesolithic, to a mixed deciduous woodland with clearings on the edge of a more stagnant, seasonal wetland. The opportunities afforded to human populations changed considerably. This shift in the environmental context is perhaps reflected by the human activity represented in the archaeological record, which indicates a reduction in occupation by the end of this broad period.

More specifically, the types of activity taking place at the Mill Lane site varied considerably throughout prehistory. The locale appears to have been highly attractive during the Mesolithic and Neolithic periods, being marked through the potentially symbolic collection and distribution of occupational waste. Furthermore, the possible early Neolithic structure represented by postholes might relate to the production of flintwork on site. This relatively intensive use of the locale appears to have continued well into the Bronze Age, although with a reduction in activity during latter half of the second millennium BC.

The reduction in activity during the later Bronze Age continued into the Iron Age. No evidence for human activity at the site during the Iron Age was recovered, although there is clear evidence of human activity during this period within the immediate locality with the presence of the hillfort of Borough Hill. Whilst there is no direct evidence that the Iron Age inhabitants of Borough Hill occupied the site, the proximal evidence does demonstrate that the area was not abandoned during this period.

The evidence for human activity during the Roman period is also extremely limited. The recovered ceramic building material from this period does not appear to represent any structures on site, although it does indicate that there might have been Roman period buildings within the local area. This is perhaps also reflected by the discovery of a single coin dating to the 5th century AD. It is possible that ditches, particularly on the western edge of the site, reflect agriculture during this period.

CHAPTER 11

ANGLO-SAXON, MEDIEVAL AND POST-MEDIEVAL ACTIVITY

11.1 Introduction

The evidence from the later prehistoric and Roman periods suggests a reduction in human activity on the site of Mill Lane, although with indications of interactions with the wider landscape. Following this apparent hiatus in activity, the evidence from the early Anglo-Saxon period suggests a more permanent, if rather small, settlement. By the medieval period, this domestic occupation of the landscape had been replaced by agricultural use, dominated by pastoral farming, a practice that persisted into the post-medieval period. This chapter discusses the archaeological evidence from the excavations, artefact analyses and palaeoenvironmental analyses in relation to occupation and use from around the 5th century AD to the post-medieval period.

11.2 The Roman/Anglo-Saxon transition

In terms of settlement patterns, the transition between late Roman Britain and the Anglo-Saxon period has been highlighted as a significant research theme for the region (Medlycott and Brown 2008, 79). The presence of the Roman coin within an Anglo-Saxon feature, which may date to the early 5th century (see Chapter 6), in addition to several sherds of late Roman pottery recovered from the Anglo-Saxon period sunken-featured buildings (SFBs), raises questions regarding the continuity and origins of Anglo-Saxon settlement at Mill Lane. The majority of the Roman tile from the site was recovered within four of the SFBs (see Chapter 6) and it is possible that the tiles were chosen purposefully to line hearths in buildings of this date.

Previous research has suggested that the earliest Germanic settlements within England were closely connected with former Romano-British towns and settlements (*e.g.* Addyman 1972). Within SFB 1322 a number of residual Roman pottery sherds were retrieved, notably including a mortarium stub flange which provided a direct cross context join with one recovered from the infill of the adjacent SFB 1170. It may be possible that the site at Mill Lane reflects some degree of continuity with Romano-British settlement patterns based on the artefactual evidence, although the focus of any such earlier settlement remains unknown. The data from the site does, nevertheless, contribute to the growing corpus of knowledge regarding the Roman/Anglo-Saxon transition.

Elsewhere, the discovery of Roman material within early Anglo-Saxon contexts has provided some insight into the transition between the two periods. For example, at Fordham, Cambridgeshire, residual Roman pottery sherds were recorded within early Anglo-Saxon sunken-featured buildings, although this was interpreted as having been imported into the site with turves for building construction (Patrick and Ratkai 2007, 8). Furthermore, the presence of a significant Saxon settlement on the site of a former Roman settlement at Bloodmoor Hill, Calton, Colville, Suffolk, can also be highlighted, although the author did not consider that occupation was continuous between the Roman and Anglo-Saxon periods (Tipper 2009, 428).

11.3 Reclaiming the floodplain – an Anglo-Saxon settlement

A significant phase of archaeological activity relating to the early Anglo-Saxon period was highlighted by a number of very distinctive features situated in the southeastern area of the site (group 101, Fig. 3.6). Three of the structures from within this area, each interpreted as a sunken-featured building (1170, 1132 and 1074, see Figs 11.1 and 11.2) were positioned on an east–west axis very close to the southern edge of palaeochannel 1299/1302. By the Anglo-Saxon period, palaeoenvironmental evidence indicates that this former river channel had already been cut off from the main river (see Chapter 9).

The location of the sunken-featured buildings in relation to the river may indicate that this specific location had once again become important. The palaeochannel may well have been gradually filling in by the time the Anglo-Saxon structures were built, yet the positions of the structures does indicate that it remained a significant feature in the landscape, with the natural resources it provided creating a focal point for the reoccupation of this locale. The possible presence of a Roman settlement nearby could be a further indicator for the choice of this location as an early Saxon village (Fig. 11.3).

Radiocarbon dates (see Appendix 5, Table A5.1) obtained for several of the Anglo-Saxon sunken-featured buildings indicate that at least three of the structures may have been occupied at roughly the same time. The upper fill (1221) of the SFB located on the northeast edge of the palaeochannel was dated to cal AD 430–590. The fill (1207) of one of the postholes within SFB 1170 on the southern edge of the palaeochannel was dated to cal AD 410–550 indicating that these two features were at least backfilled at roughly the same

Figure 11.1 Sunken-featured building 1132 under excavation, facing east.

time. The fill (1017) of the possible SFB located close to the eastern edge of the site (1018) produced the slightly later data of cal AD 540–620, though there is still a possible temporal overlap with the SFBs to the west. The final date however was obtained from the fill (1343) of the linear gully 1433 which was truncated by SFB 1074. Grains from the fill of the gully were dated to cal AD 710–750 which implies that this feature filled at a much later date than SFBs 1170, 1223 and 1018. Hence, it cannot be discounted that all the features may have been in use at the same time, although the results do indicate that one of the structures at least post-dated the main phase of activity. This could simply be the result of successive generations living and re-building in the same locale rather than completely separate phases of occupation.

Palaeoenvironmental evidence suggests that the Anglo-Saxon sunken-featured buildings were probably constructed within a predominantly open landscape. However, the small number of shade-loving molluscs which appeared to have colonised the derelict features of structure 1123 may indicate the presence of adjacent areas of open woodland (Fryer 2009). It was also indicated that the occupants of the site were exploiting nearby wetland habitats for the provision of flooring or roofing materials, and that while there was evidence for cereal utilisation, there does not appear to have been any intensive agricultural activity in the immediate area.

At Fordham four Anglo-Saxon sunken-featured buildings were recorded within an enclosure system and associated with evidence for textile production (Cuttler *et al.* 2011). There is no evidence that any of the ditched enclosure systems at Mill

Figure 11.2 Sunken-featured building 1074 facing northwest.

Figure 11.3 Reconstruction of the small early Anglo-Saxon village at the site, looking northwest to SFBs 1074, 1132 and 1170.

Lane are contemporaneous with Anglo-Saxon activity, which may suggest an open settlement existed here. The linear axis of the buildings at Mill Lane does, however, indicate some form of planned settlement morphology (*cf.* Tipper 2009). The possible trackway leading to the SFBs (1183, Fig. 3.6), may potentially indicate that the houses were part of a more extensive settlement which extended to the south beyond the edge of the excavated area, although no further evidence was recorded in evaluations or to the south of the site.

The artefactual and environmental data recovered from the early Anglo-Saxon features indicates that the inhabitants of the site led a lifestyle largely typical of a small self-sufficient settlement within a seasonally wet environment. However the diet does seem to have been more at the privileged end of the scale as indicated by the animal bone assemblage (see Chapter 7). As well as food production there are also hints of craft production at Mill Lane. The presence of a spindle whorl, for instance, along with several other artefacts can be associated with the activities of women (see Chapter 7).

11.4 Medieval and post-medieval ditch systems

The medieval ditch system identified at Mill Lane may provide a useful insight into land division, drainage and land management in this period. The ditches were also recorded during the evaluation with recovered artefacts dating to between the 12th and 14th centuries (JSAC 2001). During the excavation, at least two ditched enclosures were identified along with several apparent drainage channels which emptied into palaeochannel 1584 (Fig. 3.11). The palaeoenvironmental evidence suggests that while the palaeochannels were largely filled by the medieval period, they would still have held water, and that the area would have been subject to regular flooding (see Chapter 9). These enclosures may have either been part

of a much larger agricultural landscape extending beyond the excavation area, or formed a small paddock system for an isolated farmstead. It is not possible to determine the full nature of the medieval farming activities in the area from the excavated remains, but it does seem likely that they indicate that pastoral, rather than arable, practices were taking place, and with the exception of a single assemblage of possible charred cereal processing waste there is nothing to indicate the presence of any nearby arable activity during these periods (see Chapter 9). The continued re-cutting during the 12th–14th centuries of the enclosure ditches and drainage channels which empty into palaeochannel 1584 was probably as a result of the exceptionally wet nature of the locale. This work could have taken place at regular intervals, once the ditches had silted up to a point when they were no longer able to function as drainage channels, or it may have been the case that the site was only used for grazing on a seasonal basis, with the re-establishment of the enclosure system and drainage channels occurring before each season.

Such ditch systems may provide a useful contribution to the knowledge of medieval land division on a small scale, complementing large scale multiple parish field system studies across East Anglia (Martin and Satchell 2008). Comparable sites have been excavated in the region, such as the medieval field systems recorded in a seasonally wet environment at Longstanton and Striplands Farm, northwest of Cambridge. At Longstanton the earlier medieval enclosures and fields have been largely interpreted as paddocks with drainage ditches and features believed to be associated with animal husbandry practices (Paul 2010). Converging paddocks and animal enclosures on channels or areas which held water would have removed the necessity to regularly bring water to animals or dig wells to fulfil such a need. At Longstanton early medieval pit wells were recorded within enclosures which were on slightly higher ground and therefore not located close to a natural water source (Paul and Hunt 2015). No wells were recorded within the adjacent enclosures which came into contact with flooded areas, implying that placing animal paddocks so close to an area prone to flooding such as at Mill Lane was a deliberate decision. However, at Longstanton much of the medieval landscape was later given over to arable agricultural practices, with ridge and furrow in some cases superseding the earlier enclosure system (Paul and Mann 2012). At Mill Lane, no evidence for ridge and furrow was recorded. This may be the result of later ploughing and truncation removing all evidence, or that the area was just too wet to attempt arable farming during the medieval period.

In some parts of Cambridgeshire elements of pre-medieval field systems and land boundaries can be seen to have survived in the medieval layout (Williamson 2003) but there is no evidence for this at Mill Lane. The post-medieval phase at the site appears to show some continuity with medieval ditch systems and land-use. The entire ditch forming the western enclosure group 109 (Fig. 3.11) was re-cut and enlarged during the post-medieval period (Fig. 3.12) signifying the prolonged use of the site and probable continuity between the medieval and post-medieval farmers using the area. It is therefore likely that the site continued to be used for pastoral purposes during the post-medieval period and that water management was still an issue as the drainage channels were replaced by one large ditch during this period.

11.5 Conclusions

For perhaps a millennium prior to the Anglo-Saxon period, the site of Mill Lane appears to have been abandoned, although there are indications that human activity persisted within the locality, demonstrated by the nearby fort of Borough Hill and by the Roman period finds identified from early Anglo-Saxon features. Perhaps during the 5th century AD there was a renewed interest in the site, as occupation was established through the construction of a group of buildings, represented archaeologically as sunken-featured structure adjacent to the palaeochannel of the River Cam. At the edge of the wetlands this occupation was situated within a relatively open landscape with grazing for livestock and wild animals. Based on faunal remains, the standard of living for the Anglo-Saxon population appears to have been relatively high, and there seems to have been clear spatial patterning of waste disposal away from settlement.

Human activity at the edge of the wetlands continued, and focused on agricultural production. The ditch systems and enclosures identified on the site imply some level of water management during the medieval period. Re-cutting of these ditches seems to reflect a continued re-use of this landscape until the formalisation of drainage evidenced in the post-medieval period. The function of the Mill Lane site during the medieval and post-medieval periods focused on pastoral farming practices, and this seems appropriate given the wetness of the landscape.

CHAPTER 12

CONCLUSIONS: LIFE ON THE WETLAND EDGE

12.1 Introduction

This book has detailed the results of research undertaken at Mill Lane near Sawston, Cambridgeshire. As outlined in Chapter 1, the aims of this project centred on the investigation of human occupation within the wetland fringes of a river system, with the associated potential for preservation. Specifically, the study aimed to explore the occupation of the floodplain edge to establish the chronological range of activity and themes of continuous or non-continuous human activity, and to understand any factors that influenced the visibility of archaeological remains which might have an impact on understanding these types of landscapes. Secondly, the study aimed to understand the landscape and environmental context of the site in relation to environmental change in terms of both physical changes and shifts in vegetation to establish a clearer picture of the relationships between people and their changing environments. Finally, the project aimed to establish the nature of preservation across the site, particularly within the context of more recent land use and water abstraction activities. This chapter begins with a chronological summary of the site from the early Holocene through to the post-medieval period. This is followed by a re-consideration of the aims of the project in relation to these findings.

12.2 Narrative

The excavations at Mill Lane, Sawston, have provided the opportunity to study human activity and environments on a site at a wetland-dryland interface over a span of around 10,000 years. During the late glacial to early Holocene the palaeo River Cam incised a channel or channels into the western edge of the excavation area and it is probable that the earliest phases of archaeological activity were taking place adjacent to active water courses, within a landscape dominated by Scots Pine woodland on the dryland soils. The earliest finds recorded at the site consisted of a collection of rare late glacial flintwork dating to the period between *c.* 14,700 and 7,700 BC, reflecting the significance of the location during early prehistory (see chapter 4). The tools recovered indicated that they had been manufactured elsewhere and brought to site, with one late glacial blade having been deliberately broken prior to deposition. The small number of finds might reflect only transitory visiting, perhaps related to hunting animals

grazing around the palaeochannel, although it is possible that they erected temporary shelters that have left no trace in the archaeological record.

A subsequent phase of activity during the Mesolithic is marked by evidence for tool making, hunting activities and perhaps even deliberate, ritualised deposition. The discovery of a fine Mesolithic axe, which had been discarded at the site without ever being used, might encourage a votive interpretation, although the presence of microliths within specific areas suggests that hunting tools were produced at the site. This might indicate short-term settlement within the area, although no excavated evidence for this was found. Certainly, the rich diversity of environments, including the river, woodland, open pasture, and wetlands, would have provided a wealth of resources for a small Mesolithic hunting camp. Within the broader region, evidence for Mesolithic activity is relatively limited (Medlycott 2011), and so the material from Mill Lane indicates that this might be due to archaeological invisibility rather than an absence of human activity (*cf.* Medlycott and Brown 2008).

A range of features and the artefact assemblage from Mill Lane suggest several episodes of settlement activity at the floodplain edge during the early Neolithic period. At that time, some of the palaeochannels may have still contained flowing freshwater, but it is clear that others had been cut off from permanent flow, probably surviving as sinuous waterlogged depressions containing areas of open water colonized by sedges, rushes and other wetland vegetation. The adjacent dryland vegetation included lime, elm, ash and oak. Although this woodland may have been fairly dense, the insect record indicates somewhat disturbed vegetation and plants including nettles and docks (see Chapter 9). This may reflect disturbance by human activity, the grazing of wild animals or the naturally unstable soils that can be a feature of an ecotonal boundary between wet and dryland. It can be proposed that this interface between the floodplain and dryland edge was a preferred location, with a range of natural resources available in what may also have been a slightly more open woodland environment. The presence of relatively large flint and pottery assemblages accumulated within spreads or layers, together with evidence for postholes and other ephemeral features, indicates a relatively sustained period of occupation or reflect the residues of repeated occupational activity. Rare evidence for the primary deposition of several flint knapping episodes from within one possible structure, along with exceptionally large groups of burnt flint and pottery, indicate a significant focus of early Neolithic activity at Mill Lane. Deposits of this nature are usually dispersed through ploughing and erosion but the example at Mill Lane, being concealed and protected by colluvial deposits, could provide an example for what may well be a more common feature than is currently recorded nationally. The location continued to be marked by the apparently intentional, structured deposition of flint and pottery into pits, possibly as a symbolic process.

The general development of settlement during the Neolithic within the region is poorly understood and, in particular, finding evidence for human impact on the environment, including woodland management and clearance, presents a significant challenge (Medlycott 2011). Within this context, the early Neolithic activity recorded on the site significantly contributes to our understanding of the landscape context of settlement and associated activities in the region for this period. Traditional expectations of long-houses and permanent settlements associated with the introduction of farming have not been realised across much of southern England and the record is instead largely characterised by flint scatters and ephemeral features indicating relatively short-lived episodes of activity (*cf.* Thomas 1991). This has led to influential interpretations of mobile forms of residency in the period (Thomas 1991; Whittle 1997) and the evidence from Mill Lane appears to reflect such models. Within the context of the potential variety in their form, the identification of settlement structures has, nevertheless, been highlighted as a research priority for the region (Medlycott and Brown 2008). The features and artefacts from this site therefore provide a useful contribution to the debate on modes of settlement in this period and the extent to which settlement was transitory, sustained or permanent. Such an understanding can make a significant contribution to the broader context of settlement in this period beyond known and more readily identifiable monument sites.

Similar themes of settlement mobility exist for the late Neolithic and early Bronze Age, for which periods evidence of settlement structures is both ephemeral and rarely encountered across much of England and Wales, with occupation being considered to be episodic in nature (Whittle 1997; Brück 1999a). The examination of 'shifting' and 'settled' landscape processes and settlement types has been identified as a priority for the region (Medlycott 2011). Hence, the presence of a possible stake-built roundhouse (see Chapter 3; Fig. 3.3, Insert A) at Mill Lane may therefore be significant, albeit representing a somewhat ephemeral and perhaps temporary structure. The palaeoenvironmental data provides a context for contemporaneous artefact assemblages on the site, indicating periods of occupation within a mosaic of habitats including woodland, scrub, grassy clearings, and areas of flowing and still water (see Chapter 9).

Several deposits identified across the site from earlier periods have been interpreted as middens or 'midden-like' accumulations, and it is possible that these were still visible as low mounds during the late Neolithic/early Bronze Age periods. It is likely that these midden deposits were a more

common settlement indicator than current data suggests due to subsequent farming practices, but also as a result of excavation methods such as those that aim to 'strip, map and record'(a process that uses mechanical diggers to remove modern overburden and topsoil to the level of archaeological remains therefore increasing the possibility that surface finds or features are lost). Several of the later Neolithic features also contained what appeared to be deliberate deposits of material which, in many cases, included flint and pottery dating from earlier periods. Given the residual nature of much of the material found within these features and the midden deposits, it could be stated that the late Neolithic and early Bronze Age populations visiting the site specifically undertook the collection of these artefacts, and that this process may have been a symbolic act marking the significance of this place in the landscape. The surface scatters and middens may have been left as 'markers', reflecting activities and events that had taken place during previous seasons. Elsewhere, a large number of known Neolithic sites comprise 'monuments', while flintworking sites and unenclosed settlement are underrepresented (Medlycott 2011). The archaeological deposits at Mill Lane go some way towards remedying this imbalance, and the middens may indicate a more organic or temporary form of monumentality not as easily identified as the banks and ditches traditionally associated with ceremonial activity. The Mill Lane site may therefore indicate a possible 'monument sub type'; a more local or specific indicator of place, territory or even family or clan groups.

The use of the site appears to have changed following the early Bronze Age, and the focus for later prehistoric settlement activities shifted away. No features or artefacts dating to the Iron Age were identified despite the presence of a significant lowland fort, Borough Hill, directly to the south of the excavated area. The palaeoenvironmental analyses indicates that a more open, cultivated landscape persisted from the later Bronze Age into the Iron Age along with continued evidence for grazing animals, suggesting a high likelihood of human activity within the area. However, there is also evidence for the infilling of channels and the generation of wetlands rather than flowing water which will have altered the ecological and economic potential of the site itself. Given the importance of the location during earlier periods, it is probable that the inhabitants of Borough Hill may have visited the site regularly to take advantage of the hunting and gathering opportunities that this environment would have provided. Rather than the site being abandoned during later prehistory, it seems more likely that the types of activities taking place were refocused, for example to hunting game or the gathering of wetland plants, and away from those which would leave a clear archaeological signature.

The lack of evidence for human activity during later prehistory is matched by a similar absence of onsite occupation during the Roman period. The principal evidence for this period consists of a small assemblage of ceramic building material representing different buildings or phases of building, and a single coin dating from the fourth century. The quantity of material reinforces the lack of evidence for any Roman period structures on site, although it does suggest the presence of buildings within the locality. The majority of these finds were from secondary, Anglo-Saxon period contexts indicating that this material was brought to site during this later re-occupation.

The discovery of a small Anglo-Saxon settlement at Mill Lane indicates that this specific location had once again become important by this period, with the natural resources it provided perhaps creating a focal point for reoccupation. The positioning of the sunken-featured buildings near to one of the Roman crossings of the River Cam and close to the earlier, Iron Age, site of Borough Hill raises questions about the significance of the earlier landscape to the Anglo-Saxon population. Anglo-Saxon buildings are difficult to detect using aerial photography and so their identification can be problematic. Hence, the discovery of Anglo-Saxon settlement remains near Sawston not only provides a significant contribution to the regional distribution and context of settlement in this period but may also provide a settlement location indicator to be applied to future surveys. The evidence from Mill Lane contributes to current understanding of economic production and consumption in a rural context and this can be used as a basis of comparison with both rural and urban sites elsewhere. Specifically, the evidence provides a picture of a mixed economy, including both stored arable food products and meat. Evidence of pests (especially *Oryzaephilus surinamensis* and *Typhaea stercorea*) provides an indication of stored food products in the Test Pit B sequence, whilst the animal bone assemblage from the sunken-featured buildings implies that the diet of the inhabitants was at the more 'privileged' end of the scale for this period. In addition to food production and storage, the presence of a spindle whorl indicates that textile production was also taking place on site. Together, this indicates a successful community engaged in a diverse range of economic and craft activities.

Medlycott (2011) has highlighted the importance of exploring the impact of Anglo-Saxon settlement upon the medieval landscape. The broadly east–west alignment of the Anglo-Saxon building group at Mill Lane shares a comparable axis to the arrangement of the medieval ditches. This may, however, have been influenced by the local topography and there is nothing to suggest direct continuity between the early Anglo-Saxon activity and the medieval field system. The later re-configuration of the enclosures during the post-medieval period, on the other hand, seems to be a direct continuation of the animal husbandry practices of the 12th–14th centuries. It is notable that water management and land reclamation have also been highlighted as an important avenue for future research in the region (Medlycott and Brown 2008, 96), along with the importance of relating archaeology with palaeoenvironmental data. The medieval and post-medieval enclosures and drainage channels at Mill Lane provide such evidence of long term land management.

12.3 Reconsidering the aims of the project, and recommendations for future research

12.3.1 Chronology of occupation the wetland/dryland interface

Chronological range

The research at Mill Lane has presented a strong chronological overview of floodplain activity from the late glacial period through to the post-medieval period. Scrutiny of the archaeological features and deposits, alongside the associated specialist analyses, has demonstrated that occupation at the locality extended from the late glacial through to the post-medieval period. The small but significant collection of late glacial flint extends previous understanding of the site back to around the 15th to the 8th millennium BC. While late glacial flint is rare, the material recovered at Sawston is comparable to two small collections found to the south at Hinxton, and to the northeast at Great Wilbraham (see Chapter 4). This material reflects an apparent focus of late glacial activity related to the River Cam, which is also seen at Hinxton (on the River Cam) and at Great Wilbraham (which lies on a tributary). In addition to strengthening our understanding of early activity associated with this river, the evidence also indicates how river valleys might have been used as corridors to access inland locations (Chapter 10) and that the landscape surrounding the margins of the River Cam witnessed considerable human activity during the late glacial period.

Continuity of settlement

Whilst the late glacial flint recorded during the Mill Lane excavations can by no means be interpreted as indicating settlement, from that point on there is evidence for fairly continuous activity along the river margins over a considerable period of time. The palimpsests of Mesolithic flintworking episodes that may well have represented short-term settlement, was replaced by early Neolithic seasonal occupation. The rare example of a small early Neolithic structure containing primary deposition material is an important discovery both regionally and nationally. Such deposits have been cited as the sources for the structured pit fills recorded throughout the period, though very few examples of the original features have previously been uncovered (Garrow 2006). The early Neolithic structure at Mill Lane therefore provides evidence for a form of seasonal occupation which may have been more prevalent than current evidence suggests. The late Neolithic and early Bronze Age activity at the site also appears to have been seasonal and, while the only structural evidence identified was ephemeral, visits to the locale appear to have been repeated and sustained.

During earlier prehistory, the area of Mill Lane was relatively dry with flowing river channels providing water and opportunities for hunting and fowling. However, by the end of the Bronze Age the channels had infilled and no longer held flowing water leading to a much wetter environment generally. It may be that the environmental changes apparent in the palaeoenvironmental record at the end of the Bronze Age made the site less suitable for settlement. This less habitable landscape, coupled with wider climate deterioration during the period, may explain the apparent lack of human activity on site until the early Anglo-Saxon phase. The palaeoenvironmental data, however, do indicate human activity, if not on the site itself, then nearby, suggesting that activities within the wider landscape changed rather than ceased. This indication of human influence on the wider landscape is reflected by the presence of the Iron Age fort of Borough Hill directly to the south of the excavated area. The hiatus in occupation at Mill Lane during later prehistory continued throughout the Roman period, although the recovery of Roman ceramic building material from within the later Anglo-Saxon features might indicate that there was settlement within the wider landscape at this time in addition to the known crossing of the River Cam.

For perhaps a millennium, human activity probably persisted within the wider landscape despite there being an apparent hiatus on site. However, the significant growth in activity during the early Anglo-Saxon period indicates that the locale had once again become a suitable choice for settlement. The inhabitants of the small cluster of houses appeared to live well within the Sawston landscape, undertaking a range of activities including crafts in addition to enjoying a diet that was perhaps indicative of relative wealth. Activity at the site continued into later periods, though the actual settlement was no longer within the Mill Lane site, taking instead the form of medieval and post-medieval field systems and enclosures relating to pastoral farming.

Occupation within the wider landscape of Sawston appears to have been continuous. Whilst the intensity of activity during earlier periods cannot be known, the evidence indicates repeated activity on the site of Mill Lane from the late glacial period through to the early Bronze Age. For the subsequent Iron Age and Roman periods, activity on site reduced, although the evidence indicates human activity within the near landscape. The re-occupation of the site of Mill Lane during the early Anglo-Saxon period appears to have undergone multiple phases of activity before the landscape became one of pastoral agriculture. During the medieval period, this was represented by a network of enclosures and ditches, later replaced by the modern pattern of drainage.

Deposition of 'waste' at Mill Lane

The deposition of 'waste' and objects at Mill Lane changed significantly through time. From the deliberately broken late glacial blade to the late Neolithic structured deposits, the deposition of this material raises questions about the functionality of 'waste'. The evidence from the early Neolithic includes a variety of deposits associated with a possible structure, a ditch and a midden. The pottery and flint from the midden and the curving ditch are indicative of deliberate deposition of material. Within the midden, the

collection of artefacts appears to be a primary deposition of the material, while the high levels of abrasion of the pottery from the ditch suggests that it had been broken some time prior to its incorporation indicating a particular choice over its final placing. The sizeable collection of early Neolithic pottery and flint from a primary deposition within the structure, including a large proportion of burnt flint, indicates successive episodes of tool-making within it. The pottery from this area represented the remains of two vessels. The fact that this deposit remained undisturbed through to the time of its excavation has implications beyond the rarity of finding primary deposits of such material. The accumulated assemblage, and whatever remained of the structure around it, was a stable and unchanging marker in the landscape for a considerable length of time. Why it was not disturbed and incorporated into later middens, as the Late Neolithic material was, is unclear. It could be that its age was understood, considered to be something of the distant ancestors rather than the more recent generations whose waste was readily reincorporated with that of the recent occupation episode. Conversely the changing environment may have resulted in colluvial and alluvial deposits masking the earlier feature so it was no longer readily accessible to the later inhabitants.

The deliberate deposition of pottery and flint appears to have continued into the later Neolithic and Bronze Age periods. For example, two possible middens dating to the earlier Bronze Age identified in the southeastern part of the excavated area contained large quantities of abraded early and late Neolithic pottery along with Beaker sherds. Hence, the pottery was already old and broken at the time of deposition, and so the apparent retention of old sherds of pottery into the earlier Bronze Age implies some sense of value in the objects when they were finally placed within middens. The positioning of these middens on either side of the remains of a possible roundhouse might reflect a similar pattern to that of earlier phases.

The inclusion of earlier material within these Bronze Age middens is reflected by a pattern of re-defining the 'waste' from previous periods into either middens or pits. Why some material was selected and placed in middens forming visible features in the local area, while other artefacts were placed within pits or ditches is not yet understood, but it demonstrates that the collection and re-deposition of the waste was an important activity at the site. It is clear that throughout the prehistoric activity at Mill Lane, waste, in the form of surface scatters, middens, or deliberate deposits within cut features, was used to emphasise the significance of 'place' in the landscape. The lithic material incorporated into the middens and scatters was a good mixture of debitage and tools, suggesting that acknowledging and symbolising the act of making the tools at the site was as important as the finished tool itself. However, the fine, unused Mesolithic axe deliberately discarded, possibly under ceremonial conditions, stands out as a possible example of ritualising waste. The late glacial flint recovered at the site was also re-deposited through later features, but whether this was deliberate or by chance is impossible to tell. It may well have been unknowingly collected along with the later lithic material.

The treatment of waste changed somewhat in the later phases at the site, becoming much more practical than symbolic. The palaeoenvironmental evidence suggests that at least some occupational waste from the Anglo-Saxon sunken-featured buildings was deposited within the upper fills of the palaeochannel onto the damper, more marginal soils away from the area of habitation. Evidence for medieval and post-medieval occupation in the near vicinity of the site is only apparent through the waste which accumulated within the enclosure ditches, presumably following the manuring of the fields, a common practice for the period.

12.3.2 Landscape and environmental context

Environmental change

Due to the variation in the preservation of the insect, plant microfossil and pollen remains within the palaeochannels, a detailed if sometimes enigmatic picture of the Holocene environments at Mill Lane has been achieved (Chapter 9). The Mesolithic activity at the site appears to have been taking place adjacent to one of the channels from the palaeo River Cam within a wider landscape dominated by Scots Pine woodland. At least some of the channels still contained flowing freshwater into the Neolithic period while others were areas of open water colonised by sedges and other wetland vegetation. By that time the surrounding environment was mainly woodland of Scots Pine and Lime, but with some evidence for open more disturbed soils and possibly grassy clearings; a mosaic of habitats which would have provided a plethora of hunting and gathering opportunities for the Neolithic visitors to the site. During later prehistory the flow of water became restricted as the palaeochannels gradually filled in with decaying plant matter potentially resulting in a much wetter environment. The apparent break in occupation at the site (although not in the wider landscape) may well have been a result of this change in environmental conditions.

The reoccupation of the Mill Lane site during the Anglo-Saxon period took place within what had become a drastically altered landscape, although the areas surrounding the infilled palaeochannels remained wet enough to support a variety of wetland plants. The small settlement represented by the sunken-featured buildings was constructed within a largely open landscape with an expansion of grass and evidence for open land grazing. Areas of relatively open woodland may have been exploited along with the nearby wetland areas for the provision of building and roofing materials. However, despite the open nature of the immediate environment there was no evidence for intensive agricultural activity.

The River

The unifying environmental factor for all periods seems to be the proximity of the River Cam. During earlier prehistory, human activity appears to have been closely associated with the flowing water of the palaeochannel of the River Cam. From the late glacial period, the pattern of activity from Mill Lane and other sites within the region demonstrate a clear association between human activity and the River Cam; a pattern continuing into the Mesolithic period. By the early Neolithic, not only were human populations exploiting the area, but they were also establishing markers within the landscape through both structures and middens. During the early Bronze Age, the objects placed within specific contexts adjacent to the river included those from earlier periods, which appear to have been collected and retained for a considerable time prior to their deposition. The absence of direct human activity on site during later prehistory and the Roman period might reflect the changing environment characterised by the infilling of and cessation of flow within palaeochannels and the development of a wetland landscape. However, there is substantial evidence for occupation within the wider environment, retaining a focus within this riparian and wetland edge environment. The shift in environment towards a wetland would have provided a renewed range of economic opportunities for activities such as grazing.

The reoccupation of the site during the early Anglo-Saxon period retained a focus on the river with the more permanent nature of the settlement, defined by the series of sunken-featured buildings, positioned a short distance from the palaeochannel. The precise location of the settlement was presumably chosen to avoid the worst of the flooding and wet ground but close enough to exploit the resources it provided. Hence, the changing nature of the river's palaeochannels and their associated environments through time reflect shifts in human habitation and exploitation, with the river itself changing from a series of channels spread across a considerable area to the single body that currently flows around the site to the west and south.

12.3.3 Preservation and archaeological visibility

Preservation at the site

Despite the wet nature of the site, indicated by the many flooding episodes recorded (see Chapter 1) and the proximity of the River Cam, the preservation of palaeoenvironmental evidence varied greatly across the site. Plant macrofossils were present in all the samples examined through the northern palaeochannel and there were sizeable assemblages of identifiable remains. However, pollen preservation was very poor with only the basal samples sufficient for assessment. The preservation and concentration of plant macrofossils from the southern palaeochannel was very poor and of limited value for palaeoenvironmental reconstruction. Hence, the wet-preservation of organic, palaeoenvironmental source material across the site varied in terms of both location and the nature of material itself.

No wet-preserved organic finds were recovered from the site, even from those features displaying better levels of palaeoenvironmental source material preservation, or areas where the palaeoenvironmental analyses had indicated wet conditions in the past. It seems likely that ground water levels have reduced considerably, possibly as a result of water abstraction through the Sawston Mill borehole (see Chapter 1). If this is the case, then proximity to the borehole might have an impact on the potential for preservation across the wider area. This is perhaps reflected on site by the presence of better-preserved organic material within the northern palaeochannel compared with the southern palaeochannel, given that it is located at a greater distance from the borehole.

The preservation of the inorganic archaeological remains at the Mill Lane site is, however, remarkable, as demonstrated by the earlier prehistoric middens from primary deposits. Hence, whilst water abstraction appears to have impacted on the organic preservation across the site, physical damage to the archaeological deposits has been more limited resulting in well preserved features and artefacts recorded during the excavation, presumably as a result of the protection afforded by processes such as colluviation and alluviation.

Archaeological visibility

A considerable depth of colluvium was encountered across the excavation, in particular masking the fills of the palaeochannels, but also spread across the rest of the site. Whilst it seems likely that this concealing process has assisted in the preservation of inorganic archaeological deposits, it also demonstrates the apparent invisibility of these remains from previous approaches such as aerial photography. The combination of flooding, alluviation and colluviation makes landscapes such as Mill Lane extremely difficult to assess using conventional survey methods. However, as the results of the excavations demonstrate, the challenges of identifying archaeological remains are balanced by the high levels of preservation that are afforded by these environments.

12.4 Final remarks

The site at Mill Lane, Sawston, represents millennia of human activity within a dynamic and changing landscape setting. The location of the site bridges wetlands on its western side, characterised by the infilling palaeochannels, and drylands to the east, with the boundaries between the two changing through time. It has previously been noted that archaeological research within wetlands or drylands is frequently undertaken separately, reflecting the differences in the approaches commonly used (*e.g.* Van de Noort and O'Sullivan 2006). Hence, the site at Mill Lane offered an uncommon opportunity to explore the interface between the two types of environment.

Through the integration of wetland and dryland approaches, the work at Mill Lane has revealed a rich sequence of human activity which began during the late glacial period. The presence of potential built structures dating to the early Neolithic, the early Bronze Age and the early Anglo-Saxon periods provides some sense of continuity, albeit with a hiatus in on-site occupation during the later prehistoric and Roman periods. However, the nature of these structures and the environmental context within which they were constructed varied considerably at different times, and particularly on either side of this hiatus. Starting as a riparian landscape during earlier periods, the infilling of the palaeochannels of the River Cam, which stopped taking flow by the later prehistoric period, resulted in a wetland landscape. Over these millennia, the wider landscape shifted from being a pine dominated one, to increasingly open mixed woodland and, later, to drained pasture.

The location of the site, on the interface between wetland and dryland, seems to have also enhanced preservation at the site. The exeptional evidence for ephemeral structures and a range of midden deposits appears to have been facilitated largely by processes of colluviation, wetland spread and alluviation, providing a protective mask for the archaeology. Whilst this makes the identification of archaeological remains problematic from the perspective of traditional approaches such as aerial photography and remote sensing, the benefits of preservation at Mill Lane demonstrate the value of exploring these types of landscapes.

CATALOGUE OF THE STRUCK LITHIC MATERIAL DETAILED BY INDIVIDUAL CONTEXT

Context	Reference	Decortication flake	Rejuvenation flake	Core	Conchoidal chunk	Microdebitage	Micro-burin	Flake fragment	Flake	Blade	Blade fragment	Blade-like flake	Axe	Arrowhead	Burin	Scraper	Knife	Edge retouched/serrate	Microlith	Other retouched	Burnt flint	Burnt flint (wt:g)
709	<1>					2				1												
804	<2>					2																
807	<3>							1		1												
904	<4>					11																
907	<6>					10			1													
910	<7>					2			1													
912	<8>					2																
914	<9>					1																
1001				1	1				4	8	1	1										
1023						1			1													
1025	<4>					10																
1025						3																
1035	<6>					9																
1041	SF2												1									
1041		2		2		3		5	8	7	3	1							1			
1043									1													
1044									1													
1053	<14>					1																
1057									1													
1058									1													
1064	SF1								1													
1064	SF3								1													
1064		3			1				5	4		3				1		1				
1066	<32>					11		3	2	2											4	6
1066		17	5	8	7	24	1	20	40	32	10	7								5	37	251
1067	<47>					10															4	16
1067									1	1		1										
1073		2		1	1	5		1	2	3											2	58
1077									1	3	1											
1079						2		1	1			2										
1081										1												
1088	<39>	1		1		7															2	7
1088								1														
1099								1														
1109	<35>							1													1	2
1111										2												
1133	<40>					1																

Context	Reference	Decortication flake	Rejuvenation flake	Core	Conchoidal chunk	Microdebitage	Micro-burin	Flake fragment	Flake	Blade	Blade fragment	Blade-like flake	Axe	Arrowhead	Burin	Scraper	Knife	Edge retouched/serrate	Microlith	Other retouched	Burnt flint	Burnt flint (wt:g)
1135						1															1	5
1141		1	1					1	1	3		1							1	1		
1148	<43>					7													1			
1168				1																		
1179	<53>					11																
1184										2	1										2	24
1186		5			1			4	7	6	2	2									8	198
1202											1										1	8
1204		1							1													
1207	<56>					7																
1210		8		2	2	2		7	29	12	7	3					1				34	326
1218											1											
1221		2			1			2	6	2												
1236									1	1												
1237									1												2	15
1248	<74>	1				9																
1257																					3	27
1258									1	1												
1261									3	2												
1264						1																
1268		2			1	1			4	2								1				
1269	<79>					9																
1278	<82>																				24	102
1284		1																				
1286					1																	
1288		1							1													
1290	<101>					10																
1306								1	1													
1314										1												
1316																					1	39
1335										2												
1343	<99>					7															1	8
1343									1													
1345	SF21								1													
1345									1	2		1										
1348				1			1		1	1												
1356	<112>					3			1													
1358						1																
1359		2								1						1						
1380		1				3			1		1											
1382	<102>					5																
1384	<103>										1										10	15
1390									2	3					1	1						
1390										3												
1393										1						1						
1404						1			2													
1422									1													
1424											1											
1429		1																				
1430						1			2													
1444		2																				
1459	SF35													1								

Context	Reference	Decortication flake	Rejuvenation flake	Core	Conchoidal chunk	Microdebitage	Micro-burin	Flake fragment	Flake	Blade	Blade fragment	Blade-like flake	Axe	Arrowhead	Burin	Scraper	Knife	Edge retouched/serrate	Microlith	Other retouched	Burnt flint	Burnt flint (wt:g)
1459	SF42									1												
1459	SF43															1						
1459	SF44	1																				
1459	SF45	1																				
1459	SF46									1												
1459	SF47	1							1													
1459	SF48								1	1												
1459	Surface	18	3		3	15		4	28	25	8	8						2				
1459										1												
1465	<135>					10																
1465		1						2	2	3	2											
1466	<136>					1																
1466		1	1	1	2	4		5	2	2		1									3	8
1467	<137>									1												
1467	SF36															1						
1467	SF37	1																				
1467		1				8		2	3	3	4											
1468	<138>					1															3	3
1468	SF40									1												
1468	SF41																	1				
1468		1				2				1												
1469	<139>					1																
1469									1													
1481	<127>																				1	1
1481		1							2													
1483	<128>					2																
1492	<151>					1																
1496		1																				
1498	<155>					2		1	1													
1499	<156>							1														
1503										1												
1507									1													
1510	SF38																	1				
1510		1			1	6				2		1										
1511		4	1	2	1	4		2	4	2		2				1					196	1535
1512	SF39													1								
1512			1	1					3									1				
1519			1						1	1		1										
1545		2		2		6		2	10	7	1	2									1	5
1546						1			2	5	1											
1552	>160>																				1	4
1552										1												
1583		6		1				2	19	16	5	2		1	1	2		3				
1594									1													
1596		1							1													
+									1	2		1										

PALAEOENVIRONMENTAL AND RADIOCARBON TABLES

Table A2.1 Species List for samples from palaeochannels 1584 (TPB) and 1299–1302 (TPD) – Taxonomy follows revised Lucht 1987 (Böhme 2005).

Sample	Test Pit B	Test Pit B	Test Pit B	Test Pit D	Test Pit D	Test Pit D	Test Pit D	Habitat
Depth	0.0–0.25m	0.25–0.41m	0.41–0.61m	0.5–0.7m	0.7–0.9m	1.0–1.2m	1.2–1.4m	
Genus/Species								
Carabidae								
Notiophilus biguttatus (F.)	-	1	-	-	-	-	-	Woods, meadows living in litter layer
Loricera pilicornis (F.)	-	3	-	-	-	-	1	Damp woodlands, grasslands in moss/litter
Dyschirius globosus (Hbst.)	1	-	-	1	1	-	-	Damp peaty/open ground
Trechus sp.	-	-	1	-	-	-	-	Varied habitats
Bembidion spp.	1	1	-	2	-	-	-	Varied habitats
Poecilus cupreus (Linn.)	-	1	-	-	-	-	-	Disturbed ground, fields, damp ground
Pterostichus strenuus (Panz.)	1	-	1	-	1	1	-	Damp places, woodlands, marshes
P. nigrita (Payk.)	-	-	2	-	1	-	-	Damp places, woodlands, marshes
Pterostichus spp.	1	2	-	-	-	-	2	Varied habitats
Agonum muelleri (Hbst.)	-	-	3	-	-	-	1	Damp grasslands, fields, gardens
Agonum sp.	-	-	-	-	-	-	1	Varied habitats
Anchomenus dorsalis (Pont.)	-	-	1	-	-	-	-	Disturbed/arable ground, dry habitats
Amara sp.	-	-	1	-	-	-	-	Varied habitats
Haliplidae								
Haliplus sp.	1	-	3	2	-	-	-	Aquatic habitats, particularly ponds
Dysticidae								
Hygrotus sp.	-	-	-	1	-	-	-	Lakes, ponds, ditches
Hydroporus spp.	-	10	2	-	-	-	-	Aquatic habitats
Suphrodytes dorsalis (F.)	-	-	2	-	-	-	-	Freshwater, rich in aquatic vegetation
Nebrioporus sp.	-	-	1	-	-	-	-	Various aquatic habitats
Agabus melanarius Aube	-	-	1	-	-	-	-	Shaded, spring-fed pools, ponds (inc. bogs)
A. bipustulatus (L.)	-	-	2	-	-	-	-	Ponds, pools, ditches
A. nebulosus (Forster)	1	-	-	-	-	-	-	Ponds, especially recently formed ones, ditches
Agabus/Ilybius sp.	-	2	-	-	2	-	-	Aquatic habitats
Hydraenidae								

Sample	Test Pit B	Test Pit B	Test Pit B	Test Pit D	Test Pit D	Test Pit D	Test Pit D	Habitat
Depth	0.0–0.25m	0.25–0.41m	0.41–0.61m	0.5–0.7m	0.7–0.9m	1.0–1.2m	1.2–1.4m	
Genus/Species								
Hydraena spp.	-	-	1	-	-	-	-	Aquatic habitats
Ochthebius bicolon Germ.	-	-	5	-	-	-	-	In mud beside rivers, ponds, streams
Ochthebius spp.	2	15	14	1	4	2	-	Aquatic habitats
Limnebius truncatellus Thun.	-	8	6	-	-	-	-	Stagnant water, mud beside water bodies
Hydrophilidae								
Heleophorus spp.	5	6	8	-	-	-	-	Aquatic habitats (often stagnant water)
Coelostoma orbiculare (F.)	-	-	1	1	-	-	-	Stagnant water, moss and detritus
Cercyon impressus Sturm	1	3	1	-	-	-	-	Dung, carrion, decaying vegetation
C. marinus Thoms.	-	-	-	-	3	-	-	Damp litter in marshes
C. unipunctatus (L.)	1	-	-	-	-	-	-	Rotting litter, dung, carrion
C. atricapillus (Marsh.)	-	-	2	-	-	-	-	Damp litter in marshes, dung
Cercyon spp.	-	6	-	3	3	-	3	Dung, decaying vegetation
Megasternum obscurum (Marsh.)	-	10	-	5	4	2	-	Dung, decaying vegetation
Hydrobius fuscipes (L.)	1	2	2	1	1	-	-	Stagnant water
Anacaena globosus (Payk.)	2	4	3	-	-	-	2	Aquatic habitats (often stagnant water)
Histeridae								
Saprinus sp.	1	-	-	2	-	-	-	Carrion, dead wood, birds nests
Catopidae								
Ptomaphagus sp.	-	-	4	-	-	-	-	In damp litter, on carrion, refuse
Choleva spp.	-	-	2	-	-	-	-	In damp litter, on carrion, refuse
Catops sp.	-	-	1	-	-	-	-	In damp litter, on carrion, refuse
Colonidae								
Colon sp.	-	-	2	-	-	-	-	In fungi in dead wood (mainly)
Clambidae								
Clambus sp.	-	-	2	-	-	-	-	In decaying vegetation/wood litter in woodlands, fens, bogs
Ptiliidae								
Acrotrichus sp.	2	-	-	-	-	-	-	In decaying wood/vegetation, fungi
Staphylinidae								
Siagonium quadricorne Kirby and Spence	1	-	-	-	-	-	-	Under moist bark
Megarthrus/Proteinus sp.	-	-	2	-	-	-	-	Dung, rotting fungi/vegetation
Eusphalerum minutum (F.)	-	-	1	-	-	-	-	On flowers in marshy places
Phyllodrepa floralis (Payk.)	-	-	2	-	-	-	-	On flowers, dung, moulds and fungi

Sample	Test Pit B	Test Pit B	Test Pit B	Test Pit D	Test Pit D	Test Pit D	Test Pit D	Habitat
Depth	0.0–0.25m	0.25–0.41m	0.41–0.61m	0.5–0.7m	0.7–0.9m	1.0–1.2m	1.2–1.4m	
Genus/Species								
Omalium rivulare (Payk.)	-	6	-	-	-	-	-	Rotting vegetation, carrion, dung
Omalium (type) spp.	4	10	-	2	-	-	-	Decaying vegetation, dung, carrion, in damp places
Phloeonomus pusillus (Grav.)	-	-	1	-	-	-	-	Under bark of various coniferous tree species
Acidota crenata (F.)/creuntata (Mann.)	2	1	1	-	-	-	-	In moss, decaying vegetation, in bogs, woods etc.
Carpelimus bilineatus (Steph.)	4	26	3	-	2	-	-	Damp locations in decaying vegetation/dung/litter
Carpelimus elongatus (Er.)	3	-	-	-	-	-	-	Damp locations in decaying vegetation/dung/litter
Carpelimus spp.	2	10	-	-	-	2	-	Damp locations in decaying vegetation/dung/litter
Anotylus insecatus (Grav.)	-	-	2	-	-	-	-	Dung and decaying vegetation (rare)
A. rugosus (F.)	6	12	5	-	1	-	-	Dung and decaying vegetation
A. sculpturatus (Grav.)	7	5	4	-	-	-	-	Dung, carrion, decaying vegetation
A. nitidulus (Grav.)	3	-	-	-	-	-	-	Dung, carrion, decaying vegetation
A. tetracarinatus Block	2	6	1	-	-	-	-	Dung, carrion, decaying vegetation
Oxytelus sculptus Grav.	8	8	1	-	-	-	-	Dung and decaying vegetation
Platystethus aerinarius (Four.)	2	6	1	-	-	-	-	Dung, decaying vegetation
P. cornutus (Grav.)/degener (Mul. and Rey)	4	4	5	-	-	1	-	Foul habitats, mud beside rivers/streams/ponds
P. nitens (Sahl.)	-	-	2	-	-	-	-	Foul habitats, mud beside rivers/streams/ponds
Bledius sp.	1	6	1	-	-	-	-	Sandy places, salt-marshes, exposed sediments
Stenus biggutatus (L.)	-	-	1	-	-	-	-	Sandy exposed sediments, mud beside ponds
Stenus spp.	-	-	2	1	-	-	-	Damp locations generally
Rugilus sp.	-	-	1	-	-	1	-	In damp litter in woods, bogs, fens etc.
Lathrobium spp.	-	-	-	-	1	2	-	Damp locations generally
Leptacinus pusillus (Steph.)	-	-	1	-	-	-	-	Dung, rotting vegetation
Gyrohypnus liebei Scheer.	-	-	1	-	-	-	-	Damp decaying vegetation
Xantholinus linearis (Ol.)	-	-	1	-	-	-	-	Decaying vegetation (dry habitats)
Gyrohypnus/Xantholinus spp.	2	1	-	-	-	-	-	In foul habitats generally
Othius sp.	-	-	1	-	-	-	-	Damp decaying wood and vegetation
Philonthus/Quedius spp.	2	6	3	-	-	-	-	Varied habitats
Myceteporus sp.	1	1	-	-	-	-	-	In fungi, moss, decaying vegetation in various habitats
Tachyporus hypnorum (F.)	-	-	3	-	-	-	-	In moss, decaying vegetation, occurs everywhere
T. chrysomelinus (L.)	3	-	-	-	-	-	-	In moss, decaying vegetation, occurs everywhere
Tachinus signatus	1	-	1	-	-	-	-	In woodland in litter and fungi
Tachyporus/Tachinus spp.	1	3	3	1	-	-	-	In damp litter (also dung, carrion)

Sample	Test Pit B	Test Pit B	Test Pit B	Test Pit D	Test Pit D	Test Pit D	Test Pit D	Habitat
Depth	0.0–0.25m	0.25–0.41m	0.41–0.61m	0.5–0.7m	0.7–0.9m	1.0–1.2m	1.2–1.4m	
Genus/Species								
Aleocharinae sp. indet.	6	24	5	-	-	-	4	Varied habitats
Pselaphidae								
Bryaxis bulbifer (Reich.)	-	-	1	-	-	-	-	In moss in damp locations
Brachygluta sp.	-	-	-	-	1	-	-	In moss in damp locations
Cantharidae								
Cantharis sp.	-	1	4	-	-	-	-	On flowers and shrubs in damp locations, wood, grasslands
Rhagonycha sp.	-	1	-	-	-	-	-	On shrubs, trees in woodland (mainly)
Elateridae								
Agriotes pallidulus (Ill.)	-	1	1	-	-	-	-	On young trees/shrubs in woods, woodland margins
A. acuminatus (Steph.)	-	-	1	-	-	-	-	On young trees/shrubs in woods, woodland margins
Adrastus pallens (F.)	-	-	1	-	-	-	-	On vegetation in woodlands, woodland margins
Selatosomus aeneus (L.)	-	-	1	-	-	-	-	On vegetation in grasslands, heaths, woodland margins
Elateridae (Athous?) sp. indet.	-	-	-	2	1	1	2	Woodlands, scrubland, rough grassland
Scirtidae								
Cyphon spp.	1	12	7	2	-	2	2	Damp locations
Dryopidae								
Dryops spp.	1	2	1	1	1	-	-	On mud or moss beside ponds, in fens, rivers, bogs
Elmis aenea (P. Muller)	-	3	1	-	-	-	-	Under stones in fast-flowing water
Dermestidae								
Anthrenus fuscus (Ol.)	-	-	1	-	-	-	-	In barns, out-buildings, on flowers, animal skins
Byrrhidae								
Cytilus sericeus (Forst.)	1	1	1	-	-	-	-	On moss in damp, peaty ground
Byturidae								
Byturus sp.	1	-	-	-	-	-	-	On raspberry in woodlands etc. or on dandelion/ buttercups in woodland margins etc.
Brachypteridae								
Brachypterus urticae (F.)	-	-	2	-	-	-	-	On nettles and other associated herbs
Nitidulidae								
Meligethes spp.	1	8	4	-	-	-	-	On flowering herbs/shrubs in both wet and dry locations
Cucujidae								
Oryzaephilus surinamensis (L.)	1	-	-	-	-	-	-	Pest of stored grain/foodstuffs (introduced)
Cryptophagidae								
Cryptophagus spp.	-	4	2	-	-	-	-	On mouldy plant material mainly
Atomaria spp.	-	6	1	-	-	-	-	On mouldy plant material mainly

Sample	Test Pit B 0.0–0.25m	Test Pit B 0.25–0.41m	Test Pit B 0.41–0.61m	Test Pit D 0.5–0.7m	Test Pit D 0.7–0.9m	Test Pit D 1.0–1.2m	Test Pit D 1.2–1.4m	Habitat
Genus/Species								
Phalacridae								
Olibrus sp.	-	-	1	-	-	-	-	On mugwort/chamomile/hawkbit/hawk's beard (daisy family)
Lathridiidae								
Lathridius (group) spp.	1	-	1	-	-	-	-	On mouldy plant material mainly
Corticara spp.	2	5	1	-	-	-	-	On mouldy wood/plant litter in woodlands, bogs, fens, seashores
Cortinicara sp.	-	2	1	-	-	-	-	On mouldy wood/plant litter in woodlands, bogs, fens, seashores
Mycetophagidae								
Mycetophagus spp.								In fungoid bark in woodlands etc.
Typhaea stercorea (L.)	2	-	1	-	-	-	-	In stored products/grain often indoors
Colydiidae								
Aglenus brunneus (Gyll.)	1	2	-	-	-	-	-	Generally synanthropic, mouldy vegegation
Endomychidae								
Mycetaea subterranea (Marsham)	1	4	1	-	-	-	-	Mould feeder on decaying wood/vegetation, indoor and outdoor locations
Coccinellidae								
Coccinellidae gen. et sp. indet.	-	-	-	-	-	-	1	On various flowers/herbs, predatory on aphids etc.
Anobiidae								
Dryophilus pusillus (Gyll.)	2	4	-	-	-	-	-	In pine wood debris (and in trees)
Ernobius mollis (L.)	-	2	-	-	-	-	-	In pine wood and timber of old buildings
Anobium punctatum (Deg.)	2	3	1	-	-	-	-	In dead wood
Salpingidae								
Lissodema denticolle (Gyll.)	2	3	-	-	-	-	-	Under bark in rotting trees
Anthicidae								
Anthicus spp.	-	-	1	-	-	-	-	In rotting vegetation, reed litter and seaweed
Mordellidae								
Anaspis sp.	-	3	1	-	-	-	-	On hawthorn, pine and other dead wood
Scarabaeidae								
Onthophagus sp.	1	-	-	-	-	-	-	Dung
Aphodius erraticus (L.)	1	-	2	-	-	-	-	In dung of horse, sheep and cattle
A. contaminatus (Hbst.)	3	5	3	-	-	-	-	In all kinds of dung
A. foetens (F.)	1	-	1	-	-	-	-	In cow and horse dung
Aphodius ater Deg.	-	2	-	-	-	-	-	In all kinds of dung

Sample	Test Pit B	Test Pit B	Test Pit B	Test Pit D	Test Pit D	Test Pit D	Test Pit D	Habitat
Depth	0.0–0.25m	0.25–0.41m	0.41–0.61m	0.5–0.7m	0.7–0.9m	1.0–1.2m	1.2–1.4m	
Genus/Species								
Aphodius spp.	-	4	-	6	-	1	-	Dung and decaying vegetation
Phyllopertha horticola (L.)	-	-	-	1	2	1	-	At roots of grass/herbs in meadows, woodland margins and river floodplains
Hoplia philantus (Fues.)	-	1	2	-	-	-	-	Grass roots on sandy river floodplains, banks of rivers, heaths
Chrysomelidae								
Plateumaris discolor (Panz.)	-	-	1	-	-	-	-	On sedges, cotton-grass and Sphagnum
P. sericea (L.)	-	-	1	-	-	-	-	On sedge, Iris, Club-rush, Bull-rush and Cattail
P. affinis (Kunze)	-	-	1	-	-	-	-	On sedges, Marsh marigold
Donacia/Plateumaris spp.	-	-	3	2	2	-	-	On various wetland plants
Cryptocephalus sp.	1	-	-	-	-	-	-	On various tree, shrub and herb species
Chrysolina spp.	-	-	2	-	1	-	-	On various wetland/meadow/grassland herbs
Gastrophysa viridula (Deg.)	-	-	2	-	-	-	-	On docks and knotweed species
Phaedon sp.	-	1	1	-	2	-	-	On Cabbage family species in marshes/ponds
Prasocuris junci (Brahm)	-	-	2	-	-	-	-	On Brooklime near water
P. phellandrii (L.)	-	-	-	-	1	-	-	On various aquatic plants in bogs, fens, meadows
Phratora spp.	-	2	-	-	-	-	-	On willow and poplar
Phyllotreta undulata Kuts.	6	10	5	-	-	-	-	On Cabbage family, oak and lime
Phyllotreta cruciferae (Goeze)	3	8	8	-	-	-	-	On various Cabbage family species
Phyllotreta spp.	-	-	3	-	-	-	-	On Cabbage family primarily
Longitarsus spp.	5	13	-	-	-	-	-	On a great variety of field herbs
Chaetocnema concinna (Marsh.)/hortensis (Goeff.)	2	6	7	-	-	-	-	On various field herbs including wetland plants
Chaetocnema sp.	1	-	-	-	-	-	-	On various field herbs including wetland plants
Bruchidae								
Bruchidius villosus (F.)	-	1	1	-	-	-	-	In woodlands, pasture/parkland etc on broom, gorse, birch and other scrub species
Curculionidae								
Apion spp.	3	6	8	-	1	-	-	On a wide variety of ground herbs
Otiorhynchus spp.	-	-	1	-	-	-	1	On herbs, shrubs and trees
Phyllobius virdicollis (F.)	1	-	-	-	-	-	-	Polyphagous on wide variety of herbs, shrubs and occasionally trees
P. pyri (L.)	-	2	-	-	-	-	-	Leaf defoliator of birch, oak and other tree species
Phyllobius spp.	-	-	2	-	-	-	-	Defoliators of wide variety of shrub and tree species
Polydrusus sp.	-	1	-	-	-	-	-	Defoliators of wide variety of shrub and tree species inc. coniferous species

Sample / Genus/Species	Test Pit B 0.0–0.25m	Test Pit B 0.25–0.41m	Test Pit B 0.41–0.61m	Test Pit D 0.5–0.7m	Test Pit D 0.7–0.9m	Test Pit D 1.0–1.2m	Test Pit D 1.2–1.4m	Habitat
Genus/Species								
Barypeithes sp.	-	-	1	-	-	-	-	Polyphagous on vegetation in woods and grassland
Barynotus obscurus (F.)	-	-	2	-	-	-	-	Polyphagous on vegetation in grasslands, occasionally woods
Sitona striatellus Gyll.	3	-	-	-	-	-	-	Heaths, woodland margins etc on gorse
S. hispidulus (F.)	2	-	-	-	-	-	-	On species of clover in grasslands, cultivated ground, damp ground
Sitona spp.	2	6	-	-	-	-	-	Wide variety of habitats
Notaris acridulus (L.)	2	1	1	-	2	-	-	On sedges, rushes by ponds, rivers, marshes
Curculio spp.	-	1	-	-	-	-	-	On oak, willow, birch primarily
Hypera nigrirostris (F.)	1	3	-	-	-	-	-	On spiny restharrow and clover species
Limnobaris t-album (L.)/dolorosa (Goeze)	-	-	-	-	1	-	-	on sedges and rushes
Pelenomus comari (Hbst.)	-	-	3	-	-	-	-	On Marsh cinquefoil and Purple loosestrife (in damp areas)
P. quadrituberculatus (F.)	-	-	2	-	-	1	-	On knotweed and dock species in damp places
Hadroplontus litura (F.)	1	-	1	-	-	-	-	On Creeping thistle in damp and dry places
Ceutorhynchus contractus (Marsh.)	1	3	13	-	-	-	-	On various Cabbage family species, in damp and dry places
Ceutorhynchus ersymi (F.)	-	-	2	-	-	-	-	On Shepherd's purse, in both damp and dry places
Ceutorhynchus spp.	2	-	-	2	-	1	-	Various ground herbs
Nedyus quadrimaculatus (L.)	-	-	2	-	-	-	-	On nettle
Gymetron sp.	1	5	2	-	-	-	-	On Toadflax/Plantain in disturbed ground, Brooklime/Marsh speedwell in damp locations
Rhynchaenus alni (L.)	-	-	3	-	-	-	-	Leaf miner of elm (Wych Elm, in particular)
Rhynchaenus quercus (L.)	1	1	-	-	-	-	-	Leaf miner of species of oak
Scolytidae								
Scolytus scolytus (F.)	1	-	-	-	-	-	-	Chiefly on elm
Hylastes angustatus (Hbst.)	-	1	-	-	-	-	-	Pine and spruce
Hylesinus oleiperda (F.)	-	2	-	-	-	-	-	Chiefly in recently dead ash
Leperisinus fraxini (Panz.)	-	2	-	-	-	-	-	Chiefly in dead ash wood
Preleobius vittatus (F.)	-	1	-	-	-	-	-	In thin barked elm and ash
Ernoporicus caucasicus Lind.	-	-	-	-	-	1	-	Almost exclusively on lime (endangered)
Hymenoptera: Formicidae								
Ants (indet.)	3	1	1	-	-	-	-	

Table A2.2 Basic habitat statistics for insects identified from Sawston sample.

SAMPLE	Test Pit B 0–25cm	Test Pit B 25–41cm	Test Pit B 41–61cm	Test Pit D 50–70cm	Test Pit D 70–90cm	Test Pit D 1–1.2m	Test Pit D 1.2–1.4m
Minimum number of individuals (MNI)	142	364	246	39	39	18	20
Species	70	76	107	20	23	13	11
Index of diversity	56	29	73	18	26	-	-
MNI (exc. aquatics/varied)	122	295	198	31	32	16	11
Species (exc. aquatics/varied)	61	66	91	14	20	12	7
Index of diversity (exc. aquatics/varied)	50	27	66			-	-
Habitat groups							
Aquatics	12	42	41	6	7	2	2
Wetland inc. mud	10	28	35	4	8	7	2
Dist. ground/humus	1	5	4	1	1	0	2
Decay vegetation	25	63	22	3	2	2	0
Moulds/synanthropes	8	23	8	0	0	0	0
Dung/foul	29	67	33	16	8	3	3
Plant feeders	32	63	72	5	12	2	1
Sandy habitats	1	7	4	0	0	0	0
Woodland/dead wood	16	39	20	2	1	2	3
Varied habitats	8	27	7	2	0	0	7
% Habitat groups (exc. aquatics/varied)							
Wetland inc. mud	8.2	9.5	17.7	12.9	25.0	43.8	18.2
Dist. ground/humus	0.8	1.7	2.0	3.2	3.1	0.0	18.2
Decay vegetation	20.5	21.4	11.1	9.7	6.3	12.5	0.0
Moulds/synanthropes	6.6	7.8	4.0	0.0	0.0	0.0	0.0
Dung/foul	23.8	22.7	16.7	51.6	25.0	18.8	27.3
Plant feeders	26.2	21.4	36.4	16.1	37.5	12.5	9.1
Sandy habitats	0.8	2.4	2.0	0.0	0.0	0.0	0.0
Woodland/dead wood	13.1	13.2	10.1	6.5	3.1	12.5	27.3

Table A2.3 Complete list of taxa recorded from Test Pit B at Sawston.

SAMPLE NUMBER	TPB: 0–25cm	TPB: 25–41cm	TPB: 41–61cm	
LATIN BINOMIAL				**COMMON NAME**
Ranunculus flamula L.		3	2	Lesser spearwort
Urtica dioica L.	32	42	17	Common nettle
Urtica urens L.	9	11	9	Small nettle
Betula spp.		1	5	Birch
Corylus avellana L.		22		Hazel
Chenopodium spp./*Atriplex* spp.		6	8	Goosefoot/ orache
Scleranthus L.		1		Knawels
Persicaria hydropiper (L) Spach		3	9	Water-pepper
Polygonum aviculare L.			2	Knotgrass
Rumex L.			2	Docks
cf. *Populus* spp. (bud scale)		28	19	Poplar
Lepidium L.	11		13	Pepperworts
Vaccinium L.			1	Bilberries
Rubus spp.	4			Bramble
Potentilla spp.	5	4	67	Cinquefoils
Scandix pectin-veneris L.			36	Shepherds needle
Solanum spp.		9		Nightshades
Lycopus europaeus L.			32	Gypsywort
Sambucus nigra L.	47	72	1	Elder
Sagittaria sagittifolia L.			9	Arrowhead
Alisma plantago-aquatica L.			33	Water plantain
Lemna spp.			4	Duckweeds
Knautia arvensis (L.) Coult.	13		5	Field scabious
Carduus L./*Cirisium* Mill.	1		26	Thistles
Lapsana communis L.			1	Nipplewort
Sonchus L.		2		Sow thistles
Senecio L.			80	Ragworts
Eleocharis palustris (L.) Roem. and Schult./*uniglumis* (Link) Schult.	1	5		Common/ slender spike-rush
cf. ?*Cladium mariscus* (L.) Pohl			12	?Great fen sedge
Carex spp.			88	Sedge
POACEAE			10	Grass
Unidentified bud	17			
Indeterminate	2	8	1	

Table A2.4 Habitats of taxa recorded from Test Pit B at Sawston.

Latin Binomial	English Common Name	WOODLAND	HEDGEROW/SCRUB	ROUGH GROUND	WASTE GROUND	CULTIVATED GROUND	CORNFIELDS/ARABLE LAND	GRASSLAND	OPEN GROUND	FENS/MOORS	WET/DAMP GROUND	WATERSIDE	WATER
Ranunculus flamula L.	Lesser spearwort										✓	✓	✓
Urtica dioica L.	Common nettle	✓				✓							
Urtica urens L.	Small nettle				✓	✓							
Betula sp.	Birch	✓									✓		
Corylus avellana L.	Hazel	✓	✓										
Persicaria hydropiper (L) Spach	Water-pepper										✓		✓
Polygonum aviculare L.	Knotgrass								✓				
Rubus spp.	Bramble	✓			✓			✓					
Scandix pectin-veneris	Shepherds purse				✓		✓						
Lycopus europaeus L.	Gypsywort									✓	✓	✓	
Sambucus nigra L.	Elder	✓	✓	✓	✓								
Sagittaria sagittifolia L.	Arrowhead										✓	✓	✓
Alisma plantago-aquatica	Water plantain										✓	✓	✓
Lemna sp.	Duckweed										✓	✓	✓
Knautia arvensis (L.) Coult.	Field scabious							✓					
Lapsana communis	Nipplewort	✓	✓		✓				✓				
Eleocharis palustris (L.) Roem. & Schult. / *uniglumis* (Link) Schult.	Common spike-rush type											✓	✓
cf. ?*Cladium mariscus* (L.) Pohl	? Great fen sedge									✓	✓	✓	✓

Taxa and nomenclature follow Stace (2000)

Table A2.5 Components of subsamples from Test Pit B, Sawston.

COMPONENT	TEST PIT B: 0–25CM	TEST PIT B: 25–41CM	TEST PIT B: 41–61CM
Bud Scales	3	3	3
Herbaceous detritus	3	4	4
Insect fgts.	4	3	4
Moss fgts.	1	-	2
Plant Macrofossils	3	3	3
Snails	1	-	2
Wood fgts.	2	2	-

Quantitative score on a scale of 1–4: from '1' – one or a few (less than an estimated six per kg of raw sediment) to '4' – abundant remains (many specimens per kg or a major component of the matrix).

Table A2.6 Complete list of taxa recorded from Test Pit D, Sawston.

SAMPLE NUMBER	50–70cm	70–90cm	100–120cm	120–140cm	
LATIN BINOMIAL					**COMMON NAME**
Ranunculus subg. RANUNCULUS				✓	Buttercup
Urtica dioica L.					Common nettle
Urtica urens L.					Small nettle
Betula spp.		✓			Birch
Corylus avellana L.					Hazel
Chenopodium spp./*Atriplex* spp.					Goosefoot/ orache
Persicaria hydropiper (L) Spach					Water-pepper
Polygonum aviculare L.					Knotgrass
cf. *Populus* spp. (bud scale)					Poplar
Rubus spp.		✓			Bramble
Potentilla spp.	✓	✓		✓	Cinquefoils
Solanum spp.					Nightshades
Lycopus europaeus L.					Gypsywort
Sambucus nigra L.	✓		✓		Elder
Lemna spp.					Duckweeds
Eleocharis palustris (L.) Roem. and Schult./*uniglumis* (Link) Schult.	✓				Common/slender spike-rush
Carex spp. (three-sided)	✓				Sedge
Carex spp. (two-sided)	✓				Sedge
Unidentified bud					
UNIDENTIFIED	✓	✓		✓	

Taxonomy and nomenclature follow Stace (2000).   ✓ = presence within sample

Table A2.7 Results of the Sawston pollen assessments. TLP=total land pollen.

MONOLITH TIN AND SAMPLE	CONCENTRATION	PRESERVATION	TLP	MAIN POLLEN SPECIES
TPD 0.50m	Medium (3)	Medium (3)	131	Cyperaceae (64%) Poaceae (21%) Pteropsida
TPD 0.66m	Low (1)	Low (1)	2	Single grains of Cyperaceae and *Alnus*
TPD 0.88m	Low (1)	Low (1)	n/a	5 grains of Pteropsida
TPD 1.12m	Medium-Good (3/4)	Medium (3)	131	*Pinus* (82%) *Corylus* (10%) Pteropsida
TPB Sequence 2 0.00m	Medium (3)	Medium (3)	126	Cyperaceae (71%) Poaceae (14%) Lactuceae (9%) Pteropsida
TPB Sequence 2 0.24m	Low (1)	Low (1)	6	Some grains of *Tilia, Corylus, Pinus* and Cyperaceae
TPB Sequence 2 0.40m	Low (1)	Low (1)	7	Some grains of *Alnus, Corylus, Pinus* and Cyperaceae
TPB Sequence 2 0.64m	Medium-Good (3/4)	Medium (3)	131	*Pinus* (89%) Cyperaceae (5%) Pteropsida
TPC 0.00m	Low	Poor	17	Raw Counts – Cyperaceae (12), *Corylus avellana*-type (2), Poaceae (2), Apiaceae (1)
TPC 0.16m	Low	Poor	20	Raw Counts – *Corylus avellana*-type (11), *Alnus* (8), Cyperaceae (1)
TPC 0.32m	Excellent	Medium-Good	138	Percentages – *Corylus* (59%), *Pinus* (12%), *Tilia* (12%), *Ulmus* (5%), *Quercus* (5%)
TPC 0.48m	Good	Good	143	Percentages – *Corylus* (30%), *Betula* (27%), *Pinus* (27%)
TPC 0.62m	Low-Medium	Poor	139	Percentages – *Pinus* (99%)
TPC 0.80m	Medium	Poor	127	Percentages – *Pinus* (94%)
TPC 0.96m	Low	Poor	3	Raw counts – *Pinus* (1), Pteropsida (2)
TPC 1.12m	Medium	Medium	148	Percentages – *Pinus* (95%)
TPC 1.28m	Low	Poor	2	Raw counts – Cyperaceae (2), Pteropsida (3)
TPC 1.43m	Low	Poor	2	Raw counts – *Pinus* (1), Cyperaceae (1)

Table A2.8 Radiocarbon dates from Mill Lane, Sawston.

SAMPLE/DEPTH (M)	LAB CODE	MATERIAL	Δ13C O/OO	RADIOCARBON AGE BP	CALIBRATED RANGE 2Σ
TPD – 0.38m	Beta-260583	Wood	-27.1 o/oo	3370±40 BP	Cal BC 1750 to 1590 (Cal BP 3700 to 3540) and Cal BC 1590 to 1530 (Cal BP 3540 to 3480)
TPD – 0.91m	Beta-260584	Wood	-28.6 o/oo	4420±40 BP	Cal BC 3320 to 3220 (Cal BP 5280 to 5170) and Cal BC 3180 to 3160 (Cal BP 5130 to 5110) Cal BC 3120 to 2920 (Cal BP 5070 to 4870)
TPB – 0.03–0.05m	Beta-280638	Peat	-27.2 o/oo	260±40 BP	Cal AD 1520 to 1590 (Cal BP 430 to 360) and Cal AD 1620 to 1670 (Cal BP 350–280), Cal AD 1770 to 1800 (Cal BP 180 to 150) and Cal AD 1940–1950 (Cal BP 10-0)
TPB – 0.25–0.27m	Beta-280639	Peat	-27.6 o/oo	2590±40 BP	Cal BC 810 to 760 (Cal BP 2760 to 2710) and Cal BC 680 to 670 (Cal BP 2630 to 2620)
TPB – 0.38m	Beta-260585	Wood	-29.8 o/oo	3310±40 BP	Cal BC 1690–1500) Cal BP 3640 to 3450)
TPB – 0.58–0.63m	Beta-260586	Wood	-30.1 o/oo	3490±40 BP	Cal BC 1920 to 1730 (Cal BP 3870 to 3680) and Cal BC 1720 to 1690 (Cal BP 3660 to 3640)

Table A2.9 Plant species indicated by plant-dependent insects from all samples, Sawston.

PLANT SPECIES	INSECT ASSOCIATES	TOTAL NO. OF SPECIES
Oak	*Rhynchaenus quercus, Phyllobius pyri, Curculio* spp.	3
Elm	*Rhynchaenus alni, Scolytus scolytus, Ptelobius vittatus*	3
Ash	*Hylesinus olieperda, Lepersinus fraxini, Ptelobius vittatus*	3
Lime	*Ernoporicus caucasicus*	1
Pine	*Hylastes angustatus, Dryophilus pusillus, Ernobius mollis*	3
Willow	*Phratora* spp., *Curculio* spp.	2
Birch	*Phyllobius pyri, Curculio* spp.	2
Tree/dead wood generalists	*Phyllobius* spp., *Polydrusus* spp., *Anobium puncatum*	3
Hawthorn/other Rosaceae shrubs	*Anaspis* sp.	1
Rasberry (*Rubus* spp.)	*Byturus* sp.	1
Gorse (Ulex)/Broom (Cytisus)	*Bruchidius villosus, Sitona striatellus*	2
Nettle (*Urtica* spp.)	*Brachypterus urticae, Nedyus quadrimaculatus*	2
Dock (*Rumex* spp.)	*Gastrophysa viridula, Pelenomus quadrituberculatus*	2
Dandelion (*Taraxacum* spp.)	*Byturus* sp.	1
Knotweed (*Polygonum* spp.)	*Gastrophysa viridula, Chaetocnema concinna, Pelenomus quadrituberculatus*	3
Clover (*Trifolium* spp.)	*Sitona hispidulus, Hypera nigirostris*	2
Cabbage family (Brassicaceae)	*Phaedon* sp., *Phyllotreta undulata, P. cruciferae, Ceutorhynchus contractus, C. ersymi*	5
Daisy family (Asteraceae)	*Olibrus* sp.	1
Creeping thistle (*Cirsium avense*)	*Hadroplontus litura*	1
Spiny restharrow (*Ononis spinosa*)	*Hypera nigirostris*	1
Marsh cinquefoil (*Potentilla palustris*)	*Pelenomus comari*	1
Purple loosetrife (*Lythrum salicaria*)	*Pelenomus comari*	1
Brooklime (*Veronica beccabungae*)	*Prasocuris junci*	1
Other Veronica spp.	*Gymetron* sp.	1
Marsh marigold (*Caltha palustris*)	*Plateumaris affinis, Prasocuris phellandri*	2
Sedges (*Carex*)	*Plateumaris discolor, P. sericea, P. affinis, Limnobaris* spp., *Notaris acridulus*	5
Cottongrass (*Eriophrum*)	*Plateumaris discolor*	1
Bulrush/reedmace (*Typha*)	*Plateumaris sericea, Limnobaris* spp., *Notaris acridulus*	3

Appendix 3

Animal Bone Tables

Table A3.1 Number of bones and teeth identified to species and/or anatomy from each feature.

Date	Feature	Number
Early Anglo- Saxon	Pit in SFB	139
Anglo-Saxon	Pit ?SFB	164
Anglo-Saxon	SFB	79
Anglo-Saxon	Posthole	2

Table A3.2 Condition and taphonomy affecting the preservation of the assemblage.

Condition		Early Saxon	Saxon
Fresh	1		
Good	2	2	8
Fair	3	40	64
Poor	4	53	77
Very Fragile	5	1	1

Taphonomy	Early Saxon	Saxon
Butchery	5%	10%
Burning	3%	1%
Gnawing	15%	26%
Fresh Break	6%	11%
Refitted Fragments	4=9	6=3
Loose molars: Molars in mandibles	3.5:1	1.8:1

Table A3.3 Species representation (NISP) from the hand collected assemblage.

Species	Early Saxon	Saxon
Cattle	60	79
Sheep/Goat	31	77
Sheep	3	4
Pig	9	57
Horse		3
Dog	1	1
Red Deer		4
Deer	2*	
Domestic Fowl	1	3
Goose	1	1
Total Identified	108	229
Unidentified Mammal	147	143
Large Mammal	112	122
Medium Mammal	119	188
Unidentified Bird	4	1
Total	490	683
* includes antler		

Table A3.4 Fragment count sieved sample (NISP).

Date	No.	Species		
Early Anglo-Saxon	1	Ox		
Early Anglo-Saxon	2	Frog		
Early Anglo-Saxon	1	Dog		
Anglo-Saxon	1	Frog		
Anglo-Saxon	1	Mouse		
Anglo-Saxon	1	Pig		

Table A3.5 Fragment representation (epiphysis count) early Anglo-Saxon assemblage.

Anatomy	Cattle	Sheep	Pig
Horn core			
Mandible**			2
Occipitale			
Zygomaticus	1	2	
Atlas	2		
Axis			
Cervical vertebrae	1		
Thoracic vertebrae	2		
Lumbar vertebrae			
Sacrum			
Scapula	2	2	
Humerus P			
Humerus D	1	1	1
Radius P	1	1	
Radius D		2	
Ulna			
Pelvis			1
Femur P			
Femur D			
Tibia P			
Tibia D			
Calcaneum	3	1	
Metacarpal P		1	1
Metatarsal P			1
Metacarpal D			
Metatarsal D	1	1	
1st phalange*	2	1	
2nd phalange*	1		
3rd phalange*			
Total	17	12	6

* Phalanges have been divided by four to compensate for frequency bias
** Only mandibles with molars are included

Appendix 4

Roman pottery tables

Table A4.1 Overall Roman pottery quantification.

Context	Desc.	Fabric	Form	Rim	Body	Base	Count	Wgt (g)	Join	Date	Group/ date
1001	Subsoil	Cream	Flagon			1	1	44		C1–C2	
		Red/yell	Dish	1			1	10		C1–C2	
		Grey	Jar	1			1	12		C1–C2	
							3	66			
1017		Dk grey	Jar		1		1	2		C1–C2	
1065		Dk grey	Dish?			1	1	24		C1–C2	
1067	Fill SFB1	Grey	Jar/bowl	1			1	60		C3–C4	101 – AS
		Red/yell	Mortarium	1			1	50	1088	C4	
		Red/yell	Candlestick?			1	1	92		C4	
1073	Fill SFB3	Grey			4		4	26		C2–C3	101 – AS
		Grey	Jar	1			1	4		C2–C3	
		Red/yell			1		1	6		C2–C3	
		Red/yell cc			2		2	14		C3–C4	
							8	50			
1088	Fill SFB2	Grey			4		4	36		C2–C3	101 – AS
		Grey	Jar		2		2	76		C3–C4	
		LNVCC	Dish/bowl			1	1	30		C4	
		Red/yell	Mortarium	1			1	24	1067	C4	
							8	166			
1221	Fill SFB4	Grey			1		1	6		C2–C3	101 – AS
1248	Posthole	Grey			1		1	1		C1–C2?	101 – AS
1264		Grey				1	1	12		C1–C2?	
1267		Grey			1		1	2		C2–C3	
1343	Gully SFB3	Grey	Jar		1		1	6		C1–C2	101 – AS
1390	Spread	Dk grey	Jar		1		1	16		C1–C2	104 – med
1444	Ditch	Grey			1		1	14		C1–C2	
1481	Ditch	Red/yell	Mortarium			1	1	66		C1–C2	
		Red/yell			25		25	26		C1–C2	
							26	92			
1503	Ditch	Red/yell	Mortarium	1			1	66		C1–C2	104 – med
TOTALS				7	45	6	58	725			

Table A4.2 Roman Pottery: Quantification by fabric series.

FABRICS	Rim	Body	Base	Count	Wgt (g)	Forms
Grey	3	15	1	19	255	
Dk grey		2	1	3	42	
Red/yell	4	28	2	34	354	
Cream			1	1	44	
LNVCC			1	1	30	
	7	45	6		725	

APPENDIX 5

RADIOCARBON DATING AND ANALYSIS
FROM THE ANGLO-SAXON SUNKEN-FEATURED BUILDINGS

Table A5.1 Radiocarbon results.

Sample	Lab Code	Material	δ13C o/oo	Radiocarbon Age BP	Calibrated Range 2σ
BA1886-1017-3	Beta- 296052	(Charred material): acid/alkali/acid	-21.8 o/oo	1450 +/- 30 BP	Cal AD 540 to 620 (Cal BP 1420 to 1330)
BA1886-1207-56	Beta- 296053	Charred material): acid/alkali/acid	-21.2 o/oo	1520 +/- 30 BP	Cal AD 410 to 550 (Cal BP 1540 to 1400)
BA1886-1221-64	Beta- 296054	Charred material): acid/alkali/acid	-21.1 o/oo	1490 +/- 30 BP	Cal AD 430 to 590 (Cal BP 1520 to 1360)
BA1886-1343-99	Beta- 296055	Charred material): acid/alkali/acid	-23.5 o/oo	1190 +/- 30 BP	Cal AD 710 to 750 (Cal BP 1240 to 1200) and Cal AD 760 to 890 (Cal BP 1190 to 1060)

REFERENCES

Addyman, P. V. (1972) The Anglo-Saxon House: A new review *Anglo-Saxon England* 42, 273–307.

Air Photo Services (2000) *Spicer Estate, Area Centred TL4 72494, Sawston, Cambridgeshire.* Air Photo Services Report No. 200/24.

Alexander, K. N. A. (2002) *The Invertebrates of Living and Decaying Timber in Britain and Ireland: A provisional annotated checklist.* English Nature Report (ENRR467), Peterborough.

Amorosi, T. (1989) *A Postcranial Guide to Domestic Neo-natal and Juvenile Mammals.* BAR International Series 533. Oxford: Archaeopress.

Anderson, S. (1998) *Station Road, Gamlingay (HAT 257): Assessment of the pottery.* Archive report for Hertfordshire Archaeological Trust.

Anderson, S. (2009) Ceramic Building Material'. In S. Lucy, J. Tipper and A. Dickens *The Anglo-Saxon Settlement and Cemetery at Bloodmoor Hill, Carlton Colville, Suffolk.* East Anglian Archaeology 131, 33–35.

Anderson, S. (2010a) *Longstanton, Cambs (BA 1138, 1242, 1587, 1738 and 1987): The pottery.* Archive Report for Birmingham Archaeology, University of Birmingham.

Anderson, S. (2010b) The Finds. In S. Anderson, Boulter and A. ThorpeExcavations at Priory Farm, Preston St Mary. *Proceedings of the Suffolk Institute of Archaeology and History* 42 (2).

Anderson, S. (2014) Pottery. In S. Boulter and P. Walton Rogers, *A Landscape of Monuments, Burial and Settlement: xcavations at Flixton, Vol. 1.* East Anglian Archaeology 147.

Anderson, S. (forthcoming) The pottery. In T. Woolhouse *Medieval Activity on the Suffolk Clay at Stowmarket.* East Anglian Archaeology.

Anderson, S., Caruth, J. and Gill, D. (1996) The Late Medieval Pottery Industry on the North Suffolk Border *Medieval Ceramics* 20, 3–12.

Anderson, S. and Tester, C. (2000) *The Priory, St. Ives, Cambridgeshire (HAT 268): the pottery.* Archive Report for Hertfordshire Archaeological Trust.

Anderson, S. and Tester, C. (2001) *Lordship Farm, Hinxton (HAT 385): The pottery.* Archive Report for Hertfordshire Archaeological Trust.

Ashby, S. (2007) *Bone and Antler Combs The Finds Research Group AD 700–1700 Datasheet 40.*

Austin, L. and Sydes, R. (1998) Potential ecognition: Evaluating lithic scatters – curators' concerns. *Lithics* 19, 19–23.

Avery, M. (1982) The Neolithic ausewayed nclosure, Abingdon. In H. J. Case and A. Whittle (eds) *Settlement Patterns in the Oxford Region: Excavation at the Abingdon causewayed enclosure and other sites,* CBA Research Report 44. London: Council for British Archaeology, 10–50.

Baker, D., Baker, E., Hassall, J. and Simco, A. (1979) Excavations in Bedford 1967–1977. *Bedfordshire Archaeological Journal* 13.

Barrett, J., Bradley, R. and Green, M. (1991) *Landscape Monuments and Society: The prehistory of Cranborne Chase.*

Barton, N. (1991) Technological nnovation and Continuity at the End of the Pleistocene in Britain. In N. Barton, A. J. Roberts and D. A. Roe (eds) *The Late Glacial in North-west Europe: Human adaptation and environmental change at the end of the Pleistocene.* CBA Research Report 77. London: Council for British Archaeology, 234–245.

Barton, N. (1998) Long Blade Technology and the Question of British Late Pleistocene/Early Holocene Lithic Assemblages. In N. Ashton, F. Healy and P. Pettitt (eds), *Stone Age Archaeology: Essays in honour of John Wymer.* Lithics Studies Society Occasional Paper 6, Oxbow Monograph 102. Oxford: Oxbow Books, 158–164.

Barton, R. N. E. and Roberts, A. (1996) Reviewing the British late Upper Palaeolithic: New evidence for chronological patterning in the Late Glacial record. *Oxford Journal of Archaeology* 15 (3), 245–265.

Birks, H. J. B. and Birks, H. H. (1980) *Quaternary Palaeoecology.* London: Edward Arnold.

Bishop, B. J. (2010) Lithic assessment: Archaeological excavations at Spicers Ltd, Borough Hill, Sawston, Cambridgeshire. In Colls and Burrows 2010.

Bishop, B. J. (forthcoming) The Lithic Material. In S. Kenny and P. Spoerry, *Excavations at the Hinxton Genome Complex, Cambridgeshire, Part 1: the prehistoric occupation.* East Anglian Archaeology.

Böhme, J. (2005) *Die Käfer Mitteleuropas. K. Katalog* (Faunistiche Übersicht), 2nd edn. Munich: Spektrum Academic.

Bradley, R. (1990) *The Passage of Arms: An archaeological analysis of prehistoric hoards and votive deposits.* Cambridge University Press.

Bradley, R. (1993) The Microwear Analysis. In R. Bradley, P. Chowne, R. M. J. Cleal, F. Healy and I. Kinnes, *Excavations On Redgate Hill, Hunstanton, and Tattershall Thorpe, Lincolnshire.* East Anglian Archaeology 57, 106–110.

Brayshay, B. A. and Dinnin, M. (1999). Integrated Palaeoecological Evidence for Biodiversity at the Floodplain-forest Margin. *Journal of Biogeography,* 26(1), 115–131.

Brodribb, G. (1987) *Roman Brick and Tile.* Gloucester: Alan Sutton.

Brown, A. G. (1997) *Alluvial Archaeology: Floodplain archaeology and environmental change.* Cambridge University Press.

Brown, N. and Murphy, P. (2000) Neolithic and Bronze Age. In N. Brown and J. Glazebrook (eds), *Research and Archaeology: A framework for the eastern counties 2. Research agenda and strategy* East Anglian Archaeology Occasional Paper 8, 9–13.

Brück, J. (1999a) What's in a Settlement? Domestic practice and residential mobility in Early Bronze Age southern England. In J. Brück, and M. Goodman (eds), *Making Places in the*

Prehistoric World: Themes in settlement archaeology London: UCL press, 52–75.

Brück, J. (1999b) Houses, Lifecycles and Deposition on Middle Bronze Age Settlements in Southern England. *Proceedings of the Prehistoric Society* 65, 145–166.

Brugmann, B. (2004) *Glass Beads from Early Anglo-Saxon Graves.* Oxford: Oxbow Books.

Brunning, R. (1996) *Waterlogged Wood: Guidelines on the recording, sampling, conservation and curation of waterlogged wood.* London: English Heritage.

Buckland, P. C. (1981) The Early Dispersal of Insect Pests of Stored Products as Indicated by Archaeological Records. *Journal of Stored Product Research* 17, 1–12.

Buckland, P. C. (1982) The Malton Burnt Grain: A cautionary tale *Yorkshire Archaeological Journal* 54, 53–61.

Buckland, P. I. (2007) *The Development and Implementation of Software for Palaeoenvironmental and Palaeoclimatological Research: The bugs coleopteran ecology package (BugsCEP)* PhD thesis, University of Umeå, Sweden. Archaeology and Environment 23, 236 pp. + CD. Available online: http://www.diva-portal.org/umu/abstract.xsql?dbid=1105.

Buckland, P. I. and Buckland, P. C. (2006) *Bugs Coleopteran Ecology Package* (Versions: BugsCEP v7.63; Bugsdata v7.11; BugsMCR v2.02; BugsStats v1.22). www.bugscep.com.

Bullock, J. A. (1993) *Host Plants of British Beetles: list of recorded associations.* Amateur Entomologist 11a, 1–24.

Buteux, S. and Chapman, H. (2009) *Where Rivers Meet: The archaeology of Catholme and the Trent-Tame confluence* CBA Research Report 161. York: Council for British Archaeology.

Carey, C. J., Brown, A. G., Challis, K. C, Howard, A. J. and Cooper, L. (2006) Predictive Modelling of Multiperiod Geoarchaeological Resources at a River Confluence: A case study from the Trent-Soar, UK. *Archaeological Prospection* 13, 241–250.

Chapman, H. P., Hewson, M. and Wilkes, M. S. (2010), The Catholme Ceremonial Complex, Staffordshire, UK. *Proceedings of the Prehistoric Society* 76, 135–163.

Chatterton, R. (2006) Ritual. In C. Conneller and G. Warren (eds), *Mesolithic Britain and Ireland: New approaches.* Stroud: Tempus, 101–120.

Clark, J. G. D., Higgs, E. and Longworth, I. (1960) Excavations at the Neolithic Site at Hurst Fen, Mildenhall, Suffolk (1954, 1957 and 1958). *Proceedings of the Prehistoric Society* 26, 202–245.

Colls, K. and Burrows, B. (2010) *Land at Spicers, Mill Lane, Sawston, Cambridgeshire: Assessment of potential and updated project design.* Birmingham Archaeology Report 1886.

Conneller, C. (2009) Investigation of a final Palaeolithic Site at Rookery Farm, Great Willbraham, Cambridgeshire. *Proceedings of the Prehistoric Society* 75, 167–187.

Cooper, L. P. (2006) Launde, a terminal Palaeolithic amp-site in the English midlands and its north European context. *Proceedings of the Prehistoric Society* 72, 53–93.

Cotter, J. (2000) *Post-Roman Pottery from Excavations in Colchester, 1971–85* Colchester Archaeological Report 7, Colchester Archaeological Trust.

Cox, M. L. (2001) Notes on the Natural History, Distribution and Identification of Seed Beetles (Bruchidae) of Britain and Ireland. *Coleopterist*, 9 (3), 113–147.

Cunliffe, B. (2005) *Iron Age Communities in Britain*, 4th edn. London: Routledge.

Cuttler, R., Martin-Bacon, H., Nichol, K., Patrick, C., Perrin, R., Ratkai, S., Smith, M. and Williams, J. (2001) *Five Sites in Cambridgeshire: Excavations at Woodhurs, Fordham, Soham, Buckden and St. Neots, 1998–2002.* BAR 528. Birmingham Archaeology Monograph Series 6.

Darvill, T. (1987) *Prehistoric Britain.* London: Routledge.

Donahue, R. (2002) Microwear Analysis. In J. Sidell, J. Cotton, L. Rayner and L. Wheeler, *The Prehistory of Southwark and Lambeth.* London: Museum of London Archaeology Service Monograph 14, 81–88.

Drummond-Murray, J. (Forthcoming) *Excavations at Main Street, Stow-cum-Quy, Cambridgeshire.*

Drury, P. J. (1993a) The Later Saxon, Medieval and Post-medieval Pottery. In W. Rodwell and K. Rodwell, *Rivenhall: Investigations of a villa, church and village, 1950–1977, Vol. 2.* Chelmsford Archaeological Trust Report 4.2, CBA Research Report 80. York: Council for British Archaeology, 78–95.

Drury, P. (1993b) Ceramic Building Materials. In S. Margeson, *Norwich Households.* East Anglian Archaeology 58, 163–168.

Edwards, D. and Hall, D. (1997) Medieval Pottery from Cambridge: Sites in the Bene't Street – market area. *Proceedings of the Cambridge Antiquarian Society* 86, 153–168.

Ellis, C. J., Allen, M. J., Rhodes, E., Bevean, N. and Groves, C. (2004) *Absolute Chronology in a Prehistoric Ritual Complex at Eynesbury, Cambridgeshire: Excavation of a multi-period site in the Ouse Valley 2000–2001.* Wessex Archaeology Project Report.

English Heritage (2002) *Environmental Archaeology: Guide to the theory and practice of methods, from sampling and recovery to post-excavation.* London.

English Heritage (2004) *Geoarchaeology: Using earth sciences to understand the archaeological record.* London.

Evans, C. (1988) Excavations at Haddenham, Cambridgeshire: A 'planned' enclosure and its regional affinities. In C. Burgess (ed.) *Enclosures and Defences in the Neolithic of Western Europe.* BAR International Series 403. Oxford: British Archaeology Reports, 127–148.

Evans, C. (1993) *Archaeological Excavations at Hinxton Quarry Cambridgeshire* Cambridge Archaeological Unit Report.

Evans, C., Pollard, J. and Knight, M. (1999) Life in Woods: Tree-throws, 'settlement' and forest cognition. Oxford: *Oxford Journal of Archaeology* 18, 241–254.

Evans, C. and Knight, M. (2002) A Great Circle: Investigations at Arbury Camp, Cambridge. *Proceedings of the Cambridge Antiquarian Society* 91, 22–53.

Evans, C. and Hodder, I. (2006) *A Woodland Archaeology: Neolithic sites at Haddenham.* Cambridge: McDonald Institute.

Evans, C. and Knight, M. (1997) *The Barleycroft Paddocks Excavations, Cambridgeshire.* Cambridge Archaeological Unit Report.

Evans, C. and Webley, L. (2003) *A Delta Landscape: The over lowland investigations (II)* Cambridge Archaeological Unit Report.

Evans, J. (1990) The Cherry Hinton Finewares. *Journal of Roman Pottery Studies* 3, 18–29.

Evans, J. (1991) Some Notes on the Horningsea Roman Pottery. *Journal of Roman Pottery Studies* 4, 33–43.

Evans, J. (2011) Roman Tile and Building Materials. In R. Cuttler, H. Martin-Bacon, K. Nichol, C. Patrick, R. Perrin, S. Rátkai, M. Smith and J. Williams, *Five sites in Cambridgeshire: Excavations at Woodhurst, Fordham, Soham, Buckden and St. Neots* Birmingham Archaeology Monograph Series 6, BAR British Series 528. Oxford: Archaeopress, 70.

French, C. and Pryor, F. (2005) *Archaeology and Environment of the Etton Landscape.* East Anglian Archaeology 109.

Fryer, V. (2009) An Assessment of the Charred Plant Macrofossils, Mollusc Shells and Other Remains from the Spicers Warehouse Site, Sawston , Cambridgeshire. In Colls, K. and Burrows, B. (2010) *Land at Spicers, Mill Lane, Sawston, Cambridgeshire: Assessment of potential and updated project design.* Birmingham Archaeology Report 1886.

Garrow, D., Lucy, S. and Gibson, D. (2006) *Excavations at Kilverstone, Norfolk: an episodic landscape history* East Anglian Archaeology 113.

Garrow, D. (2006) *Pits, Settlement and Deposition during the Neolithic and Early Bronze Age in East Anglia* BAR British Series 414. Oxford: Archaeopress.

Gdaniec, K., Edmonds, M. and Wiltshire, P. (2007) *A Line Across the Land: Fieldwork on the Isleham to Ely pipeline, 1993–4.* East Anglian Archaeology 121.

Grace, R. (1992) Use Wear Analysis. In F. Healey, M. Heaton and S. J. Lobb, Excavations of a Mesolithic Site at Thatcham, Berkshire. *Proceedings of the Prehistoric Society* 58, 53–63.

Grant, A. (1982) The Use of Toothwear as a Guide to the Age of Domestic Ungulates. In B. Wilson, C. Grigson, and S. Payne (eds), *Ageing and Sexing Animal Bones from Archaeological Sites*. BAR British Series 109. Oxford: British Archaeological Reports, 91–108.

Green, H. S. (1980) *The Flint Arrowheads of the British Isles: A detailed study of material from England and Wales with comparanda from Scotland and Ireland. Part I.* BAR British Series 75. Oxford: British Archaeological Reports.

Greenwood, M. and Smith, D. (2005) Changing Fluvial Conditions and Landscape in the Trent Valley: A review of palaeoentomological evidence. In Smith *et al.* 2005, 53–67.

Greig, J. (1982). Past and Present Lime Woods of Europe. *Archaeological aspects of woodland ecology*, 146, 23–55.

GSB Prospection (2000) *Borough Hill, Sawston*. Geophysical Survey Report 2000/108.

Guido, M. (1999) *The Glass Beads of Anglo-Saxon England c. AD 400–700.* Woodbridge: Boydell.

Haselgrove, C., Armit, I., Champion, T., Creighton, J., Gwilt, A., Hill, J. D., Hunter, F. and Woodward, A. (eds) (2001) *Understanding the British Iron Age: An agenda for action* Salisbury: Iron Age Research Seminar and Prehistoric Society.

Halstead, D. G. H. (1993) Keys for the Identification of Beetles Associated with Stored Products II: Laemophloeidae, Passandridae and Silvanidae. *Journal of Stored Product Research* 29, 99–197.

Hamerow, H. (1991) *Anglo-Saxon England*. Cambridge University Press.

Hamerow, H. (1993) *Excavations at Mucking Volume 2: The Anglo-Saxon Settlement*. London: English Heritage/British Museum Press.

Harrison, S. 2003. The Icknield Way: Some queries. *Archaeological Journal* 160, 1–22.

Healy, F. (1988) *The Anglo-Saxon Cemetery at Spong Hill, North Elmham. Part VI: Occupation during the seventh to second millennia BC.* East Anglian Archaeology 39.

Higgs, E. and Jarman, M. (1977) Yeavering's Faunal Remains. In B. Hope-Taylor (ed.) *Yeavering, An Anglo-British Centre of Early Northumbria*London: HMSO.

Hodder, M. A. and Barfield, L. H. (eds) (1990) *Burnt Mounds and Hot Stone Technology: Papers from the 2nd International Burnt Mound Conference, Sandwell, 12–14 October 1990.*Sandwell Metropolitan Borough Council.

Holmes, M. A. (2011) *Food, Status and Complexity in Saxon and Scandinavian England: An archaeozoological approach*. PhD thesis, University of Leicester.

Howard, A. J., Smith, D. N., Garton, D., Hillam, J. and Pearce, M. (1999) Middle to Late Holocene Environments in the Middle to Lower Trent Valley. In A. G. Browne and T. A. Quine (eds), *Fluvial Processes and Environmental Change*. London: John Wiley and Sons, 165–178.

Hughes, T. McK. (1902a) On the Potter's Field at Horningsea, with a Comparative Notice of the Kilns and Furnaces in the Neighbourhood *Proceedings of the Cambridgeshire Antiquarian Society* 10 (for 1898–1902), 174–194.

Hughes, T. McK. (1902b) The War Ditches at Cherry Hinton *Proceedings of the Cambridgeshire Antiquarian Society* 10 (for 1898–1902), 174–194.

Hurst, J. (1956) Saxo-Norman Pottery in East Anglia, Part I. *Proceedings of the Cambridgeshire Antiquarian Society* 49, 43–70.

Jacobi, R. (1976) Britain Inside and Outside Mesolithic Europe. *Proceedings of the Prehistoric Society* 42, 67–84.

Jacobi, R. (1978) The Mesolithic of Sussex. In P. L. Drewett (ed.) *Archaeology in Sussex to AD 1500*. CBA Research Report 29. London: Council for British Archaeology, 15–22.

Jacobi, R. (2004) The Late Upper Palaeolithic Lithic Collection from Gough's Cave, Cheddar, Somerset, and Human Use of the Cave. *Proceedings of the Prehistoric Society* 70, 1–92.

JSAC (2001) *An Archaeological Evaluation Excavation at Borough Hill, Sawston, Cambridgeshire*. John Samuels Archaeological Consultants Report JSAC 685/01/07.

JSAC (2003) *An Archaeological Evaluation Excavation at Borough Hill, Sawston, Cambridgeshire* SMNO24407, John Samuels Archaeological Consultants Report JSAC 685/03/09.

Jennings, S. (1981) *Eighteen Centuries of Pottery from Norwich.* East Anglian Archaeology 13.

Kenward, H. K., Hall, A. R. and Jones A. K. G. (1980) A Tested Set of Techniques for the Extraction of Plant and Animal Macrofossils from Waterlogged Archaeological Deposits *Science and Archaeology* 22, 315.

Kenward, H. K. and Allison, E. P. (1994) Rural origins of the urban insect fauna. In A. R. Hall and H. K. Kenward, *Urban-Rural Connexions: Perspectives from environmental archaeology.* Symposia of the Association for Environmental Archaeology 12.Oxford: Oxbow Books, 55–79.

Koch, K. (1989) *Die Käfer Mitteleuropas*. ÖkologieV – Bands 1–2. Krefeld: Goecke and Evers.

Knight, D. and Howard, A. (2004) *Trent Valley Landscapes: The archaeology of 500,000 years of change* King's Lynn: Heritage.

Lamdin-Whymark, H. (2008) *The Residues of Ritualised Action: Neolithic depositional practices in the Middle Thames Valley.* BAR British Series 466. Oxford: Archaeopress.

Lauwerier, R. (1988) *Animals in Roman Times in the Dutch Eastern River Area.* Nederlandse Oudheden 12. Amersfoort: ROB.

Lethbridge T. C. (1948) Further Excavations at the War Ditches *Proceedings of the Cambridgeshire Antiquarian Society* 42, 452–481.

Levi-Sala, I. (1992) Functional nalysis and ost-depositional lterations of icrodenticulates. In R. N. E. Barton, *Hengistbury Head Dorset Volume 2: The late Upper Palaeolithic and early Mesolithic sites.* Oxford University Committee for Archaeology Monograph 34, 238–246.

Lucht, W. H. (1987) *Die Käfer Mitteleuropas* (Katalog). Krefeld: Goeck and Evers.

Luff, M. L. (2007) *The Carabidae (Ground Beetles) of Britain and Ireland*. Handbooks for the identification of british insects 4, part 2, 2nd edn. London: Royal Entomological Society.

Lyman, R. L. (1994) *Vertebrate Taphonomy.* Cambridge: Cambridge University Press.

Lucy, S., Tipper, J. and Dickens, A. (2009) *The Anglo-Saxon Settlement and Cemetery at Bloodmoor Hill, Carlton Colville, Suffolk.* East Anglian Archaeology 131.

MacGregor, A., Mainman, A. J. and Rogers, N. S. H. (1999) *Bone, Antler, Ivory and Horn from Anglo-Scandinavian and Medieval York*. The Archaeology of York 17: 12. York: Council for British Archaeology.

MacKreth, D. F., Esmonde Cleary, A. S., Bamford, H., Shepard, J., Perrin, J. R., Wild, F., Rollo, L., Cameron, F., French, C. A. I., King, J., Powell, F., Bramwell, D., Harman, M. and Gurney, D. (1988) Excavation of an Iron Age and Roman Enclosure at Werrington, Cambridgeshire. *Britannia* 19, 59–15.

Martin, E. and Satchell, M. (2008) *'Wheare Most Inclosures Be'. East Anglian Fields: History, morphology and management*. East Anglian Archaeology 124.

Marzinzik, S. (2003) *Early Anglo-Saxon Belt Buckles (late 5th to early 8th centuries AD): Their classification and context*. BAR British Series 357. Oxford: Archaeopress.

McKenna, R. (2010) A Full Analysis of the Palaeoenvironmental Remains From a Series of Deposits from Excavations at Sawston. In Colls and Burrows 2010.

McOmish, D., Field, D. and Brown, G. (2002) *The Field Archaeology of the Salisbury Plain Training Area*. Swindon.

Meaney, A, 1981, *Anglo-Saxon Amulets and Curing Stones*. BAR British Series 96. Oxford: British Archaeological Reports.

Medlycott, M. (ed.) (2011) *Research and Archaeology Revisited: A revised framework for the east of England*. East Anglian Archaeology Occasional Paper 24.

Medlycott, M. and Brown, N. (eds) (2008) *Research Agenda Framework for East Anglia*. www.eaareports.org.uk.

Menotti, F. (2012) *Wetland Archaeology and Beyond.heory and Practice*. Oxford University Press.

Merritt, R. (2006) *Atlas of the Water Beetles (Coleoptera) and Water Bugs (Hemiptera) of Derbyshire, Nottinghamshire and South Yorkshire, 1993–2005*. Sorby Record Special Series pp. 14.

Moore, P. D., Webb, J. A. and Collinson, M. E. (1991) *Pollen Analysis*. London: Blackwell.

Mortimer, R. and Evans, C. (1996) *Archaeological xcavations at Hinxton Quarry, Cambridgeshire, 1995, the North Field*. Cambridge Archaeological Unit Report 168.

Mortimer, R. (2006) *Bronze Age Enclosures on Land at Rear of 16–20 Cambridge Road, Sawston, Cambridgeshire (the Police Station site): An evaluation and excavation*. Cambridgeshire County Council Archaeological Field Unit Report.

MPRG, (1998) *A Guide to the Classification of Medieval Ceramic Forms*. Medieval Pottery Research Group Occasional Paper 1.

Myres, J. (1977) *A Corpus of Anglo-Saxon Pottery of the Pagan Period*. Cambridge University Press.

Needham, S. (2005) Transforming Beaker Culture in North-west Europe: Processes of fusion and fission. *Proceedings of the Prehistoric Society* 71, 171–217.

Noddle, B. (1970) Animal bones.n P. Fowler, K. Gardner and P. Rahtz (eds) *Cadbury Congresbury, Somerset, 1968*. Department of Extra-Mural Studies, University of Bristol, 37–40.

Paul, S. H. (2010) *Longstanton Field 7, Phase 2a*. Birmingham Archaeology Report 1987.

Paul, S. H. and Hunt, J. (2015). *Evolution of a Community: The colonisation of a clay inland landscape. Neolithic to Post-medieval remains excavated over sixteen years at Longstanton in Cambridgeshire*. Oxford: Archaeopress.

Paul, S. H. and Mann, P. (2012) *Longstanton Field 11, Phase 3: Assessment of potential and updated project design*. Birmingham Archaeology Report 2146.

Patrick, C. and Rátkai, S. (2007) *Hillside Meadow, Fordham, Cambridgeshire: Archaeological Investigations 1998*. Birmingham Archaeology Report 565.

Payne, S. (1985) Morphological Distinctions Between the Mandibular Teeth of Young Sheep and Goats *Journal of Archaeological Science* 12, 139–147.

Perrin, J. R. (1996) The Roman Pottery. In D. F. Mackreth, *Orton Hall Farm: Roman and early Anglo-Saxon farmstead*. East Anglian Archaeology 76, 182, 189–190.

Pollard, J. (1998a) Prehistoric Settlement and Non-settlement in two southern Cambridgeshire River Valleys: The lithic dimension and interpretive dilemmas. *Lithics* 19, 61–71.

Pollard, J. (1998b) *Excavations at Over: Late Neolithic occupation (Sites 3 and 4)*, Cambridge Archaeological Unit Report 281Pollard, J. (1999) 'These Places Have Their Moments': houghts on settlement practices in the British Neolithic. In J. Brück and M. Goodman (eds), *Making Places in the Prehistoric World: Themes in settlement archaeology*. London: University College of London Press, 76–93.

Pollard, J. (2000) Ancestral Places in the Mesolithic Landscape *Archaeological Review from Cambridge* 17 (1), 123–138.

Poppy, S., Propescue, S. and Drummond-Murray, J. (2006) *Fieldwork in Cambridgeshire 2005*. Proceedings of the Cambridgeshire Antiquarian Society V.95.

PCRG (1995) *The Study of Later Prehistoric Pottery: General policies and guidelines for analysis and publication*. Prehistoric Ceramics Research Group Occasional Papers 1 and 2.

Pryor, F. (1974) *Excavations at Fengate, Peterborough, England: The first report*. Royal Ontario Museum Archaeology Monograph 3.

Pryor, F. (1998) *Etton: Excavations of a Neolithic causewayed enclosure near Maxey, Cambridgeshire 1982–7*. London: English Heritage Archaeological Report 18.

Pryor, F. (2001) *The Flag Fen Basin: Archaeology and environment of a fenland landscape*. Swindon: English Heritage.

Prummel, W. and Frisch, H. (1986) A Guide for the Distinction of Species, Sex and Body Side in Bones of Sheep and Goat. *Journal of Archaeological Science* 13, 567–577.

Pullinger, E. J. and White, P. J. (1991) *Roman-British Sites at Hinton Fields, Teversham, Cambridgeshire* Privately printed.

Pullinger, J. and Young, C. J. (1982) Obelisk Kilns, Harston. *Proceedings of the Cambridgeshire Antiquarian Society* 71, 1–24.

Reynolds, T. and Kaner, S. (2000) The Mesolithic of Southern Fenland: A review of the data and some suggestions for the future. In R. Young (ed.) *Mesolithic Lifeways: Current research from Britain and Ireland*. Leicester Archaeology Monograph 7, 191–197.

Riddler, I. and Trzaska-Nartowski, N. 2013, Artefacts of Worked Bone and Antler. In C. Hills and S. Lucy, *Spong Hill Part 9: Chronology and synthesis*. Cambridge: McDonald Institute Monographs, 92–155.

Riley, D. N. (1944) The Technique of Air-archaeology. *Archaeological Journal* 101, 1–16.

Robinson, M. A. (1991) The Neolithic and Late Bronze Age Insect Assemblages. In S. Needham, *Excavation and Salvage at Runnymede Bridge 1978: The late Bronze Age waterfront site*. London: British Museum, 277–325.

Robinson, M. A. (1993) The Iron Age Environmental Evidence. In T. G. Allen and M. A. Robinson (eds) *The Prehistoric Landscape and Iron Age Enclosure Settlement at Mingies Ditch, Hardwick-with-Yelford, Oxon*. Thames Valley Landscapes The Windrush Valley, Volume 2, Oxford: Oxford Archaeological Unit, 101–120.

Saville, A. (1980) On the Measurement of Struck Flakes and Flake Tools. *Lithics* 1, 16–20.

Serjeantson, D. (1996) The Animal Bones In S. Needham and T. Spence (eds), *Refuse and Disposal at Area 16 East Runnymede*. Runnymede Bridge Research Excavations 2. Oxford: Oxbow Books.

Schlee, D. and Robinson, B. (1995) *An Aarchaeological Evaluation of Land Adjacent to Duxford Mill, Duxford: Late Mesolithic/ early Neolithic activity on the floodplain of the River Cam.* Cambridgeshire Archaeological Unit Report 113.

Schleifer, N., Weller, A., Schneider, S. and Junge, A. (2002) Investigation of a Bronze Age Plankway by Spectral Induced Polarisation. *Archaeological Prospection* 9, 243–253.

Sidell, E. J. and Wilkinson, K. N. (2004) The Central London Thames: Neolithic river development and floodplain archaeology. In J. Cotton and D. Field (eds) *Toward a New Stone Age: spects of the Neolithic in south-east England.* CBA Research Report 137. York: Council for British Archaeology, 38–49.

Silver, I. A. (1969) The Ageing of Domestic Animals. In D. R. Brothwell and E. S. Higgs (eds), *Science and Archaeology.* London: Thames and Hudson, 283–382.

Slesin, S., Rozensztroch, D. and Cliff, S. (1997) *Kitchen Ceramics.* London: Abbeville Press.

Smith, D. N., Brickley M. B. and Smith, W. (eds), *Fertile Ground: Papers in honour of Susan Limbrey.* Oxford: Oxbow Books, 53–67.

Smith, D. N. and Whitehouse, N. J. (2005) Not Seeing the trees for the Woods: A palaeoentomological perspective on Holocene woodland composition. In Smith *et al.*, 136–162.

Smith, D. N., Roseff, R., Bevan, L., Brown, A. G., Butler, S., Hughes, G. and Monckton, A. (2005) Archaeological and Environmental Investigations of a Late Glacial and Holocene River Valley Sequence on the River Soar, at Croft, Leicestershire. *The Holocene* 15 (2), 353–377.

Spoerry, P. (2008) *Ely Wares.* East Anglian Archaeology 122.

Stoodley, N, (1999) *The Spindle and the Spear: Critical enquiry into the construction and meaning of gender in the early Anglo-Saxon burial rite.* BAR British Series 288. Oxford: Archaeopress.

Sykes, N. (2007) *The Norman Conquest: A Zooarchaeological Perspective.* BAR International Series 1656 Oxford: Archaeopress.

Taylor, A. (1998) *Archaeology of Cambridgeshire Vol. 2: South east Cambridgeshire and the Fen Edge.* Cambridge: Cambridgeshire County Council.

Thomas, J. (1991) *Rethinking the Neolithic.* Cambridge University Press.

Thomas, J. (1999) *Understanding the Neolithic: A revised second edition of Rethinking the Neolithic.* London: Routledge.

Tipper, J.(2004) *The* Grubenhaus *in Anglo-Saxon England.* Yedingham (N.Yorks): The Landscape Research Centre.

Tipper, J. (2009) The Anglo-Saxon Pottery. In J. S. A. *et al.* 2009.

Van de Noort, R. (2004) *The Humber Wetlands: The archaeology of a dynamic landscape.* Macclesfield: Windgather Press.

Van de Noort, R. and O'Sullivan, A. (2006) *Rethinking Wetland Archaeology.* London: Duckworth

von den Driesch, A. (1976) *A Guide to the Measurement of Animal Bones from Archaeological Sites.* Harvard University Press.

Wainwright, G. (1972) The Excavation of a Neolithic Settlement on Broome Heath, Ditchingham, Norfolk. *Proceedings of the Prehistoric Society* 38, 1–97.

Walker, H. (2012) *Hedingham Ware: A medieval pottery in north Essex; its production and distribution.* East Anglian Archaeology 148.

Walton Rogers, P, (1997) *Textile Production at 16–22 Coppergate.* The Archaeology of York 17/11. York: Council for British Archaeology.

Walton Rogers, P. (1998) Textiles and Clothing. In G. Drinkall and M. Foreman, *The Anglo-Saxon Cemetery at Castledyke South, Barton-on-Humber.* Sheffield Excavation Reports 6, 274–279.

Walton Rogers, P. (2001) The Re-appearance of an Old Roman Loom in Medieval England. In P. Walton Rogers, L. Bender Jørgensen and A. Rast-Eicher (eds), *The Roman Textile Industry and its Influence: Birthday tribute to John Peter Wild.* Oxford: Oxbow Books, 158–171.

Walton Rogers, P. (2007) *Cloth and Clothing in Early Anglo-Saxon England, AD 450–700.* CBA Research Report 145. York: Council for British Archaeology.

Watkinson, D. and Neal, V. (1998) *First Aid for Finds* 3rd edition RESCUE and the Archaeology Section of the United Kingdom Institute for Conservation.

Webley, L. (2007) Prehistoric, Roman and Saxon ctivity on the Fen interland at Parnwell, Peterborough. *Proceedings of the Cambridge Antiquarian Society* 96, 79–114.

Wells, J. (2007) Appendix 9: eramic building material. In J. Abrams and D. Ingham, *Farming on the Edge: rchaeological evidence from the clay uplands to the west of Cambridge.* East Anglian Archaeology 123, CD Rom, 162–163.

Whimster, R. (1989) *The Emerging Past: Air photography and the buried landscape.* London: RCHME.

Whitehouse, N. J. (2006) The Holocene British and Irish Ancient Forest Fossil Beetle Fauna: Implications for forest history, biodiversity and faunal colonisation. *Quaternary Science Reviews* 25, 1755–1789.

Whittle, A. (1997) Moving on and Moving Around: Neolithic settlement mobility. In P. Topping (ed.), *Neolithic Landscapes* Neolithic Studies Group Seminar Paper 2, Oxbow Monograph 86. Oxford: Oxbow Books, 15–22.

Wilkinson, D. (2011) Cambridge Water Company v. Eastern Counties Leather plc: Diluting liability for continuing escapes *The Modern Law Review* 57 (5), 799–811

Williams, H. (2003) Material Culture as Memory: Combs and cremation in early medieval Britain. *Early Medieval Europe* 12 (2), 89–128.

Williams, D. F. (1994) The Petrology of the Pottery. In V. Evison, *An Anglo-Saxon Cemetery at Great Chesterford, Essex,* CBA Research Report 91 81–82.

Williamson, T. M. (2003) *Shaping Medieval Landscapes: Settlement, society, environment* Macclesfield: Windgather.

Wilson, D. R. (1982) *Air Photo Interpretation for Archaeologists.* London: Batsford